*"Few books in the marketplace these days that offer general advice on how to live a peaceful, productive, and meaningful life are worth the time to even peruse their cover much less their relatively thin content in terms of its practical utility. And fewer still are ones I care to endorse. But this book is clearly the exception. Thankfully, it does not focus on pursuing happiness for its own sake - a vapid goal in life if ever there was one, as the field of happiness psychology quickly discovered. Instead, it focuses on clear thinking, pursuing meaning, and doing so in the most effective ways known. It contains the wisdom of not just a life well lived by its author but also securely based in the scientific evidence and philosophical work that help lead us to the essential guiding principles of really living that also really work. Clearly written and with an economy of words that respects the reader's valuable time and life left to live, this book can serve as life's desk reference for not only how to think about but how to fully live a complete, effective, and meaningful life with true peace, strength, and the common sense needed to achieve them. Simply brilliant! I plan to recommend it widely to family, friends, and strangers alike."*

**Russell A. Barkley, Ph.D.**
*Clinical Professor of Psychiatry,*
*VCU Health Center, Richmond, VA.*

# PEACE, STRENGTH & COMMON SENSE

# PEACE, STRENGTH & COMMON SENSE

THIS MAY BE THE MOST VALUABLE BOOK YOU EVER READ

## JAMES STEAMER

**PEACE, STRENGTH & COMMON SENSE**
**THIS MAY BE THE MOST VALUABLE BOOK YOU EVER READ**

*iUniverse books may be ordered through booksellers or by contacting:*

*iUniverse*
*1663 Liberty Drive*
*Bloomington, IN 47403*
*www.iuniverse.com*
*1-800-Authors (1-800-288-4677)*

*Because of the dynamic nature of the Internet, any web addresses or links contained in this book may have changed since publication and may no longer be valid. The views expressed in this work are solely those of the author and do not necessarily reflect the views of the publisher, and the publisher hereby disclaims any responsibility for them.*

*Any people depicted in stock imagery provided by Thinkstock are models, and such images are being used for illustrative purposes only.*
*Certain stock imagery © Thinkstock.*

*ISBN: 978-1-5320-3966-9 (sc)*
*ISBN: 978-1-5320-3967-6 (e)*

*Library of Congress Control Number: 2017919070*

*Print information available on the last page.*

*iUniverse rev. date: 01/25/2018*

# CONTENTS

Introduction ..................................................................... vii

Chapter 1   Numbers Don't Lie: The Basics of Rules and Order .......... 1
Chapter 2   The Nature of Contentment and Order ............................ 7
Chapter 3   Making the Best of Our Mental Capacity ....................... 37
Chapter 4   Our Spirituality ................................................. 56
Chapter 5   Fast Guide to the Best Financial Management ............... 84
Chapter 6   Healthy Behaviors and the Family ............................ 118
Chapter 7   Going For it .................................................... 151
Chapter 8   What to Stand For & Why ...................................... 174

Conclusion ..................................................................... 259
Summary of Highlights ..................................................... 261
Bibliography .................................................................. 267

# INTRODUCTION

**M**Y FIRST BOOK, Wealth on Minimal Wage, substantiated that with relatively basic knowledge and determination most anyone can manage their personal finances in a manner that is highly rewarding regardless of how much one earns, their level of formal education or one's occupation. This book is even more useful and worthy since it is aimed right at the reader *personally* to achieve the greatest level of satisfaction life can bring through not merely practical advice but useful opinions. I am taking the most appropriate aspects from the past work along with considerable fresh writing to not merely make this my best work but close in on only that which readers can strictly benefit from the most yet more broadly than only finances.

I am sitting here at age sixty writing this work as decades have passed in my life without needing to seek the help of a medical professional for anything significant and take no medications, still have my wonderful wife at my side after thirty-five years together, have a healthy, productive son, several great friends I have had for well over forty years, have had no debt since the age of forty and now pursue passions beyond what I dreamed of when younger. What else can I ask for? Nothing to be quite honest! Having achieved this great level of satisfaction while living such a comparatively modest lifestyle has me now very passionate to share with others the principles of precisely how I reached this point.

I will accomplish this goal by focusing my mind writing here in the same manner in which I personally live my own life while also making an honest attempt at empathizing with others. While experiencing life's adventures, good parenting and the personality I was born with, I have, with considerable effort and persistence, managed to achieve a healthy, satisfying level of balance and contentment. I realize that we all differ in many areas with greater and lesser abilities, unique learning styles and interests, varying personalities and an endless variety of environments we are raised in. I insist however, that there is a basic methodology to reap the best, most positive and productive outcomes from all human life.

While indeed how I define what is positive, negative, most or least destructive, healthy, efficient, etc. may have subtle and even not so subtle differences of opinion among others; I believe that generally most of my definitions apply to nearly everyone. This is why this book has a place on many bookshelves around the country and beyond. I firmly believe that application of the principles presented here work for virtually all of us which are my primary goals – to receive the *maximum returns* from living. These principles are what provide our lives with meaning and purpose – to experience, learn, produce and share and give back. To not do so is to waste and to those who knowingly waste – I ask: What you are here for? Since life without a purpose has little if any meaning.

It is my belief that an enormous portion of the human population is not living anywhere near its potential in terms of being rewarded with the greatest return from the maximum of health, longevity, education, prosperity, freedom, friendship, intimacy, love and marriage, personal accomplishment, religious and spiritual contentment and ultimately self-satisfaction. My purpose here is to introduce and precisely demonstrate the pathways necessary to achieve a near state of nirvana in which we grow old and comfortably approach the end of our existence as we know it here on earth while experiencing that our life has been exquisitely "packed to the max" with all that we wanted to be exposed to and achieve while leaving a legacy we hope the world will gain from. By no means does this imply that I have or one is able to live a perfect life and avoid all the traps, temptations, hurdles, accidents and misfortunes in life, some of which are essential to occur in order to ultimately improve life. True perfection does not exist in life and perhaps not anywhere as I believe this is only a theoretical concept but this book will bring readers as close as they can get.

In fact when *apparent* perfection or an ideal state of being is attempted to be implemented in humans it often creates dysfunction and failure as we so often observe in movies, music and sports stars who enter the "pot of gold" at such an immature age that it covers up and deviates their lives from the necessary trials and tribulations that are essential ingredients of character building and maturity. Over and over we sadly see the deplorable repercussions of huge windfalls of fame and fortune on the young as they bungle through their twenties and beyond with poor quality relationships and sexual experimentation, decadence, alcohol and drug abuse, divorces and substandard parenting, spiritual emptiness, goal-less futures and worse – with *some* exceptions. It is my goal here to offer and provide a pathway which yields the maximum potential of one's life to become the absolute most healthy, interesting, stimulating, rewarding and satisfying it can be though not necessarily the pathway with the resistance. Eliminating too many hurdles and making life excessively easy can cause it to become unproductive, boring, confusing and less meaningful – hence the danger of enabling.

In addition to supplying worthy, practical advice to reach great levels of contentment I also give clear, strong opinions on worldly social and political and spiritual philosophies. I am all too aware in today's world that almost every reader here will significantly appreciate and/or feel disgust at some of these opinions, much as I may insist that I can back them up through rational common sense, moral and ethical values or from those with far greater legacies on the topics. I am a natural teacher with an enormous amount of passion to make the world the best it can be. I have discovered that once one reaches a plateau in which he or she is spending most of their time engaged in what they fully enjoy, then the next step is to demonstrate to others how they can relish in the same. Hopefully many people will benefit from reading further into this book since there is *nothing I want more* than for people the world over to be more content and at peace.

# CHAPTER 1

# Numbers Don't Lie: The Basics of Rules and Order

L IFE CAN BE viewed as a clock. Every one of us only has just so many seconds, minutes, hours, days, weeks, months and years to exist alive here on earth. We take a limited number of breaths and our heart beats for a limited period of time. When it's over, it's over as we know it to be. There are no second chances. *This is it!* Another aspect of viewing life is being aware that one's brain has virtually an unlimited sponge of storage capacity for knowledge and experience which given time and exposure to the world becomes ever wiser with a deeper vault of material to base continued existence on. There are just so many units of not only time but energy and money as well. It is important to maximize their use. Why is it important? Because the more efficiently and effectively we use all resources, the more we benefit the same way a more economical car obtains better gas mileage while still permitting its occupants to be comfortable and arrive safely at their destination in a timely manner. The computer organizes text, photographs, charts and data far more efficiently than the typewriters and paper files of the past saving us enormous amounts of time and storage space while allowing us to have more time and space in our lives for other pursuits.

Being able to accomplish more with our lives with all of this time and space saving technology, however, does not necessarily bring about greater happiness in everyone since many people do not choose to maximize their potential in ways that directly contribute to further satisfaction.

Some choose to fritter away their time channel hopping through 100s of cable channels and sending frivolous text messages for hours on end while paying a couple of thousand dollars a year for this privilege as they teeter on bankruptcy. I firmly believe life should be as meaningful, productive, and satisfying as possible while living in a manner that encourages others to do the same. We cannot forget that *life is sacred*, especially human life. Therefore, it deserves the ultimate respect in its maintenance, productivity, reproduction and moral grounding – hence the challenge of living prosperously in every area or at least achieving such prosperity with age.

Some readers of this work may think I am obsessive about this simple fact, perhaps being in a constant state of anxiety that the sand is running out of the top of the hour glass. Yes, most every day I am aware that it could be my last since there always is that chance of being in a car accident, having a heart attack or stroke, breaking a hip on the ice walking in the winter, my house burning down, or God knows – an earthquake, war or other unpredictable catastrophe that halts my life goals/desires. This awareness does not consciously manifest itself in a part of my mind that interferes with or suppresses my present enjoyment of life. Actually, quite the contrary since maintaining such awareness *improves* my quality of life because it motivates me to focus and concentrate on making such improvements. Growing up with a grandmother living in my home may have had some effect on me being extra alert to the fact that my life is only once and no more. I saw her wrinkling up into her nineties, losing her faculties and finally bed ridden and losing her mind during her final days. And now I have experienced my brilliant parents very sadly failing into old age and passing which has set off an alarm in my head that I am next though I certainly do not dwell on this fact.

I acquired a passionate appreciation for life early on, particularly human life. In part this may be my natural love of science and arriving at the realization that who we are and what we are is a result of the growth and interaction of trillions of cells continually performing countless chemical reactions and transformations that literally create the action and grand mystery of being alive and conscious. Though I am not one who believes in miracles, a living human mind and body is as close as it gets other than the formation of the universe itself. And the more I appreciate life the more I respect it and wish to maintain and preserve it to operate as effectively as possible for as long as I am alive – within reason. Frankly I find it hard to relate to those who choose not to make the most of their health and potential longevity, and actually consider such behavior to be downright self-destructive. And worse yet, we all pay a fortune in much higher taxes, health care costs, crime and other social ills due to poor physical and mental health. There is quite a complexity of reasons why a substantial percentage of the population does not take on the job of being the captain of their own ship and maintaining it in the best possible condition, unfortunately enough to require another volume or more of writing.

After spending a couple of weeks touring around one of the poorest countries in the world yet taking note that almost 100% of the inhabitants there were cheerful, not loaded with class envy despite their desperate predicaments as perceived by me and in no way making me feel uncomfortable or unsafe, I have some solid opinions. These extremely hard-working natives in Africa cannot be lazy because they must survive. They primarily eat the fresh fish they catch and the fresh fruits and vegetables they grow. Diabetes, depression, suicide, gun violence and crime other than war are virtually unheard of. For example, Africans in Sierra Leone and several other countries live on less than a dollar or two a day; yet, I never have met such polite, warm, cheerful and friendly people in my life! The need to survive forces one to work proudly which we Americans need to more closely identify with.

My parents who were born in and lived in the United States provided my brother and me with a solidly middle class life. It included a secure, decent family income, long-term overall satisfying parent marriage, safe, beautiful places to grow up as a child and formal education through the university level. I don't take this for granted and am thankful daily for being so fortunate yet also realize we all are challenged in life no matter. So, what did I want as I grew up? Naturally I also desired a comfortable middle-class life, and a healthy, satisfying marriage. This is no real surprise. It is very normal to desire at least what one's parents have and usually more. And most parents want their children to flourish beyond where they went in life. I love the great examples of children who have had very few advantages in life and overcame their many disadvantages while moving up several socioeconomic levels from their parents. I don't merely mean entertainment stars who made $millions before they completed their teens. I am referring to children who endured significant economic and social hardships who have become healthy, productive and prosperous exemplary citizens.

The clock begins ticking basically the moment we are born or I could even say upon conception. In recent times more and more research has been done by doctors, child psychologists and other scientists that have proven that our environment in utero, infancy and early childhood is equally as essential to our future development into healthy or unhealthy human beings as our genetics. Additionally, permanent patterns of how the brain is wired and formatted are created during these crucial formative years. While some structures are genetically passed on and not easily altered others are very malleable and apparently some more or less in different people. Certain aspects of brain neurology are very dependent on their environment to properly shape them during infancy. We sadly know from a few isolated cases that children not exposed to light may never develop proper eyesight or those who have been left in near complete isolation for years never learn to speak properly.

Human personalities start like pianos. All pianos have 88 keys in exactly the same pattern but no two sound *exactly* alike when played. It is similar to the way no two people have precisely the same voice except perhaps identical twins. As we grow our environment stimulates us to learn and respond. And quite naturally our response is based upon that which we are exposed to. A loud, argumentative household is most certainly going to bring about a significantly different personality outcome than a quiet one. A parent who regularly disciplines softly and does not set behavioral limits with their children will have quite a different older child than the one who is more structured and follows through with firm enforcement. We all unfortunately know the negative results of abusive and neglectful parenting – no need to discuss this in detail!

I strongly believe that much of who we are now as adults, that is how we respond to the world and others for the better or worse, revolves around how our environment shaped us during our first five years of life. Studies are regularly being carried out to further explore and discover more precisely how our neurophysiology works and why. Also science has established that genetics play a very significant role with various traits that may manifest themselves under the right stimulation that triggers such action with all of us being different. The thrill I obtain when my plane touches down in a foreign country for the first time may well be insecurity and fear to someone else.

The manner in which numbers emerge as the ultimate dictate of life is in how we deal with and manage our utilization of resources of all types. Yes, the clock keeps ticking no matter but we can make more of those ticks count toward that which we enjoy and wish to accomplish through the choices we make. Getting at the roots of why we make the choices we do may bring us to some of the more complexities of psychology so critical to our understanding of why we behave the way we do. We cannot all be the next Albert Einstein, Alexander Bell, Thomas Edison or a future president but most of us can significantly improve the quality, quantity and efficiency of our lives to fill our 80-100 years with more lasting satisfaction which will be described in much further detail later. Reaching celebrity status is rarely the goal of celebrities. Most simply have great talents and enthusiasm for a particular field whether it be singing, dancing, engineering, leadership, painting, sports or whatever which in some cases leads to such status.

When it comes to thinking about mathematics in general one could very nearly say that numbers dictate how lives and the entire universe evolved and operates because pure math explains *everything* from atomic and molecular structure to all types of motions, forces, mass, time, biological activity, forecasting and extrapolating, classifying, charting and otherwise organizing and describing reality. Numbers by default force boundaries on our behaviors. For example, one can only spend so much money until they have none. One may borrow money but this also has limits. One can only run so fast, carry so much, eat so much or go so long without sleep. Each model of automobile has a peak performance point in which it uses the least amount of fuel to adequately perform the job, the peak of efficiency. However, to say that all reality consists of nothing other than the manifestation of mathematical formulas certainly is a stretch. The challenging philosophical question which arises is not *how* mathematics describes reality but *why* the math exists. Following the title of this chapter, yes, numbers don't lie because they cannot in reality as we know it to be. When there are 10 apples on the table there cannot be 11, 9 or 142 – only 10.

The periodic table of the elements describes via the mathematics of the known science of chemistry precisely how they all exist and potential interactions with other elements under various conditions. Matter can only behave in a specific manner depending on the environment that it exists in. A chunk of pure sodium behaves very differently in water than submerged in kerosene. It all can be described by mathematical formulas that precisely demonstrate how molecules, atoms and atomic particles such as electrons, neutrons and protons seek a state of equilibrium because equilibrium represents stability and stability is what nature continually seeks. Human beings behave very differently as well but even human behavior can be traced back to the atomic and molecular configurations of genes and countless billions of chemical reactions taking place in the brain. And again we seek stability, the result of satisfying our needs from hunger to sex, sleep, solving curiosity, etc. There is nothing more stable than numbers since math describes the most basic foundation of all reality as we know it. Numbers provide accuracy of measurement; accuracy provides irrefutable reliability which in turn provides infallible benchmarks we can depend on. When numbers appear not to follow this irrefutable path this is due to human misinterpretation or intended bias as with how statistics are frequently used to slant news and ideas to one's benefit or in peculiar cases of esoteric particles and cosmological physics where matter and energy can act in unknown ways. Numbers are the most pure form of logic due their irrefutable, factual reliability.

# CHAPTER 2

# The Nature of Contentment and Order

**W**E EXIST WITHIN and perhaps as an aspect of billions of years of a time/energy/matter continuum. How we act and behave during our infinitesimal though certainly significant (to us) lifetimes is what makes our lives what they are. We have various resources from which to draw from such as time, intellectual and cognitive capacity, creativity, physical strength and coordination, self-discipline and determination, money, food, water and energy. To what degree we make use of order and efficiency in managing these resources has a *very dramatic* effect on how successful, productive, healthy and satisfied we become. In fact *how we manage* our lives is actually more critical than whether or not we achieve high grades in school or earn over $100,000 a year.

Certainly, it is a note-worthy accomplishment to attain top academic achievement and financial success in the work world. Success however, is measured in human beings by *how satisfied they feel* via their perception of life more than by the grades or the money they acquire because doing so is a more honest, objective assessment. This is because achieving satisfaction and contentment along with assisting others in experiencing the same is much of our purpose in living and what ultimately generates happiness over the long term. Though school performance and financial success may often be components of the creation of good feelings, completing the construction of a well that provides drinking water and the growing of fruits and vegetables for the neighborhood may offer the same to others. How we define success is very relative.

I have observed people from around the world and seen happy and content people from all socioeconomic levels. There are satisfied people who get up before 5AM daily to milk their cows living in a simple 2-3 bedroom ranch house with a mortgage who when asked feel equally as content with their lives as others earning over a $million a year who own properties around the world paid for in cash and appear to "have it all". I find it most amusing to meet families living in straw huts who must haul their own water, grow their own food, have no or minimal access to electricity and live on less than a dollar a day, yet the kids are happily kicking a ball made from rolled up old socks and the hard working parents are smiling – not that poverty is a pretty picture by any means. Poverty often is created by one's *perception* of their lifestyle in comparison to others. For those with adequate shelter, food and clean water most cope well with life until they become corrupted with images of large, affluent homes, new cars, high end appliances and electronic devices, etc. though some choose to keep their simple life no matter. However, those who are malnourished, do not have access to clean water and reasonable shelter are considered by community observers to be in true poverty since at this point people's health and emotions are affected negatively due to *suffering*.

One's sense of satisfaction or happiness arises from *within* which is why the big houses and CEO salaries or cow milking and straw huts are largely irrelevant in comparison. A characteristic that is built into our well-being is called hedonic adaptation which is defined as the tendency for humans to return to a stable level of contentment – no matter the big raise or loan pay off, new baby, new car or latest electronic gadget, grand vacation or sexual experience. The new computer is not what brings on happiness but my writings, beauty and intrigue of my photographs and videos and the sharing of information with others does over the longer term. Higher pay from that new job may provide an initial euphoria but before long all will become humdrum as we usually increase our lifestyle proportionately and soon acquire more concerns about our ability to maintain it. Studies have shown that lottery winners are not significantly happier eighteen months later than before they won their giant windfall of cash. The same goes for the purchase of a new, fancier, roomier house. Once one adjusts to all the new features the thrill languishes. A new $800,000 Lamborghini sitting in my garage makes me no happier than a new $20,000 Honda and in fact may actually be more of a burden.

So what do we do to keep the happiness alive for the long term? We must accept that we cannot be in euphoria all the time. Being engaged in something we *genuinely* enjoy accomplishing and often helping others, normally brings about great satisfaction in life, whether it be carrying a bucket of water from the well for three miles through the desert for the family or completing a PhD thesis – though it is what we do with that PhD that ultimately is the most rewarding. Making choices such as using recreational drugs, alcohol in excess, smoking, or sexual relations with strangers due to boredom or addiction may indeed bring about temporary intense highs but these experiences are merely artificial highs. Such behaviors do not bring about the deeper, long-term satisfaction which humans need and desire in their lives. Our healthy interaction with others is certainly one critical area that increases satisfaction. But ultimately we need regular variety in our lives to obtain a sense of appreciation for the good quality of life we have in comparison to our past or others in lesser circumstances. Gratitude for our circumstances is a great emotion to relish in as well.

Too much predictability can generate a sense of dullness and boredom from work to romance and marriage to chatting with the same Facebook friends or watching similar television programs. Creating a sense of individuality and uniqueness can also play a key role in satisfaction for many people as there is a certain type of excitement in being the only person who wins a race, takes a unique photograph, paints a unique picture, composes unique music, engineers a new device or is one of the few who ever travels to Antarctica or meets the Bushmen of the Kalahari. Breaking away from the humdrum of everyday life does not mean we must necessarily take huge risks climbing vertical cliffs; cheat on our spouse or try heroin either. Whether it is simply taking a different route home from work even if longer occasionally, taking a walk or bike ride to new neighborhoods, taking a work break at a different time and interacting with another set of people, mowing the lawn in a different direction, reading a new book, eating out at a new restaurant or cooking a unique meal or driving a relatively short distance to explore a new place, we need variety for our brains to feel more stimulated. There is an ideal balance of variety, yet in certain areas of our lives dependability and predictability are crucial. When one starts their car they do not need the "variety" of it not starting nor the "variety" of a tire going flat or having the flu either. The expression, variety is the spice of life, is largely true when healthy choices are made. I relish in the exposure to other cultures, languages, foods, wildlife and scenery upon traveling yet also love returning to my predictable life back home.

Managing our lives in ways to receive the most rewarding and satisfying returns also require involvement in work and responsibility. To achieve the point of realization that work – effort, concentration, focus and diligence – and responsibility which is the understanding that one has a moral conscience of what is right (good) and wrong (bad) takes *maturity*. If we are not mature we cannot properly manage our lives no matter how intelligent we may be. I know people who barely completed high school but they have a high degree of emotional and moral maturity that has led them to an abundance of contentment with their lives while others with near genius level IQs whose lives are in disarray. Why? Because they are nearly 40 years old but never matured much past the age of 17. Of course I am using an extreme example to make a point here but I conclude that ideally we hope to be intelligent and emotionally and morally mature. There are plenty among us who are.

Emotional and moral maturity rise as we move through our childhood and adolescence, usually involving a fair amount of "ups and downs" to reach a healthy plateau which many acquire as early as our teens. However, some almost never seem to mature though most do by their mid to late twenties. With greater age an even higher level can be reached as we realize more and more that our time here is limited and that we should make the most of life with fewer mistakes and regrets. Dedicated parents who provide a healthy level of love, attention, discipline and resources to their children will most certainly on average produce more mature children though some of the best parents I know who appear to have "done everything right" end up with adult children who fail at life. Observing one's own offspring reach adolescence with nothing but the sheer determination to become involved with peers with poor values, decadence, crime, drug and alcohol use, early sex or even terrorism is among the most trying times of parenting. And in rare cases, highly mature, successful children arise from horrendous circumstances which I took particular note of when substitute teaching in rough urban schools. A young person's life was often positively impacted by the ongoing support from a close and concerned person such as a school teacher, neighbor, mentor, coach or pastor.

Maturity has a direct relationship to happiness and satisfaction because those with a high level of maturity have a stronger understanding of how to effectively manage their lives in a manner in which higher levels of rewards are brought to fruition. By most definitions a well-rewarded life is a better life. Since we cannot have a rewarding, happier life without maturity just how do we mature to achieve the good life? This can be complex and involves several factors including genes which science attributes to about 50%, parenting, other environmental stimuli, and finally the conscious choices we make as we move into our teens and adulthood. Regardless of genes and environment once we all reach a certain level of maturity in which decisions are being consciously made we also have the ability to *exert control* over them. Depending on how deeply certain patterns of behavior are entrenched creating perception by the individual, one can learn to step back, think and reason, and then perhaps make a better, more informed choice for the circumstance being confronted. This is the higher level ability of self-analysis that humans have over animals. We can say no when consuming more than three drinks, a second piece of pie or to an offer of illegal drugs because we are able to understand the consequences of our behaviors, while animals do not, though they may avoid some temptations or indulgences based on instinct instead of reason.

Religious influence plays a role in the maturation of humans in the majority of societies. While anyone may take various quotes from religious books such as the Bible, Koran or the Buddhist Tipitaka out of context and perhaps misinterpret them for the worse, for the most part such works are intended to make human societies more ordered, peaceful and moral though often at the exclusion of other religions and even antagonistic toward them. Ancient monks and priests, etc. who wrote these books and even theologians presently attempt to bring people together via their religious messages. Traditionally the Christian perspective of going to heaven or hell depending on what moral choices one makes throughout life has had some effect on people. But there are other teachings in the Bible and other religions along with the rule of law arising from Christianity that has had the most beneficial impact. There is also the concept of *natural law* which in my opinion is simply the result of life naturally having the propensity to sustain itself. In order to do so, human life requires a minimal level of structure, order and morality to exist. Conceptions of natural law can vary; however, there is general agreement on this point of natural law: Human beings are capable with sound reason to perceive what is morally right and wrong. Many of the religious may call this God's laws with the message being the same. Natural law is therefore viewed as the foundation of all human laws.

We learn that there are consequences to our actions and choices well before we are taught any understandable aspects of religion. So, *in theory* religion is not an absolute requirement for humans to be moral but societies in which religion is banned or for whatever reason hardly exists, political leaders tend to exert tyrannical control on their populations over a spiritual or godly belief system. We can observe the deterioration of personal freedoms as is exhibited by heavily communist regimes, theocracies forcing religious belief on populations and dictatorships around the world. America has thrived largely due to personal freedoms granted by our Declaration of Independence and Constitution – something we should never take for granted because much of the rest of the world does not operate the same way. Condemning political leaders in many countries around the world can quickly land one in jail and worse. Due to maintaining a strong military which I am grateful for every day we continue to have such freedoms for the time being.

Theories of natural rights led by great philosophers such as John Locke (1632-1703) made it clear that everyone is born with certain types of rights no matter the country of their origin. This is because John Locke's theory of natural law was applied to government in the context of people's natural rights. He believed that government existed to uphold natural law; therefore, governmental tyranny violated the natural rights of man. In other words, natural rights were not given to the people by kings or governments but belonged solely to the people by nature. Such freedoms continue to cause much social and legal conflict which keeps the American judicial system alive and flourishing. However, we have a far better quality of life as a nation and a republic with the Declaration of Independence and other founding documents than operating as a country without them. I am of the opinion that having a strong level of individual freedoms that do not suppress the freedoms of others brings about a greater level of contentment among the general population yet realize this is a delicate balance to maintain in a society.

## Never Be Complacent

Making the right choices for our lives to become the absolute best they can be does not always come naturally, particularly during youth when middle or old age appear to be so far away and irrelevant. An eighteen-year-old is not naturally going to be thinking about maintaining healthy cholesterol and sugar levels in their blood or packing away substantial portions of their work pay into retirement accounts. Most believe alcohol will not hurt them and that they can drive well over the speed limit because they are "young and in control". Sure, their reflexes may be sharper but the risks involved in drunk driving and speeding are not significantly less. The body may be able to digest hot fudge Sundaes, salty potato chips, candy, soft and hard drinks and cheese balls better at age 19 than at age 68 but forming poor habits when young increases our risk for poor health with age.

Even though just a one-time placement of a couple of thousand dollars from that part-time cashier job or neighborhood lawn mowing work in one's teens could grow to hundreds of $thousands by middle age in a Roth IRA tax free, the need for more immediate gratification dominates costing a fortune of what is called *lost opportunity cost*. Most young people simply believe they will either get a good paying job which in their mind negates the need to save early on, may have the security of cheap living at home or due to immaturity have not analyzed the enormous benefits of becoming financially independent. Also many young people in American society have been given the message through television, entertainment, friends and the internet that acquiring wealth will always be a struggle so who cares. This negative attack simply provides the social reinforcement that young people are not yet able to move past their overwhelming need for present gratification and nor should they pursue delayed gratification.

This concept of lost opportunity cost is extremely critical to having a great life because of how we behave and the actions and decisions we engage in early on enormously multiply their effects over time. The more time we have remaining in our lives the more these effects manifest themselves for the better or worse depending on one's choices.

To make matters worse our culture being loaded with "instant everything" as we all know in the technology revolution only exacerbates and extends immaturity in the young. We almost never have to place a stamp on an envelope and walk it to the mailbox anymore. We can chat on the phone anywhere at any time and even quietly text so privately that parents have no idea of what the intentions or plans of their children are. Movies including pornography may be watched at home for free. Paper checks are vanishing and moving money, photos and entire books anywhere in the world in seconds require nothing more than the click of a mouse. Telephone directories have largely vanished along with landlines. We can instantly communicate with friends and relatives anywhere in the world for nothing more than internet cost. Not all of this innovation is negative as I cannot imagine hardly a day passing without the use of texting or email. Of course like others, I enjoy the freedom to chat with a good friend while I am way out in the forest hiking. The role of cell phones for emergencies literally saves lives. And hopefully soon paper checks will vanish in place of secure electronic transfers and postal mail will be delivered about three days a week which will save considerable amounts of money and energy for the U.S. Postal System.

The problem that arises with all of this instant technology is the lack of in-person contact and voice as well as the tendency for people to become addicted to computer/phone use causing significant sleep deficits and throwing us out of emotional balance. We also have become so attached to this stuff that we are detached from nature and I don't simply mean green fields, forests, birds and frog ponds but the *forces* of nature. We should never become overly complacent. Earthquakes, volcanoes, hurricanes and tornados, tsunamis, floods, power outages and even war can occur at any time most anywhere and though we should not obsess about such possibilities, we do need to be able to cope and survive should we have to confront such events. I find it troubling to observe people in public constantly staring down at their mobile phones while literally bumping into trees, street lamps and other people as they lose touch with their natural environment.

Another troubling aspect of the techno culture is that, along with ever more popular professional and college sports and the relatively decadent Hollywood movie following is again having all of this entertainment right at one's fingertips plus simply endless websites from gardening, photography, cooking, travel, science, pornography, millions of videos, online books, Facebook, gaming, job hunting and applying, dating, house locating, endless shopping sites and far more. No matter what it is one needs, it is online. So whether it is a date, a book, a camera, information on fishing, watching police chases, booking a flight, taking a class, cooking one's Thanksgiving turkey, researching one's ancestry, getting sexual thrills, or checking live to see the traffic flow in Istanbul it's *all online*. This in a practical sense is wonderfully convenient and is able to bring people together from far away, permits people to shop online, and learn about an endless variety of fascinating topics.

For me to realize that within moments I can check my stock portfolio's performance, football scores, the latest military skirmish in Afghanistan, zoom down on satellite photos and check out a neighborhood in Antananarivo Madagascar or Beijing, chat with people all the way back to preschool, translate languages instantly, send and receive emails from around the world, instantly make payments, etc. is mind boggling when I can so easily recall such different times. Scientists are having their first glimpses of indications that our brains are rewiring and forming new patterns oriented toward computer use. Such social isolation is now well documented to be problematic. This social change leads to both physical and psychological problems since the behavioral changes necessitated by this technology have occurred at a rate hundreds of times faster than biological evolutionary adaptations can take place. For those who are highly conscious of such changes and understand the health of balance in life I think it may be highly stimulating to the brain and create significant enhancement to life. However, face to face interaction or at least voice and video calling will always be a more significant, deeper and broader form of communication, particularly for serious relationships and important business transactions.

JAMES STEAMER

# High Quality Families are Critical for a High Quality Society

We have had in person social interaction going on more frequently for tens of thousands of years, something that is rapidly diminishing. Taken a step further many young people are even avoiding the responsibility of committed relationships, marriage and parenting. This along with the liberalization of the meaning and purpose of sexual activity and birth control has the population seriously declining in various parts of mostly the western world from Japan to much of Europe. Even in the United States many young people are choosing to avoid marriage, not have children if and when they marry and replace the overall healthy stresses of raising children with pets, smart phones and computers. Most certainly the world is overpopulated in some areas but I think the choice to opt out of parenting is not based on the need to cut down on resource utilization but to be lazy, avoid maturing and take on the stress of such responsibilities. Unfortunately those with the most education, better jobs and availability of quality medical care, clean water and food are generally the ones making such choices. This means that those with fewer resources and education to properly raise a family under healthier conditions are increasing in numbers much faster.

If those at the lower end of the socioeconomic scale are having the most children how can this bode well for our future? Given enough time this phenomenon will naturally generate a larger underclass of lessor skilled people when it surely is more desirable for the population to become more educated and therefore, more able to enjoy a prosperous life. Perhaps ironically one aspect of becoming well educated is the increased desire for a highly coveted, more productive and lucrative career which in turn may cause such people to view parenting as a great inconvenience and loss of significant income. And in these economic times giving up a high level career position is very risky. Another aspect is sheer self-centeredness – the desire to advance in one's career, accumulate ever greater wealth and perhaps hop on planes to Zanzibar or Bangkok upon a whim instead of dealing with Tommy's wet diaper, Susan's math homework or Johnny's $250 a month asthma medication. Such negative views of parenting are destined to significantly affect population demographics. It is no coincidence that pet ownership has significantly increased in recent times since people still have the need to care for someone so they substitute with dogs, cats and others instead of children who are less stressful emotionally and financially.

As many of these career and money focused couples reach middle age at least some will experience regret that they chose to not have a family, though not all. As for the happiness factor this is complex but having children most certainly is a deeply maturing and mind broadening experience, not to mention the obvious benefit of creating the next generation. Something to consider is that the underclass population of the ghetto and crime culture including radical terrorists are reproducing at a much faster rate. Several anthropological sociologists speculate that civilizations come and go in cycles with the most educated elite reaching a peak of intellectual capacity and awareness while reproducing at such a low rate that the world becomes overrun by thuggery and tyranny starting the cycle over again. With much of the world in comparative poverty compared to the U.S. and terrorism running rampant, this is an issue to seriously contemplate and perhaps take action on though realistic solutions are very complex. It is no wonder that young people feel insecure about parenting with horrific student loan burdens, health insurance payments that rival the cost of a home mortgage not long ago and tiny apartments renting for over $1,000 a month! But read on. There *are* solutions.

## Thrift and Simplicity Only Make Life Better

Maturing in awareness of what truly makes life the best it can be is what will give us the keys. This is the awareness of how to maximize the use of all resources while experiencing the most rewards in return. Naturally the younger we attain such consciousness the more we will benefit but it is almost never too late. Some people realize this as young as age 10 and begin acquiring an orderly habit of thrift – not only applied to money and the material world which is essential and imperative for a better life but to time and efficiency as well. This consciousness means learning and desiring to attain the *maximum return for the minimum* of output and this does not mean cheating, stealing, engaging in dangerous short cuts, and not respecting others or the environment – actually quite the opposite in most circumstances.

For example, packing down the trash firmly in one's trash can save space, alleviates having an extra trash can to put out, clean and buy, is faster for the trash hauler to dump into the truck, and may save money if the sanitation company charges per can for pick up. The same applies to saving time and gas by combining errands, saving water with shorter showers and planting drought tolerant grass, filling dishwashers or washing machines rather than running them half empty, keeping a fridge full which uses less power, driving a smaller more economical car that is also easier to park, keeping most records on backed up computer files or in the cloud rather than paper, paying bills securely online or by automatic withdrawal instead of using paper checks, stamps and waiting days for postal mail to reach its destination, keeping computers in sleep mode to save power, using LED light bulbs, keeping the house comfortable though cooler inside during the winter and warmer in the summer, maximizing the cost of phone usage, learning more self-care and natural methods to take care of the majority of medical issues and understanding risk reward potentials regarding the purchase of various types of insurance and investments.

By living and applying the principles of thrift, simplicity and minimizing one's use of resources and being comfortable doing so one assuredly can live well below their means. The most important words in that last sentence are "being comfortable doing so" because life is not about being miserable. It may be very lean for a period of time but when one has realistic goals living lean and simply generates enormous levels of anticipation and incredible future rewards. I recall living with my wife very cheaply through our twenties and thirties earning around $3.00-8.00 an hour. We were willing to work extra jobs, live in very small yet comfortable places that cost as little as $250 a month including utilities and lived by these principles of thrift, almost consistently saving close to half of our take-home earnings while teaching ourselves how to invest it. By the age of 40 we were debt-free, taking annual family vacations, owned a nice home and vehicles paid for in cash, were raising a child and continuing to build our retirement savings which led me to publish my first book, *Wealth on Minimal Wage.*

What we implemented to achieve this feat was not complicated, does not require a financially related degree or license and is surprisingly simple for most anyone to succeed at. Learning the basics of financial planning is something that should be an essential requirement in every high school and mostly involves common sense and simple math that most anyone can understand. It all begins with our emotions, desires and attitudes in terms of what we want from our lives. Once we realize that minimizing life to only residing in the square footage that we need while still being comfortable, having only the number of children we desire, owning only that which either increases in value over time, offers a truly pleasing level of quality in the home or is a necessary possession such as a basic, dependable car, appliances and a computer or things that are honestly sentimental, we will cope far more effectively.

Whenever I pass by a house with an open garage that is at least half full of stuff that if it were my place I would immediately dispose of, I think of what a burden it must be to have all that junk. However, I know that many such people actually feel comfortable with fifty-year-old rusted out appliances, bikes, car parts and broken garden tools occupying their space or at least don't stress over it but I still insist that human life is easier and less stressful when we only have what we need and truly acquire regular enjoyment from. Being a hoarder is most certainly a sign of an emotional/psychological dysfunction since hoarding primarily subtracts from one's quality of life, if not in the present certainly in the future. Anything that does not have value in some form does not need to be part of our life. Now, to be a bit more empathetic some hoarders may have come from a background of a style of poverty from times of the Great Depression when people deliberately saved almost everything in case it could be repaired or parts taken from it to be used for alternative purposes. But in today's world I ask if one would carry a brick in their backpack while hiking up a mountain in addition to their lunch and water bottle? The answer is obvious.

What is so special about minimizing one's life is that one soon becomes wonderfully conscious of how much greater life can be. What began occurring to me as a very young child, though not so consciously as in adulthood is that by allocating and focusing my space and time to more of what brought about personal feelings of reward I was literally creating more of these resources to pursue even further exploration in my life. By my twenties I diligently pursued this philosophy at an even greater level which made raising a family and being debt-free by the age of forty, even on work paying minimum wage, less challenging than I anticipated yet startling to the public – so much so that I easily was received by a publisher of that first book.

My obvious point here is that by sheading the unnecessary stuff out of one's life that uses up space, time, energy and money with mostly a negative return we generate so much of the opposite or positive. We quickly realize that we have far more of these resources than we thought we had. My gosh, now I have the time and money to go back to school, perhaps work a second job, take those trips to the Amazon or Congo jungles I dreamed about as a kid, fix up an antique car, or start that online business I have been visualizing. *Life is truly incredible* and totally amazing when we manage it to the maximum potential! We must get rid of that which is little more than waste, clutter, unnecessary, excessively costly with minimal or a negative return and instead truly focus on that which we most sincerely care about in order to become productive, prosperous and content. This rule applies for how we use the internet and television as well – stay focused on what reaps the greatest return.

Certainly most of us desire good health, good school grades, interesting, high paying work and wealth creation, satisfying relationships of all types with others, a comfortable place to live, perhaps parenting, travel and the pursuit of some hobbies. While the majority of people may say they are reasonably happy when asked in the moment, if examined more deeply are frequently found to not be fulfilled or have satisfied most or all of these desires regardless of their socioeconomic status. The main reason is because they are somehow not tuned in to the preciousness and fragility of life, especially at a young age. I believe that when we do acquire a heightened awareness of this preciousness and fragility we then also place a greater value on our individual lives. We realize that anything can happen anytime and that the clock keeps on ticking forward no matter. At this level of consciousness we are stimulated to place a high enough value on our lives to live in ways that reward us with the most return. With such a higher level of consciousness one may also experience *gratitude* in which we feel fortunate for our existence, good health and relationships, material well-being, accomplishments, etc. Gratitude adds to our contentment, perhaps our ties to our spirituality and is further enhanced by demonstrating it to others whose attitudes and accomplishments we appreciate.

## Delayed Gratification has Incredible Rewards

Though it may not appear this way on the surface in the moment life *is* fragile. As for life being precious viewed objectively it may not be but from the standpoint of the individual it most certainly is or else we might as well walk in front of a roaring train. Again, our genes and our environment more or less equally play a role in making us who we are and how we react to the world (our behavior) so explaining here how readers can acquire the greatest rewards from life is not easy – hence the challenge of my message. While some genetic factors are very hard wired in terms of how we behave I am of the belief that through learning to become *aware* of who we are and our built-in tendencies to react we are able to transform ourselves significantly for the better. Will the procrastinator suddenly start jumping out of bed at 6AM, make a to do list and immediately start racing around knocking stuff out as if this is the last day in time, the obsessive compulsive person quickly change to a more relaxed mode, or the type A personality within days learn to reward themselves at a more graceful pace? No, but all of us can read what I am writing here, think seriously about what is stated, consider the reward/effort ratio required to change for the better and then seriously contemplate the value of doing so. Will I convince every smoker to quit? Again, no but if I reach some who do then my time is well spent. I am not writing this book as much to earn money but for the benefit of readers and the world.

The earlier one learns to anticipate the future and experience the rewards of being orderly and exercising restraint in the present the larger a head start one has on life in terms of both planning and increasing prosperity which also leads one to more wholesome moral values. Experiments conducted on personalities tell a lot about who we are and how our behaviors develop. The child left alone who at the age of nine grabs the chocolate brownie or ice cream before the meat, potatoes and vegetables is far more likely to be the adult at the age of thirty-five who when asked if they want $100 now or $120.00 a month from now when most any investment can never be assured to receive this level of gain in value over this short a time period will take the $100 now. In contrast the nine-year-old who has learned to experience the joy of a reasonably balanced meal while also feeling pleasure in the act of anticipation of the sugar high of consuming the dessert will be far more likely as an adult to realize that earning a 20% return in a month is irresistible.

Though genes obviously play a role in personality development most certainly appropriate parenting directs and focuses our natural tendencies. Children left to rip open all of their Christmas presents within moments of getting out of bed are being given a very different message by parents than families who have breakfast together, clean up the table, perhaps get dressed and then take turns opening gifts one at a time while cherishing each other's gifts. These experiments of course only create generalizations while there are plenty of exceptions where personalities are so strong willed in the genes that even the most ideal parenting environment does not bring about anticipated results leaving parents in great disappointment and asking themselves what they did wrong when it is clearly not their fault. We all know of cases in which parents probably did "everything right" yet one or some of their children ended up in dysfunctional situations such as involvement in crime, illegal drug use, alcoholism, teen pregnancy, etc. There are always going to be some who sadly go down the ill-fated path in life but I firmly believe that much of this is preventable and some individuals mature later in life and manage to repair much of the damage.

Fortunately I learned at a very young age to engage in a high level of order and to appreciate and enjoy anticipation of greater pleasure and satisfaction to come with the passing of time. Along with intensely passionate hobbies of collecting, preserving and identifying a large variety of biological specimens and seeing my live-in grandmother age into her nineties, it occurred to me that life of all types is fragile and precious and that *we only live once* with no second chance. It became self-evident that in order to obtain exposure to the most I could touch, feel, smell, taste, hear, observe and record that I had to prioritize and create order. The more I did so, the more enriched life became. Unfortunately the rules and restrictions of school stifled me for much of my first twenty-some years since much classroom style learning went at such a pathetically boring and slow pace. And it frequently covered material that I determined was impractical, irrelevant and did not enrich my life. Now 40-50 years later I regret that I did not take more interest in certain subjects back then as I feel lacking in some topics, yet I can fill in the gaps of knowledge now on my own.

To my detriment I became so rooted for example, in this pattern of passionately learning all I could about life science, philosophy and astronomy during my spare time rather than caring more about homework, quizzes and tests that my academic performance was significantly compromised. And when I entered the work world after college I perceived work just as I did school – something to do as an obligation only, get it over with, take home the paycheck and then put my passion and creativity to work to make that paycheck go absolutely as far as it possibly could with the goal of having enough money as soon as possible in order to never have to work for someone else again. Though certainly I had expectations of finding interesting professional level work I could not hide my real self on interviews because my real self only wanted to pursue my true interests such as nature, science, writing, photography, travel, etc.

Unfortunately during much of my adult life I ended up working at jobs that I have been way overqualified for, largely bored with and pathetically paying but other features of who I am led me to what is actually a very satisfying life. I know many people who performed much better in school and have the very interesting, professional level occupations and good pay that I always wanted, yet do not appear to have much gusto in their personal time or worse yet have health problems, messy divorces and have reached well into middle age and are still significantly hindered financially despite their much higher incomes. I guess I have something reversed! But one thing is certain; that *having it all* – the nearly perfect health, occupation, marriage, financial savvy, sense of simplicity and endless lust and passion to learn and engage in hobbies is virtually impossible in one life.

## Everything Has Order

Everything in the universe is orderly starting with atomic structure itself, the workings of matter and energy, and the physics of motion, the chemistry of the stars and our brains and bodies – described by mathematics at the base, mathematics being the foundation of order. The order of time is what creates change or perhaps change is what describes time. Everything is in flux all the time moving from order to disorder and returning back to order once again. The whole concept of order is a bit mysterious since even what we perceive as disorder can be classified as order if examined closely enough. But it is our *conscious mind*, not merely the brain (We all have brains made out of the same chemicals operating under the same functions of biochemistry.) that determines who we are as individuals and how and why we make the choices we make as we mature. And every one of us is unique because the brain and mind, though may have some similarities to computers in certain respects, are far from operating the same way. A million computers can be manufactured to operate identically while even identical twins have some differences. The brain uses both analog and digital methods of operating in combination to work at its best with several mysteries still not fully understood. One period accidentally placed at the end of an email address will not send or be returned while the human brain will categorize it as "similar enough" to recognize it – something I wish more software would do.

## Experiences & Relationships
## Over Money & Things

The people who tore open their Christmas gifts by 7AM as kids, grabbed the ice cream and candy before dinner and snatched that $100 rather than $120 in thirty days and otherwise live "off the seat of their pants" for the brief endorphin high usually are the least content. They have not learned to savor and cherish satisfaction, create minimal complexity to their lives, do not practice reminiscing good memories much and also do not engage in significant future planning which generates the joy of anticipation and improved future outcomes. In his great book, "The Happiness Pursuit: What Science can Teach us About the Good life", Shimon Edleman, professor of psychology at Cornell University, I quote saying "Our capacity to retain memories and develop foresight allows us to plan for the future, by using a mental "personal space-time machine" that jumps between past, present and future. It's through this process of motivation, perception, thinking, followed by motor movement, that we're able not only to survive, but to feel happy." Professor of psychology Tom Gilovich, also from Cornell, confirms exactly the same thing. I mention two ideal examples below to consider.

A friend and I planned a trip to roam around Costa Rica for two weeks. We spent many hours over several months along with a travel agent preparing the itinerary hoping to enrich our adventure by experiencing all that we can while there – walking the streets of San Jose, having tours of coffee and banana plantations, boat rides, beach and rain forest hikes, considerable photography, meeting some people related to our interests, using our limited Spanish skills, visiting native villages, observing erupting volcanoes, enjoying zip line rides, observing the southern night skies and more. We planned to get up around sunrise and still be taking in all we can until sometime after sunset. We truly wish to obtain all the experience from life we can.

This same friend of mine went to Rome and Naples Italy. He and his wife had made plans to visit and sightsee various places of interest and did all they could to have a good time. They went with some others who had apparently made no plans, spent until almost noon to get started with their day, acted bored and confused shortly after they arrived, continually complained about American style conveniences not being available to them, were a terrible drag on my friend and otherwise miserable. People of this type simply should not travel! Hell, even on airport layovers if I am not overly sleep deprived I am either loading my brain with information from reading material I brought for this purpose or I explore around the airport checking out the area, viewing various types of aircraft, chatting with a pilot next to me about flying, learning about some foreign culture or language from someone sitting near me and using Wi-Fi. Life is about *taking it all in* – learning and exposing ourselves to new knowledge and experiences while fully enriching the brain right until our last days! What else are we here for?

To quote professor Edleman again since I could not do it better he says "If you have some money to spend and you spend it on buying goods that's not nearly as effective in making you happy in the long run as buying experiences." I could not agree with this statement more! When I look back nearly 60 years I can tell you for sure that purchasing a new house, computer, car, bicycle, our first large flat screen TV or a camera do not immediately come to mind though certainly all of those things have brought about increased enjoyment to my life – the new house having more modern and convenient features, the faster computer more conveniently permitting me to save and upload my photography and writing, the car more dependably and bicycle comfortably taking me where I want to go, the TV enriching my experience viewing various shows and the camera letting me record my life and be ever more creative.

However, it is the *experiences* in my life that always jump to my mind first such as bumming around the country in an old van for months exploring all I could get my hands on, spending a year living in a 900-year-old house in a tiny English village, visiting Europe and roaming through the rain forests of Costa Rica, exposing myself to the cultures and sites of Peru, Paraguay, Chile, Vietnam, Thailand, Indonesia, Nepal and the U.A.E., roaming around the primitive, unique culture of Sierra Leone, Kenya, Zimbabwe Mozambique and Morocco, being on ship to Antarctica, other great trips and nice holiday times with my family, falling in love, biking and hiking out in the wilderness, great conversations with close friends, my hobbies of science learning, stock market investing, writing and photography, and philosophical and political debates. I do not know how it feels to be bored except under conditions when one must perform a function or duty as required by an employer that is not stimulating – what I called forced boredom.

Other studies have shown again and again that income beyond a certain point – typically around $50-75,000 a year for an American family of 3-4 in 2017 hardly gains any more "happiness points" when their household income rises much more than this. The real danger is when we falsely believe that when our income rises to $125,000 or to over $200,000 we will be ever happier. If the occupation we have offers us a more interesting *experience* with the higher income, yes we may become a notch happier on the scale but do not bet on just the money alone accomplishing this – especially if one's plans are merely to buy bigger and "better" material things. The bigger house will also cost more in property taxes, more effort to maintain and clean, more gardens to tend to, a larger lawn to mow and more insurance. Owning more costly stuff translates into more responsibility, consumption of more of one's time and money which does not necessarily increase happiness and may very well accomplish exactly the opposite outcome.

Our level of satisfaction in life is based on how we interpret/perceive the world as we experience it. And we are all different. I know someone who has several dogs and she and her husband are willing to spend countless thousands of dollars on their care no matter how old they get, will not take vacations because they have the dogs, and otherwise all but let their dogs rule their lives. This person has even said to me that she might save a suffering animal before a human child! They are happy with their choices in this regard while someone more like me would be miserable in those circumstances to say the least. And in reverse take away their dogs and put them on a plane to roam the forests of New Guinea, Sumatra or Madagascar to see beetles nearly the size of a fist and hear indigenous languages that change every thirty miles and they would be just as miserable. Others might prefer to coup themselves up in a cabin in Vermont to write poetry, practice brain surgery, be a manager somewhere, an engineer or Wall Street investor, operate their own business or whatever.

Why else do good parents, psychologists and career/life counselors notoriously tell their children or clients to stick with what you love to do and the money will take care of itself? Money is worth nothing more than the paper it is printed on if one is not happy – I repeat, *nothing*. Again it is *experiences and relationships* that contribute to our wellbeing far more than money and material goods. But let us briefly get back to the first sentence of the previous paragraph which has one very critical word in it, *interpret*. If we interpret and perceive ourselves as happy packing boxes all day at work on an assembly line, come home and do not dread going back to work the next day, so be it. We are content. If we are content being an engineer, a poet or brain surgeon, so be it as well. Of course nobody is always happy all the time as this is not even meant to be. The box packer may prefer to engage in relatively mindless work while experiencing much lower stress than the manager, despite the lower pay while acquiring satisfaction via other aspects of life, perhaps having a loving marriage and children to come home to and/or avocations of particular interest. I have sacrificed better pay for less negative stress, a shorter commute in awful traffic or to work with nicer people many times in my life.

So let us come back to the fact that how effectively we make use of the mathematical value of various resources in our lives largely determines how positive the outcomes are. People who do not have a healthy grip on foresight at a young age are at a significant disadvantage. Parents should highly encourage children to begin looking more forward as they enter their teens and far more so by the end of the teen years. Not simply being able to plan (Any young child can obey chore lists and read a calendar when required to.) but *relishing* in doing so because the rewards are so great is what stimulates people to naturally want to be planners. Without rewards there is little if any incentive to engage in most anything as occurs with the young who acquire large amounts of wealth, excessive sexual experiences and other highs. While growing up I had parents who were highly organized and planned life in a manner which enabled my family to experience life very fully which may have rubbed off on me. The old expression that what one receives from life is the result of what one puts into it is most certainly true. Those who have good foresight have learned to set goals. And setting goals opens the potential for life becoming better in the future.

Whether it is building good quality friendships, completing an academic degree or work project, publishing this book, saving a certain amount of money or paying off a debt, being able to buy a house or new car or painting the house, these are all goals that bring us to a higher plateau in life. Having a trusting, delightful mate with similar passions for life quite obviously can also enhance life *enormously* and may well exceed the pleasure of most any material purchase or accomplishment. Someone please tell me if they have more pleasure by themselves in their beautiful mansion than being with a passionate, committed soul mate. I would much prefer to be madly in love with someone and live a much simpler life than manage a large house and yard and either be alone or in a boring relationship! Then one could say the best of both might be to have the large home and yard and be madly in love with someone.

But examined more closely we might well find that this perceived ideal cannot really last long-term because the effort and responsibilities necessitated to maintain the larger estate which require very long stressful work hours may equally subtract from the passion of being madly in love. The wonderful glow of romantic love can be quickly stifled by packed, stressful work schedules needed to generate income to pay for a lifestyle that while perceived as "better" may actually create the opposite effect of the intended desire. This is the situation many people do not realize until they are up to their neck in long commutes, high taxes, difficult work challenges, college loans, complex finances and medical and car repair bills, countless trips to soccer games and music lessons, and big homes and yards to insure, maintain and clean while their relationship dries up. If passion dries up no amount of money, big houses, fancy cars or designer shirts will alleviate the dullness which castes itself over one's life. There is nothing more fulfilling beyond food and water than deep passion for another person which overshadows all material needs. This need can manifest itself as a deep friendship of intense verbal discourse, companionship and of course intense sexual intimacy. If I had to choose between living in a tent with my intimate loving partner and best friend and being alone in a comfortable large house I would take the tent living hands down!

Most certainly finishing a college education has the potential for reward as does publishing this work, accumulating wealth or paying off debt. Having a nice home to live in is plenty satisfying as well as owning dependable transportation. The paint job, once completed, should not have to be done again for many years opening up opportunities for other things to fill our time with. These accomplishments in and of themselves do not immediately bring on contentment. It is what we *create and complete* with them that matters, the *experiences* that are generated with that special person, shared times in the new house, driving the new car, enjoying a less stressful life without debt and appreciating work more after a difficult project is behind us.

Happiness and longer-term contentment also arrive from having an optimistic attitude which is something that our heredity plays some role in though can be learned to some extent as well. We can react to noticing it is snowing outside our window, become worried that our drive home or to work will be more difficult – bringing our mood down. Or we can react by looking at the weather report, taking note of what may be coming, properly prepare, allow ourselves more time to carefully drive, enjoy the beauty of the fresh snow and perhaps even interpret the drive as more of an adventure instead of a hassle. We can see a stock market downturn as an opportunity to purchase more stock at a lower price rather than feel down that our portfolio or retirement account is moving down in value. When our car exhaust system needs replacement at the same time as our mortgage payment is due along with taxes to pay, stress can build but if we have "saved for a rainy day" such times should be survivable. Dealing with conflict with our spouses, the boss, close friends and relatives whom we depend on for love, support and a paycheck is perhaps the most challenging to our spirit. There are methods of preventing and mitigating these circumstances as well.

## Less Can Be More

It is human nature to continue to keep desiring more, bigger and what we perceive as better no matter how much we have – an emotion we must learn to keep under control. Continuing to set goals to improve our lives and satisfy our curiosities is good and much of what drives us to bring us to where we are in life; yet, we must also learn to gracefully accept and be content with our lives as they are. There is just the right balance. For example, I am totally satisfied with my basic automobile and have no particular desire to replace it for I hope 15-20 years as long as it comfortably takes me where I need to go economically and dependably, something a new one would not accomplish any better. I love my home and have no interest in a fancier, larger one *no matter my level of wealth* and in fact now actually prefer to live in a smaller, less expensive home. The basics of shelter, security, convenience and comfort the home provides will not change from a $250,000 house to a $500,000 house or a million dollar house. The same principle applies to my car, hotels I travel in and restaurants I eat at. By living in this manner below my means for my income I have extra resources of time and money to spend on that which matters the most – love and friendships, reading and writing, photography, travel, charity and the pursuit of whatever curiosities provoke my mind.

Completing this book however, is different. I do want to finish it as soon as I feel it is ready for the publisher so I can move on to another project. As for increasing my net worth and getting rid of debt, this really is a goal that *does* bring about increased contentment. This is because it is self-empowering to improve one's financial status in the world. Nobody else has authority over another person when one owns everything in cash and greater wealth translates into more purchasing power, therefore increased freedom to choose and pursue that which one particularly enjoys. There is a great sense of relief upon completing an obligation whether it is a class paper, work project, building a new patio and garden, paying off a bill, cleaning something, having the car repaired or accepting a diploma. Such relief is very satisfying because completion is naturally rewarding since it frees us from the feeling of being tethered to obligation and brings us one step closer to emotional and financial prosperity.

It is this *broader opportunity to choose* how to occupy one's time and energy that greater wealth provides which makes life better – not the latest smart phone, largest flat screen TV receiving 500+ channels or the new Mercedes parked in the garage. This is because the human mind and brain crave and accumulate wisdom via *experiences and knowledge* gathering far more than merely altering one's material environment. The new TV, house and car only provide a very temporary high which shortly blend into the humdrum and background of everyday life but that summer one spent in China or Spain or taking an exciting course in a subject of desire is learned/experienced recallable information that can be accessed for the rest of one's life, forever enriching greater intellectual depth that can never be taken away. The value my wife and I receive from a wonderful evening and personal exchange with another couple has the same value whether in our home, their home, over a hundred dollar dinner in a classy restaurant, a cheap fast-food restaurant or a straw hut in Uganda.

Once one has played with the various functions of the new car and phone and scrolled through hundreds of TV channels, it soon is realized by the brain that *life is about the basics*. The car needs to take us from one place to another dependably, safely and comfortably. The phone needs to make and receive calls, text and access the internet. In all likelihood we will discover that we spend 90%+ of our television viewing time watching less than a dozen channels and the other 10% or less watching another five at the most. When I stay in a hotel or motel I need to be in a safe, clean room at a reasonable temperature with a bed that gives me seven to eight hours of sleep, an adequate breakfast, a toilet that flushes and a shower – *nothing else*. The extras simply are cost wasters and add nothing to the greatness of the experience and memory of my vacation since the purpose of traveling is the exposure to new places, people and cultures, not fancy chandeliers, chef prepared five course meals, eye popping art on the walls of my room and opulent lobbies which I can find near my home.

## Set Goals & Gain Clarity

Goal setting is a critical aspect of life if we want the most from it. To set goals we must learn to be focused. To become focused we must be at least somewhat organized. Being organized in a manner that maximizes return of our time and energy means that we have reached a full understanding of what is important, what is not, and what is waste. Waste is abhorrent to life. Waste and excess things in our lives must be reduced as much as possible to decipher, separate and focus on that which benefits us the most. Stuff that we are certain we never will benefit from again unless perhaps someone close to us can or there is real sentimental value, needs to go. Clutter just fogs up our lives. *Clarity* is what we need! Not everyone naturally trashes junk mail and spam the moment they receive it, eliminates extraneous outdated papers on their work desk, maintains a personal date/appointment calendar, keeps a running to do list, places their wallet, keys and cell phone in exactly the same place every day and backs up all important computer documents daily but their lives would be significantly better if they did.

For those not so inclined they need to put out that extra effort to practice such habits which will eventually become automatic. The clock does not stop. Would we rather be fumbling around trying to find our keys or phone for a half hour three times a week or less than once a month? That time doing so can never be returned to our life allotment. It's gone *forever*. I can make quite a list of much more interesting, amusing and productive activities I could do with that time only enriching my life further. We must learn to take swift action against the seemingly endless entities that want a piece of our attention, time and money to have more for ourselves and those we care most about. For example, I don't need to load my file cabinet with piles of financial statements from each month but can get them electronically and only save the ones with necessary income tax information and summaries for the whole year. We also must become extra aware of how various social media are creating ways to keep us glued to the internet, much of which honestly is a waste of time.

So for those who seriously want the best and most from life they must attain more than the minimal level of order to succeed and experience greater satisfaction. At this point we have to make choices. Do we want to waddle through life in disorder and hindrances which stifle us from achieving as close to our full potential as possible, be moderately orderly and focused enough to function reasonably well or climb to the top of the chart and truly fulfill our dreams? The closer to the top we reach the more easily we can accept our pending demise without regret when we are over the age of eighty and perhaps even leave a legacy of our existence to pass on to our loved ones. Despite our genes or childhood environment we must examine the previous sentence and make a decision. The vast majority of us have the potential to take life as far as we wish. For some their dreams will be more challenging to achieve than others but with sustained self-discipline and motivation inspired by desire almost anything can happen. Unfortunately for some it seems that extreme and often tragic circumstances must occur in order for them to realize that they have to become decisive and focus on their lives – better known as a wakeup call or hitting bottom. For others religion may have a positive influence in assisting people to organize their lives through finding a sense of purpose.

## Practical Resource Management Works

Regardless, we must all reach the conclusion that life has great value, it is all we have and that we must make appropriate decisions to make it productive and satisfying. Once one has direction and focus in terms of what they want from life one must then obtain a feel for being smart with their use of resources. All resources have *limits*. We only have so much time to accomplish our goals of acquiring what brings us pleasure from life so we must acquire wise time management skills. The same principle applies to money since we only have so much, earn so much and can only borrow so much. We must also look at being economical and practical in all other areas of life while still enriching and enjoying ourselves. We need to examine our use of all types of materials and energy such as gas, oil, electricity. At the extreme there are households that generate almost zero non-recyclable trash.

A lifestyle that uses the least amount of resources while not experiencing significant feelings of deprivation not only is generating less damage to the environment but is also enlarging the paycheck of everyone doing so. For every dollar saved by purchasing something at a garage sale, subscribing to less cable channels, having less cell phone features if not needed, couponing, looking very closely at the real value of various types of insurance, cooking fresh at home, carpooling, cutting out newspaper subscriptions when the news is online anyway, living in only the space one actually needs, and having an economical car, one's wage rises proportionately permitting earlier debt pay off, more retirement savings, more rewarding family vacations and ultimately a better life. This is the *principle of less being more*. One of the greatest pleasures I have now is realizing that I need virtually no more material goods in my life. My house satisfies me just fine and I certainly do not need a bigger one. I do not need new furniture, appliances, a new car, a new computer, camera or phone. I truly have to rack my brains out to come up with something I really need – sure I could use a new pair of shoes at some point.

The less time, energy and money spent in one area permits it to be allocated to another area which increases what we can enjoy and accomplish in our lives when we become aware of what areas we are wasting resources in and other areas those wasted resources can be placed. The quality of life improves as a result. And remember that it is quality experiences, special friends and relatives that count way over the power of the latest smart phone, having 300 cable channels instead of 50, owning a new high end automobile over an older model, living in a 3,000 square foot home instead of a 1,600 square foot one, having everything insured to the maximum, or staying in the Hilton instead of a Super 8 when on a road trip – the purpose of which is to admire the greatness and serenity of the Grand Canyon or amusement of Disney World over the classiness of the hotel's wallpaper. When unsure how to make such decisions we can look years into the future and ask ourselves what we will recall most vividly and fondly that we cherished the most. When I look back to my childhood the size of my house, how many television channels we had (around five I think on a thirteen inch black and white set!), how big and new the family car was and the quality of my household furniture, these items are not even on the immediate list. Life is about targeting that which we receive the greatest contentment from which is simple to accomplish when we understand the formula for doing so.

True contentment arrives from memories of *experiences* over time including those of hardship, memories presently being created and future expectations of better to come along with a sense of security, love and friendship from others. As mentioned earlier, I recently spent a couple of weeks in one of the poorest nations in the world where the average income struggles to reach one dollar a day; yet, there is virtually no rape, burglary, muggings, depression or suicide, no psychologists employed and a seemingly amazing level of contentment and peace among the natives. They were among the friendliest people I ever have experienced. After watching people carry buckets of water from a well or river for over three miles in blasting hot weather to have water for their family for the day with a smile on their face, I was humbled to say the least! Meanwhile people are fighting for places in line to buy a Play Station and in Germany a restaurant has opened for pets. In the United States we are debating whether to spend up to $1,000 on a phone while these people are content living with no running water or electricity with their kids playing soccer in the dirt using sticks to mark off goals with a ball made from rolled up, worn out socks.

Fortunately for most people the brain and mind work together to soften the roughest edges of our worst memories in life while prioritizing the more positive memories creating a healthy level of optimism. However, we must also remain balanced in regard to having full awareness of the practical sense of reality itself and the potential to cope with future hardship. As with the truth of numbers being unendingly rock solid, stable reality is what it is and cannot be avoided. As already alluded to earlier contentment, satisfaction, and happiness arrive from lifestyle choices we make and how we choose to perceive reality as we live through it with the passage of time. We can choose to hate cleaning toilets, scrubbing the kitchen floor, raking leaves, shoveling snow or grocery shopping and therefore bring our mood down or we can feel better that we are improving the quality of our immediate environment and obtaining good food we need. We could also share such work with another family member while having an interesting or humorous discussion when doing things we generally do not enjoy.

Though we may have built-in genetic tendencies toward optimism and pessimism we also have conscious control of our perception of the world via choice. Yes, to some extent we can feel better or worse by consciously choosing to use mind over matter as the old expression goes. It is also noteworthy to point out how we sometimes dread certain chores or activities of life which once engaged in we do not despise so much and may even find them to be a creative endeavor. Cooking is a great example. To some it may appear that the process of making a choice is a very simple matter which in theory it is but our minds and emotions are very complex to say the least. From biting our nails, grinding our teeth to disliking certain types of work, procrastinating or even addictions, decision making is not always easy and often may require the support of others and perhaps medical intervention in some cases. However, we must have limits when dealing with those who continue to knowingly make poor decisions because sympathy can also be enabling.

# CHAPTER 3

# Making the Best of Our Mental Capacity

T HE FOUNDATION FROM which we all exist is our physical, biological health, something we all should be critically aware of as functioning human beings. The human body and especially the brain are the most magnificent machines known and why we exist at all remains among the most mind boggling philosophical mysteries. As is true of all life our bodies operate in a constant effort to remain homeostatic – healthy and free of illness and suffering. All of our systems work together in near perfect harmony except for a comparative minority of genetically defective individuals, for decade after decade with occasional battles the immune system struggles to fight and rarely loses as with certain cancers. It is all but miraculous!

To enable us to achieve the good life as discussed in the first chapter *good health is the basic requirement.* On the surface this appears obvious because if asked anyone desires to feel good. And if we all gave ourselves the healthy quantity and quality of nutrients, exercise, sleep, social interaction, intellectual stimulation and stress levels, we indeed would have excellent health under most circumstances for eighty years or more. Our insane health care system would consolidate to perhaps a quarter or less of what it is, relieving trillions of dollars in unnecessary costs to all, permitting government to finally pay down debt, people to be far more productive at the work place, cancer and fire reduction from reduced smoking, a fortune saved on fighting the drug war and drunk driving, and a great increase in employer and shareholder profits along with higher wages by relieving employers of paying for such costly health care benefits. Sadly readers, this practically utopian scenario is not going to happen. Drug and alcohol addiction will continue. Obesity is worse than ever. Though smoking is down in the U.S. worldwide it is still at epidemic levels. Diabetics will keep eating sugar laden foods that they should not. Far more accidents than necessary will occur largely due to consciously made poor choices.

I can ask why. The answers in a sense are simple and obvious though when viewed from another angle are rather complex. The obvious answer is that we as human beings are not willing to put out the extra effort to be more careful and respectful to our bodies, therefore taking more conscious control to protect our only truly meaningful asset, us. It is sad but true. Many of us are not willing to take more self-leadership – self-control, discipline, goal setting, and the exercise of restraint for our betterment and otherwise do most all we can to feel as good as possible and live as long as we can. Simplicity says to an overweight person eat less and exercise more but complexity says it's too hard; I cannot resist the pleasure of eating, I cannot imagine a day without soda, I have obesity genes, I don't mind being fat, my spouse and friends are mostly overweight, I eat practically nothing and still gain weight, I don't like exercise or have time for it and more because we are dealing with *human emotions* rather than merely the simple science of cause and effect.

The same principle applies to alcoholism, smoking and other addictions. The simple obvious solution is of course to stop engaging in such habits but the complexities involve the myriad of human needs, emotions and chemical addiction problems. It is easy to say to a smoker or obese person, "Stop buying cigarettes and smoking or simply stop eating the junk food or overeating!" And from a highly practical, rational standpoint yes, one should be able to make the conscious choice to change. For many becoming more practical, rational, ethical and moral are the greatest challenges of life which is troubling to realize. We also must be compassionate yet only tolerant within a range toward the extreme difficulties of departing from chemical addictions in which entire parts of the brain have become programmed to crave substances that negatively affect our well-being. As many of us know the opiate drug problem recently has become an epidemic with dozens of people dying daily from this tragedy.

The intelligent, rational mind asks out of frustration why there is so much disengagement toward health awareness since the rewards of sensible, wise and healthy behaviors are so great. With some exceptions excessive wealth and comfort may explain a major aspect of why we engage in such poor choices. The poor person who cannot afford alcohol or cigarettes or to waste time must out of necessity be orderly and disciplined to survive. Someone must fetch the water from the well over a mile away. Laundry must be washed in the nearby river. Firewood must be gathered to cook the next meal. Sweet potatoes have to be dug up, washed and cut up. More water has to be brought in for the vegetable garden. The neighbor needs assistance in constructing their mud and thatch hut. Babies have to be breastfed and the elderly must be attended to. *Survival necessitates order and discipline* which naturally fall in line with moral structure. In primitive societies where most everyone lives almost continuously in survival mode a *moral base* becomes the default because nobody can afford to be ostracized by others in the group since all individuals need the social support of the rest.

The question that arises here is how we maintain high levels of order and discipline in the modern, westernized world of much greater wealth in which survival needs are taken care of at the flick of a switch, turning of a faucet, the pressing of a button, turning of a key, click of mouse and the sliding of a credit card. With the basics of survival all but taken for granted we most certainly have a very different view of our lives which generates entirely different behaviors. What comes to mind first is the sense of complacency which makes us Americans vulnerable and often lazy as well. When life is too easy and comfortable where basic survival needs of water, food, medical care and housing are provided regardless of economic status and how hard we work, our perception of productivity and work become distorted for many.

This is because when work is *required* for our survival we don't question the type of our work or what it pays because we just need food, water and shelter and are ever grateful just to survive. Unfortunately with large numbers of our population, once they have these basics and even more provided by either government "entitlements" and/or a small paycheck, are not motivated to take their lives to the next level. This occurs because doing so involves the type of effort that only comes with considerable discipline.

And for the mind to engage in self-discipline requires conscious effort to be put forth which often is perceived negatively as difficult in the present. Negative perception can truly be our enemy!

Trying to teach people to do what they need to improve their lives sometimes is analogous to trying to teach flowing water to not move in the shortest direction – no simple task. It is noteworthy to point out how frequent it is for people to continue to consciously engage themselves in that which is knowingly harmful while taking no action to change, especially when such change as perceived by others appears to be very simple and the rewards so beneficial. Yet I should never be so arrogant to assume change is so simple knowing the chemical and social factors of deeply rooted behaviors. The tough part is being on the side of the fence feeling good while being able to observe those on the other side who are not while knowing exactly what the remedy is for improvement – yet not being able to stimulate change in choices being made. This is the constant frustration of social workers and psychologists.

We all experience the temptation to presently take the easy path, grab the TV remote or computer mouse and be fed an endless amount of entertainment. While it is not totally fair to place judgment on how people spend their spare time we can all agree on some generalizations. Considering that we Americans have enormous amounts of free time at our disposal there most certainly is nothing wrong with contemplating how it is put to use. My opinion is that such spare time can largely be used to make our lives ever higher in quality. In addition to enjoying a good movie or getting some laughs from a comedy show occasionally, playing or watching a sports game, more time with our family and friends and connecting on the computer many of us can also focus on a good hobby or passion. We might even start a small business or pack away some cash from a second job to brighten our future.

With all of one's basic needs virtually guaranteed it is perhaps too easy for the mind to choose the less difficult path and not make that extra effort to improve one's life with further schooling, working a second or third job, living a more thrifty life and investing the difference, etc. Worse yet there may be more of a tendency to fall into a life of not merely stagnation and perhaps poverty but crime as well. And in a society with such an unequal distribution of wealth as the United States the perception of class division leads to class warfare where those with much less than others steal from the wealthier, if not directly by muggings and burglary by gathering enough sympathy from policy makers to increase equalization of wealth via taxing the rich ever more and increasing benefits to the poor.

The problem with this philosophy is that handing out free things and money to the poor beyond survival necessities does little or nothing to improve their predicament and most certainly does not make them happier. And more recently some of the extremely wealthy individuals such as Bill Gates and Mark Zuckerburg are forecasting that technology and robotics will cause such a loss of jobs that our country should guarantee nearly middle class incomes to everyone no matter their credentials, intelligence or motivation. Gosh what a terrible disincentive to work hard, become well educated and use our brains! What an awful world that will be if it comes true. Will the definition of "working class" change to those whose earn the most with the highest skills while the remainder sit on the couch, play with their phones and shop for stuff they hardly need while living from the high taxes the working class pay?

Money alone in many cases actually is a disincentive to move up in socioeconomic class due how most of the less educated and poor tend to live primarily in the present. For people to become motivated and passionate about increasing their status they must not merely be offered the opportunity to have a better life but *choose* to walk on a better path and leave the poverty, crime, violence and drug culture, prostitution, poor health choices, etc. behind. Note how these lines above almost precisely expose the dangers of the philosophy of socialism – the concept of everyone in a society being guaranteed adequate housing, clean water, plenty of food, affordable medical care, education through the college level, affordable TV, phone and internet service, etc. in exchange for the rest of us to pay more taxes. We all become more equal but far fewer become outstanding as the higher government taxes provide reduced incentives for the wealthy and highly talented and motivated to produce many great things such as inventions and businesses that create more jobs.

# Humans Make Conscious Choices

It certainly is most intriguing that non-conscious or low conscious life operates in a manner that continually maintains order toward survival which involves health, vitality and reproduction but when *high consciousness*, the hallmark of being human, enters the scene we have something far more complex to deal with. This is because high consciousness permits us to ask questions and make choices consciously with explicit intent more than merely instinct. Doing so has enormous benefits though detriments as well. Consciousness gives us the great ability to focus specifically on increasing our knowledge and awareness of the world and the universe, learn how and ask why things work which can make life vastly richer, healthier, more interesting and satisfying under the appropriate circumstances and unfortunately cause considerable challenges to deal with on the downside as well. This downside is when we consciously know we are making poor choices but do not decide to change for the better. I do not believe chimps, elephants, dogs or mice do this because they operate via instincts which exist for the benefit of survival and procreation.

Human consciousness with its much higher level of thought process permits us to go *against* our instincts by altering our population through the use of birth control and consciously destroying our environment rather than merely co-existing with it. And more recently we are taking the laws of physics, chemistry and biology and inventing machines that are altering how we exist every day to the extent that many of us are detaching ourselves from the practical limits of reality. The possibility of having computer chips implanted in our brains that permit us to "think our way" to the internet totally eliminating computers and smart phones is not out of the question. In recent times we can intentionally move against nature by even changing our gender – at least on the surface though we never will lose what we were born with inside.

My definition of the word practical is the description of a conscious decision made that generally uses the least amount of resources to bring about the most satisfying result, a way of living that most any intelligent person should choose to do by maximizing what can be received from the world. As much as I believe in practicality it must also be acknowledged that humans are very complex and derive satisfaction from much that is not practical. We cannot quantify everything we do in mathematical terms of strictly resource utilization nor rule out the moral aspect of our decisions. For example, someone might drive to work a somewhat longer way using a bit more gas and time because they enjoy the scenery more. It would probably be wrong to offer a derogatory opinion of this choice based solely on the fact that this person is choosing to use more gasoline and time to commute, because contentment is what life is about and if one is more content spending a little more gas and time to commute then so be it. The same goes for a person who chooses to drive a larger car with the belief that they are safer no matter the extra fuel it uses because it makes them feel better, limited as this benefit may be. Educating the person that their use of a more economical car will statistically bring about a more desired outcome than their use of a larger vehicle can be attempted but altering human perception can be extremely challenging once it is engrained into the psyche.

What about the person who nearly has a pharmacy at home of countless vitamins, mineral supplements and power foods, etc.? Though perhaps misinformed and not able to understand that simply eating a full, balanced diet of healthy foods would be plenty adequate for good health, they feel more content in their belief that spending an extra couple of thousand dollars a year and countless trips, fuel and time shopping is providing them with better health. It is so easy for marketers of food supplements, minerals and vitamins to scam people into thinking that buying their products will improve one's health when in fact this extra material is usually just excreted. We should note that such products are extremely profitable and often sold through multi-level marketing operations where various people at all levels make money. And more sadly such people are quite vulnerable to the placebo effect – believing that taking a pill makes them feel better or that they would feel worse if they did not take it even though the substance in it is benign or redundant of what they receive from healthy eating. Let's not forget that there are some people who actually are deficient in certain vitamins and minerals for medical reasons that do need some supplementation.

Pure, straight practicality in resource utilization, while sensible in calculated terms (using the least to receive the most), does not always match our human emotions. However, if one honestly wants to reach goals

43

whether they are financial, improved health, better time management, education, etc. practicality works because it involves the *measurability* of reality itself. One cannot measure the benefits of the more scenic drive to work vs. the extra time and fuel usage because this is a bit like adding apples and oranges; any more than one can measure or quantify the satisfaction one derives from attending church over the cost of tithing, time and fuel to attend. Yet we all must reach the conclusion no matter our emotions that our lives consist of resource usage – time, energy and money being the obvious examples. These three primary resources are absolutely quantifiable with every event in our lives usually making use of any one or all three. And we cannot deny that the choice we make to use of any of these resources limits usage in another area with some exceptions. If we allocate more funds for our child's education we may not be able to take the vacation we planned on. If we use up our evening helping our son with his math homework we may not be able to clean the bathrooms or read our e-mails. Every resource has natural limits.

Exceptions might be exerting energy and spending money on a university degree as the degree could blossom into a highly satisfying, good paying career. The same can be said of the investor who buys real estate or stocks that increase in value in which the time and money invested generate a more prosperous life. I am of the opinion that the more we invest our resources into places that create increased value the better our lives will become. Helping our child with his or her homework and instilling healthy values increases the chances that he or she will have a higher quality life later on. Purchasing a high quality, dependable, well priced automobile that will last many years and uses less fuel translates into more resources that can be placed elsewhere to enjoy life more. Buying things that lose value and deteriorate quickly is poor use of resources while owning things that at minimum maintain value equal to inflation or better yet, increase in value, is wise. Life is meant to only improve with time. Forget the old expression to be "over the hill". Aside from a major health calamity life can only improve with age up until we truly reach our last few years.

Unfortunately many of us are permitting our weaker emotions to dominate over our true, higher, practical awareness and intelligence as in how we have created systems of morality and economics – one example being the need to have nearly immediate fulfillment and not caring how hard the later burden is to pay for it and another being the placement of human life on such a limitless pedestal that we have become willing to almost economically destroy ourselves into bankruptcy to pay for health care. Yes, we engage in hypocritical, oxymoronic behaviors – knowing for example that if one plots a graphic line of the costs of health care, entitlement costs and college tuition as they are now into the future against other costs, complete destruction of the economy will occur at some point.

However, we dawdle and dawdle while we could easily deliver mail only three days a week, up the eligibility age for retirement benefits to sixty-eight and largely eliminate labor unions which pay unjustified far higher wages and benefits out of proportion to supply and demand. This lack of action is costing others terrible burdens in high taxes and other costs. People need incentives to force them to work and therefore produce something of value to the society in order to receive most entitlements, colleges should be incented to stop raising tuition, we must vastly improve preventive medicine and kick the greed out of health care, and otherwise cut out trillions of dollars in waste, fraud and inefficiencies.

The unconsciousness of nature does not permit such processes to occur in the natural world. If it costs too much to deliver mail six days a week it would cease to be this way. Almost nobody would be sitting around collecting a check since in the natural world production must occur for a return to sustain life. Unconscious nature would never let a hopelessly defective animal live long if there were no possibilities for it to survive on its own and there are no nursing homes for horses, skunks, rabbits or cats. We need to examine our conscious choices and intelligence to truly survive in natural prosperity because artificial prosperity can only be temporary since ultimately *nature always wins* - subjectively for the better or worse. Human consciousness is an extension of survival and while it certainly can aid survival it also causes considerable dysfunction as it can lead us astray from reality and down questionable moral paths. While animals make instinctual choices based on the need to survive and reproduce humans take their much higher level of consciousness and bend and mold choices at will to engage in nearly whatever activities they wish, going way beyond such basic, essential instincts. Animals can't consciously engage in birth control as we do though succumb to the natural forces that reduce populations – most of which us humans now find horrifying and all but unbearable such as famine, natural disasters, accidents and disease. Animals do not obtain transsexual operations.

All I am saying here is that when we use our conscious mind to alter nature on our behalf in excess and ways that deviate from its natural course there is a price to pay because nature/god are the ultimate default winners. We create antibiotics and other medications and germs create immunity to them and the drugs contaminate our water. We destroy rain forests and build more power plants and if in excess the earth's climate may change to a dangerous level. We force by mandate that families only have one child and babies end up in the trash dumps or the population becomes sexually skewed as has happened with the Chinese. We give money and food to starving areas of the world and then they temporarily become healthier and reproduce more frequently creating an even greater starving population in the future. There have even been demographers who have speculated on whether it is more or less moral to eradicate malaria in parts of the world since doing so saves lives that then reproduce only exacerbating the poverty problem in the future. Examining the future ramifications of our present implementations is not always a simple task. The least we can do is engineer and design products to not only last longer and be more efficient but be disposable in ways that are least damaging to the environment.

So we muddle through life controlled to such a level by our emotions to receive nearly immediate short-term gratification that we frequently do not do what is best for the human race as a whole or for ourselves individually. We keep on engaging in unhealthy addictive habits, avoid making decisions that others will perceive as threatening to their poor habits and short-term desires, and otherwise procrastinate implementing positive change in part because some negative consequences may ensue along the way. Meanwhile we consciously are permitting our country to head toward bankruptcy no matter the solutions that we know are at hand.

No doubt this dysfunction of human behavior is an aspect of why civilizations that rise also eventually fall. We do not take action on problems that are easily solved if done proactively but instead choose to consciously delay such action only exacerbating being able to arrive at a solution – certainly a most intriguing behavior since it dooms us toward failure which goes against the very law of the nature of life to prosper. Sadly so many of our political leaders around the world merely keep "kicking the can down the road" in their own short term self-interest of keeping their well-paid positions in part due to a system that permits these behaviors such as not having term limits on our elected officials. Isn't human behavior fascinating! Sociologists will always have their work cut out for them.

If we truly want to have the best life we can have then it is essential that we engage ourselves in some serious introspection. Yes, we must examine our own behaviors – perhaps with the help of others such as those close to us or more objective counselors – and carefully consider why we make the choices we do. For better or worse all behaviors have an explanation for their existence. We may be highly focused on obtaining an engineering degree because we are loaded with curiosity and love to create, invent and figure out how the world works – getting up early, arriving to class on time and studying until we must sleep. We may be fascinated with a large variety of topics and wish we could live 1,000 years instead of less than 100 – ever frustrated that we must sleep because we feel the burning desire to fill our bucket to the very top while we are here with of all the knowledge and experiences we can acquire. Others may complete their schooling and remain unfocused for years merely drifting from job to job not being sure where their passion is beyond merely surviving from paycheck to paycheck. And worst of all are the people who have only the minimum level of motivation to survive and truly live on the edge. I also note that there are many combinations of the above and some people who seem to grow out of certain stages of their lives and discover their passions as their lives progress over time.

As stated in the previous chapter we first must create some level of *order* in our lives. Order is what lets our minds build and move to higher levels of fulfillment because clutter stymies this process. An analogy is someone dumping a load of lumber of various sizes in our driveway. We now have a choice. We can let it sit in a pile of disarray, neatly arrange the boards in our garage for future use or start building that tool shed we wanted. We cannot make the lumber useful until we *organize* it. The human brain operates in a similar manner. We must feel that having greater order improves our lives enough to make it worth the effort to create it because energy is consumed to create order out of disorder whether it is rearranging the load of lumber to make it more useful and occupy less space or maintaining a calendar and list of our appointments, bills and other essential obligations which clears the mind permitting new stimuli to be taken in and recalled. Now there is enough space for that pallet of roof shingles to be delivered. And with the calendar we will be far less likely to forget David's piano lessons on Thursday at 7PM, the car going in for an oil change next Tuesday at 10AM, that employee meeting at 2PM Wednesday, the job interview Monday at 3PM, Susan's ballet performance on the 12th of the month, the dental cleaning on the 17th at 1:30PM, my spouse's birthday, the old friend that said she would call on Thursday evening about 8PM, the plumber coming to fix the toilet Friday afternoon and more.

Every time we write something down on a list or calendar it frees up our brains and relaxes our stress levels because that responsibility is now confirmed outside of our minds. When my work schedule differed everyday working in retail I had a sheet in my wallet or one can use their phone rather than trying to recall their schedule in their head. Wallets, phones, keys, purses, work papers, perhaps a pen, needed tools and lunches if packed need to be placed in the same place every day because doing so *makes life better* and this is what this book is about. Packing a lunch the evening before work is ideal. Order improves life because it permits one to focus on that which naturally leads to accomplishment and therefore satisfaction. In today's world order is more important than ever with the countless websites, user names and passwords, various computer commands, security hints, account numbers, etc. required both at home and work as our brains can only recall so much. I have a whole file of this stuff several pages long!

All of us operate with some level of order to at least survive and many of us take order to a higher level which enhances our life even further. As expressed above creating order requires effort or work. For this action to express itself a signal from the brain saying "This is worth doing!" must occur. The brain fires the signal; we get off our buns and go for it. Yes, our brains must interpret that an action is worth the effort for the gain. We get in trouble when we are not focused and/or have low self-confidence. Low confidence has us not believing we can properly accomplish a task whether true or not which restricts our decision making to go forward with a task within the largely self-imposed limitations of our comfort zone. Many of us feel this way when we see the inside of a commercial jetliner's cockpit with all of its many dials, buttons, switches, flashing lights and other controls even though if we put our mind to it we might very well be able to properly fly such a machine as thousands of pilots safely do every moment of the day and night. Others feel this way upon opening college physics, medical or engineering textbooks with their pages of complex formulas, graphs and charts.

Some need continued confidence boosting by others via emotional support and recognition since they tend to feel of less value without it. Though I will happily accept compliments of this writing by my wife or other close relatives, friends or coworkers, I do not depend on their feedback to continue writing. I simply enjoy writing and learning and believe I am producing something of value to others. Those who need heavy support by peers and tend to follow what they do are generally followers, not strong initiators and are more prone to self-esteem and image problems as they move into adulthood. Let's make it clear however, that appreciation and recognition by others and better yet, the production of a work actually being utilized by the world and having its intended expectation of increasing contentment among people is certainly the most rewarding. If the invention of the telephone, camera or airplane had never left the garage or back yard of the inventor it would serve little purpose. Unfortunately countless great works of writing, music and inventions have never reached the very hands of those who may benefit the most from their use due to lack of funding for research and development and publicity. It is regretful that many talented artists are either never recognized or only after their death.

## Our Emotions & Personality Are Most Critical For Success

We have all heard expressions such as "The sky is the limit" and "Anyone can do whatever they put their mind to". In theory these positive expressions are true but in reality many of us place a variety of emotional roadblocks to following through. We often believe so strongly that we will fail that such self-doubt ruins any hope of success. Sadly we are not always right. I recall being quite a technophobe many years ago and only trusting mutual fund managers paid the big bucks to invest my money. I now use computers daily and have a better rate of return than many of the well paid mutual fund managers through buying individual stocks at lower cost. To have strong amounts of order in our lives necessitates self-discipline which requires high levels of self-esteem. But when our self-image is undermined by doubt, fear and other emotional detriments our sense of discipline and focus is compromised which causes us to fall into a sort of wasteland and only do a bit over the minimum to survive. We may become ambivalent, indecisive, bored, depressed and perhaps enter into destructive habits such as drinking, recreational drug use, uncommitted sexual encounters and other cheap thrills to escape what we believe is monotony for a period of time.

Healthy self-esteem is achieved in part from our inborn personality heredity but primarily from our environment growing up. If we have teachers and parents who regularly make sure that we try a large variety of activities and disciplines with solid positive encouragement, we certainly have a higher chance of feeling better about ourselves as we enter the working world than if from upbringings full of constant criticism, mocking, doubt and fear planted in us. I find it amusing when I look back on my life and recall one of my peak experiences of being in business for myself selling my photography on the streets of Boston, loving what I was doing and making the most money in my entire life to date. Meanwhile I was being told by those closest to me that I was a "meager street peddler" comparing me to the shriveled up old man selling popcorn who ironically was a millionaire with franchises all over the city which I did not know at that time.

Examined a little further this situation is very understandable since I had parents who were highly academic, had never experienced having their own business and tended to believe that advanced formal education was close to the only path to achieving career success. Seeing a little old man selling popcorn on the street did not impress them. As another example in my recent travel to Peru I visited the floating islands of Lake Titicaca where the Uros natives live and work. Initially one sees a series of straw huts and has the impression that these people must be extremely poor but on closer examination finds that this is not true at all. By the time they sell their beautifully handmade blankets and other arts and crafts and charge groups of tourists a couple of dollars each to ride their catamaran several times a day which cost them nothing but time and labor to construct they are easily able to support themselves. Additionally because they have minimal expenses to live such as utility bills and pay practically no taxes, they can easily stash away a modest amount of cash. If they had investment knowledge they could do even better though the concept of having extra cash beyond regular living expenses is largely an unknown way of life to many of the developing cultures.

## Procrastination & Defiance Prevent Success

Having confidence and self-esteem problems is tough but can be overcome. However, when strong defiance is also a major factor in personality recognizing one's own deficits, admitting to them (humbling oneself) and taking corrective action is far more challenging but possible. Defiance or not, one way or another, the day must arrive in which we introspect longer and deeper, look at ourselves in the mirror literally and/or figuratively and honestly ask precisely what we realistically want from life. Writing down what we want helps emphasize this further. We may become aware of such goals as completing our education, finding interesting work, moving, meeting someone special, saving money, quitting a bad habit, losing weight, etc. Whenever there is something in life that we don't have but we want we must exert effort and energy to obtain it. Surely this is obvious but it is this exact point where we initiate the decision and take action where our minds perceive the most difficulty – what many use the term lazy to describe. If we tend to procrastinate with negative self-talk, ambivalence and uncertainty our ability to be decisive is hindered. So it is our own personal consciousness that so frequently hinders or encourages us to succeed or fail at our goals, often more than our ability or lack thereof. Our emotions are often more critical to our success than our intelligence.

Procrastination is caused by such issues as perfectionism, confusion over prioritizing, being poorly organized, poor sleep habits, low energy, boredom, distraction, defiance, fears and low self-worth. Psychologists generally accept that there are several cognitive distortions involved in procrastination which are irrational thoughts and assumptions. Procrastinators tend to underestimate time required to complete tasks which causes them to rush through such completion when the task must be completed and assume that they will be in a more motivated, better mood to do it later. Perfectionism is the belief that one may never meet the standards one wants and/or is demanded by others such as parents, teachers or professors and work supervisors. Impulsiveness is another related component because the desire to place lower priority, easier tasks over more challenging higher priority ones often wins in the minds of procrastinators (play now, work later). We probably all know of children, college students and unfortunately some adults as well who watch a movie or sports game, play video games, chat online, etc. before tackling the math or chemistry homework, writing a paper, or shoveling snow – when completing those more physically and cognitively challenging projects would be completed with better gusto and quality early on in the day when one has a greater store of energy. And now with social networking and text messaging instantly available one must work even harder to say no to such tempting distractions.

The recreational activities rationally should be engaged in *after* the harder, more complex tasks are finished – back to what I call the principle of "hard now, easy later". Another aspect of procrastination referred to above is boredom. Cleaning my bathroom and vacuuming my floors which must be done again and again every week or so is exceedingly boring, though I certainly enjoy the benefits of a clean, neat home. Practically anything is higher priority on my list but I have to decide how much I enjoy the result even if competing for time with other tasks I prefer, having a dirtier place to live and/or a less satisfied wife. As for rebelliousness/ defiance such emotions are most wasteful because they are largely so self-defeating and spiteful toward others and generate a poor impression of oneself. Saying the hell with that dirty bathroom, laundry or cleaning one's room only makes one feel worse about oneself, increases anger and brings out further procrastination as well as makes one less appealing to others. This is a conscious emotion that one must grab control of but when feeling down there must be a positive incentive to do so, which if lacking may not light the fire.

By taking a greater interest in one's own desire to improve and committing to becoming more organized, prioritizing and experiencing positive results via small steps one can construct positive feelings and emotions which can remove one away from excessive procrastination. Ideally procrastinators should be placed in situations in which they cannot continue their bad habit without strong consequences such as lowered grades for tardiness to class or having their ability to support themselves (their paycheck) threatened for not being timely at work. School grades and money are usually taken quite seriously. When *conscious consequences*, those produced by others such as the lowered grades, late fees, employer warnings, internet routers shutting off access, or speeding tickets do not work then *natural consequences* such as being hungry for missing lunch time, losing friendships, having very expensive dental work because of missing appointments for exams and cleanings, being arrested for not paying a speeding ticket, wrecking one's car after repeated warnings of poor driving habits, or being forced to live on the street due to not performing properly at work and poor money management. Ultimately reality forces us to live within certain boundaries of behaviors should we wish to survive.

As time management skills improve out of necessity in most cases the brain will perceive the value of procrastinating less. Most of us must experience rewards to continue to take action in order to make our lives better or else we see little purpose in the pursuit. There are a couple of theories on evolutionary adaptations also. It may be that people in times and places in which energy had to be stored for emergency survival perhaps focused on more petty tasks first saving their energy in case of a calamity. In modern societies today we clearly have vastly more spare time and energy outside of only that needed for survival – time for reading, travel, sports, socializing, intellectual endeavors, decadent behaviors, hobbies, money and wealth management and more – so we are prioritizing differently and for different reasons.

However, even with this supposedly more spare time to recreate we also have far more things to keep track of and recall – debit and credit cards, loyalty store cards and bonus points, countless user names and passwords, college loans, car and house payments, other household bills, relatives birthdays, Christmas gift buying, children's needs and appointments, batteries and commands for how many different TV and related equipment remotes and their corresponding codes, retirement and other financial accounts, car inspections, repairs and oil changes, aging parent needs, keeping cell phones charged and various apps operating, perhaps obtaining another credential for work, keeping up with the news and politics and more. I ask what could be more useful than a date calendar and pocket notebook either on paper or in one's phone in this day and age?

Simply each day referring to a to do list and glancing at a calendar can make one create a big dent in procrastination, a habit that needs to become fully entrenched just like eating and driving to work. The list needs to be continually amended and updated almost daily. This is the basis of maintaining order to one's life other than keeping one's physical environment reasonably orderly. Also noting time needed for certain tasks and then making use of that knowledge in the future when the same or similar tasks are encountered assists with timeliness. Procrastination's greatest costs are perhaps in two major areas; marriage and money management.

A severe procrastinator can drive their spouse nearly crazy if they are married to someone who bangs out chore lists like a carpenter with a hammer, bag of nails and a pile of 2X4s. And the cost of delaying financial decisions can be nearly incalculable. As it is explained with detailed examples later on simply saving 10-20% of one's income while young can reap thousands of percent return later in life bringing one to total financial empowerment and freedom well before the standard retirement age of 65. My frequent advice to college students and those in their twenties to shrink their bills through a variety of means that do not necessarily involve deep sacrifice and/or to work an extra part-time job to pack away from less than $100 to around $200 a month which would bring about rewards they would be ever grateful for later on; unfortunately, almost always falls on deaf ears. Such behavior is primarily due to their young age when being 40-70 years old appears to be so far away into the future that it seems irrelevant along with often having the expectation to soon earn such a good living that saving such a comparatively small amount feels unimportant even though it is not.

I wanted to cover our psychological and emotional health first because after living nearly 60 years it has occurred to me that this aspect of our health in many respects may actually be more important or at least equally so to our physical health. It is most noteworthy how often I observe people who are about my age, are in poor health, way overweight and make regular use of the health care system, while for the most part I continue to feel very close to the way I did around thirty years ago. And my brain functioning in some respects feels more focused, aware and sharper than it did then. It is extremely clear that well over 50% of human health problems originate with our psychological and emotional state of being which leads us to our decisions and choices so it is not hard to deduct that when one has those mental areas functioning in a healthy, practical manner much of the remainder of our health falls into place for the better. Those with good mental health – loving life, curious and enjoying learning, reaping rewards from goal setting and fully engaged in self-preservation, being orderly and disciplined, avoiding high risk and conflict with others and having a spiritual outlook balanced with practicality – usually tend toward greater physical health as well.

# CHAPTER 4

# Our Spirituality

**A**NOTHER ASPECT OF our mental health is our *spiritual* outlook on life. In my last book I wrote about 70 pages on philosophy, religion and science in the first chapter. This topic unfortunately deeply raises many people's emotions. This is because most societies have taken the natural expression of human curiosity, wonder, awe and puzzlement over the grandest questions we have regarding our existence, suffering and death, human consciousness, and the origin and evolution of the universe and organized it to generate answers to these mysteries in ways that satisfy the majority in their comfort zone.

We first drew pictures, created music, dance and festivity and then developed whole systems of organized religion with their enormous edifices (churches, cathedrals, mosques, temples, etc.) and holy books loaded with countless references to various moments in history, stories and myths that are labeled as sacred – all in the name(s) of an almighty god(s) who is or are the ultimate source of everything that is. Again, we have *strayed from nature* and reality itself using our perhaps overly conscious and intelligent minds and generated these entire systems to attempt to explain these grand questions of mystery which we may never be able to fully comprehend. Such systems have been given serious credence, depth, authority and downright sacredness over the centuries attracting billions of people, hopeful for an "ultimate explanation", in order to firmly latch on to their beliefs.

I have minimal interest in debating if one religion is "better" – more historically accurate in its holy book, more morally and philosophically true, etc. and whether stories, supernatural events (Since everything is part of nature I ask how anything can be "supernatural"?), legends and myths such as resurrections, virgin births, walking on water, the existence of an afterlife, instant healing and such are factually true or not since none of such so called events can be supported via any method in which they can be shown to be *irrefutable*. People are free to use their consciousness to believe whatever they wish and mix reality and possibility with fiction and myth as they like. But *only* reality/nature itself is objectively true and directly affects our lives. Indeed this last sentence may be the most profound of this book. Reality, reason and rationality speak for themselves. A relatively newly used expression, "It is what it is", has some real intellectually objective merit to it. Outside of our human consciousness is the world and yes, it is what it is. Sure we can temporarily create and construct our human societies, religions, economies and corresponding infrastructure but this entire civilization will be extinguished in a flash in astronomical terms of the universe in only a matter of time and there is nothing humans can do about this.

Even if we seed another planet with life, that too will eventually fall fate to cosmological evolution with no recourse. I believe that those who interpret and operate their lives via rational principles of reality though not without reverence for that which we do not and may never be able to understand, survive with the healthiest mental outcomes. When we use our human consciousness to fight or oppose rational principles of reality we are merely challenging that which cannot be challenged – a form of insanity. We can only bend certain materials just so far before they break, only drink so much alcohol before it causes us trouble, and only go without sleep for so long before we feel miserable and countless other examples. We must accept the boundaries of reality and live a healthy lifestyle within them to survive. And though spiritual reverence for that which confounds us is healthy to have it is not essential to create entire belief systems with corresponding rituals and multitudes of fantasies within them and in fact can be harmful. Sure it can be harmful because leading people down a road of fantasy or potential fantasy leads them away from healthy rational thought and operation of life based on that which we have no choice but to confront. If it is essential to cross a fence to get where we need to go we can only walk along it sideways for so long; at some point we must decide to climb it, dig a hole under it, go around it or break a hole through it.

Fantasy is healthy and important for young children to engage in and harmless in small doses to adults who may read novels and enjoy fictional shows but to permit fantasy to actually guide and/or alter one's practical existence can throw us off track. One example is belief in astrology and living by its fantasies as opposed to astronomy which is the known, empirical science of the universe as we observe it. Where celestial objects are relative to each other or oneself that are tens or hundreds of millions of miles away do not and cannot have any relevance to human behaviors or traits.

It is *only our self* that ultimately makes the choice to go to work, complete a degree, wash our clothes, cook a meal, fix the car, finalize a divorce, lose weight or cut down that dead tree in our yard. Income tax forms are not going to be completed without effort nor are another entity such as a god going to do it either. The spiritual reverence for the gap of the unknown is healthy and quite normal and indeed arriving at a philosophical conclusion to comfortably resolve a level of understanding of such issues including the god concept is OK. This is because it is a natural response to offer hypotheses to fill this gap in our lack of understanding but we must stay conscious that these ideas are *only* possibilities because we are using our human consciousness again to essentially guess at what might be since we honestly do not know for certainty. In other words God is a possibility as an explanation for the origin and fate of the universe, life and human consciousness but *only a possibility, not an irrefutable fact* because the concept of a god is created by human beings, not necessarily the objectiveness of reality itself. When human beings propose ideas or theories they become subjective instead of objective, especially when the evidence can be questioned. Without objectivity we no longer have irrefutability because for something to be irrefutable it must not be tainted by living consciousness.

The instant a human being records an event there is great potential for bias whether as an individual or a group due to the psychological and emotional operations of our minds along with knowledge accumulated to date by that person or persons. In fact nobody observes, interprets and records their observations exactly the same way. However, machines such as cameras have no emotional and psychological barriers to interfere with objectivity. Therefore assuming the camera is functioning properly and no human being has altered it or the photography or video that it produces, the camera records the world *objectively*. So it is safe to assume that if a camera had been present during the many so called miracles presented in various books and documents written by human beings who are naturally susceptible to bias and misinterpretation, the recorded photographs and videos would most certainly demonstrate a different outcome in many cases.

We can never go back in time and set up a camera to prove such accuracy of observation so we can never know for absolute certainty. However, since in present modern times such events are not being recorded by objective means and by default of how reality operates are not going to be, certainly considerable doubt can be placed upon those that make the conscious choice to believe such events actually occurred in the past. If those who insist they witnessed miracles had a collection of people snapping photos and shooting video with their smart phones such events would have clear, empirical explanations.

Contrary to the strong opinion of many people one does *not* have to spend hundreds or thousands of hours reading countless pages of the Bible, Koran and other religious works to easily reach the obvious conclusion that reality/nature is all there is in terms of what we must confront and deal with, and simply operates by very predictable laws of science/reality and that worshipping, praying, singing and dancing – as much as such activities feel satisfying to our emotions – will not change the course of reality/nature. And certain mysteries will simply remain mysterious for millennia or even forever into the future such as pre-big bang. Pre-big bang is where the potential for some enormously greater force or power comes into play and why I accept the possibility of what the religious call "God" since by default there must be a first cause of everything. The firm atheist or astronomer cannot explain the origin of everything any better than the most devoutly religious person.

The difference is that that the religious person attempts to reconcile life with meaning, once again straying from reality, using their human consciousness to invent the god concept and firmly plugs in their god idea to fill the unknown holes of mystery. In my opinion this is an intellectual failure (dishonesty) due to the fact that a humanly invented concept obviously is subjective rather than objective. An analogy might be one opening the hood of their car and having to fill various fluids but not knowing which ones go where but instead just assuming that windshield wiper fluid goes into the gas tank, and gasoline is placed into the radiator, and brake fluid is placed into the windshield fluid reservoir – hardly a good action to take with one's car! Of course religious people will normally rebuttal such an opinion saying that their sacred book is loaded with "accurate witnessing" to many miraculous occurrences while such text was written and compiled via the use of human consciousness so prone to deviating from reality, especially during such primitive times. The atheist accepts that there are confounding philosophical and scientific mysteries that are not solved and may never be. There are a variety of people, some more spiritual than others, who simply admit that they *just don't know* regarding the ultimate grand mysteries. As an analogy I would much prefer to not to place fluids into any of the chambers of my car if I am not certain which ones go where.

By now some readers who are religious are starting to become highly defensive as their blood pressure rises when my intent is definitely *not* to offend or anger anyone but to simply clarify the difference between a system that human beings have consciously created (god and organized religions) and just pure reality/nature as it is. The religious will put forth multiple arguments to demonstrate that they are "right" because they will say "God created everything including reality." or that "God is within us." or lower themselves to degrading opinions such as "You are going to hell for not believing." "I know where I am going when I die." or "My belief in Jesus Christ, Allah, Buddha, etc. sets me free" indicating that one who does not believe as they do is of lower character, perhaps has a more chaotic life and/or is emotionally chained down in some way.

Obviously it is the truly free thinker who has carefully studied science, philosophy, psychology and religion that has a healthy grasp on reality/nature that is *truly free* as such people are aware of the *constraints* of religious beliefs. They have learned to realize that living under an umbrella of religious confinements is highly restricting to their lives and freedom and that they can live healthy, moral lives no matter whether they believe in a god, attend a church, formally pray, read a holy book or not and that they are equally as good human beings regardless. Believers and nonbelievers can be good or evil.

Believing in a supreme being under an organized religion offers such adherents a set of moral boundaries to operate within, which in their sense may be perceived as freedom from having to be uncertain where to draw behavioral boundaries. I lean in the direction of having clarity of my moral boundaries while not deeply adhering to any particular religion – taking the best of the moral values offered by most religions while not regularly participating in rituals or necessarily believing in what I feel justified in saying are mostly fictional beliefs and stories. Once one completely knows the size, temperature, composition, lighting, and other characteristics of a room and they stay in that room all the time, they can make the claim that they are free. This is because all boundaries and limits are totally defined leaving little or nothing to question. But let's face the fact that such freedom only applies for one living in this room so obviously the room is confining.

Another manner in which many of the religious may *feel* that having their religious beliefs has freed them is because now that they have an "emotional handle to grab onto" they appear to experience improved direction in their lives. They now know where the curbs are in the streets and which streets to travel on so to speak. They may feel more at peace living because their belief in a higher power reinforced by rituals such as praying and church attendance and other group activities, reading the book of their religion and even contemplation of the order of the universe from the perspective of their religion further instills their beliefs. Having such beliefs does indeed appear to guide very large numbers of human beings and in many cases significantly benefits them.

In an ideal world the religious of *any* persuasion who treat the world and others equally with dignity and respect as well as those who consciously choose to not adhere to a belief system *all deserve* to be respected equally. The sense that some experience a feeling of freedom through adhering to an organized religion derives from how religious concepts stand for benchmarks and defined boundaries. For many the delineation of boundaries sends the message that they now are free because they have a defined comfort zone. And indeed stress is relieved upon being able to gracefully accept rules which mark certainty over uncertainty. With certainty one can live *freely within* the rules. For others they view such demarcation as confining and believe that nearly every person who has differing needs, opinions and ideas should be able to live however they wish with the only boundary perhaps being blatant crime or murder.

The problem is that when humans congregate into groups based on a particular belief system that organizes, differentiation and separation occur which frequently leads toward bigotry and arrogance with exceptions of course. Though many may not directly behave in ways that degrade those that are not members of their group this is often the result. My Jewish neighbors on the surface appear just as pleasant and friendly as my Methodist, Catholic, Baptist, Muslim, Buddhist, Mormon, and agnostic or atheist neighbors. However, if I should have a more extended conversation, perhaps spend time in their homes and develop a deeper relationship with any of them the lines of demarcation become ever more evident. Pushed a step further such a conversation has the ever higher chance of becoming downright hostile as people defend their religious beliefs – the worst case scenario being when someone might pull out a weapon.

Countless people have died in defense of their religions; an astounding, pathetically irrational behavior, especially when taking into account that so many religious tenets are intended to promote peace. Religious persecution has been around for at least a couple of thousand years. Roman historians have shown that thousands of Christians suffered severe persecution that led to their being imprisoned, tortured and executed during the church's first three hundred years merely because they refused to honor pagan gods and engaged in more self-restraint in regards to food, drink and the pursuit of justice. And what has changed now as Christians are being slaughtered by barbaric people who claim to be Muslims, different Muslim groups are killing each other, and other religions are being discriminated against around the world?

So is all organized religion just a fairy tale based on a fluff of fantasies and legends? Though many of the highly unrealistic stories of events and sightings of miracles may well be, many of which either were misinterpretations of reality/nature due to humans more limited understanding of the world in the distant past or deliberate altering of observations to attract the gullible population at large to increase numbers of religious adherents, it is the *moral values* put forth in terms of our behavioral boundaries that have practical importance since they directly affect the present operation of our society. How respectful we are of each other, how we take care of our health, our charitableness toward others, how fiscally responsible we are, our qualities as husbands, wives and parents, our level of respect for authority, our sexual behavior, our orderliness and respect for the environment is what actually matters. We should also keep in mind that one's concept of God being divine or merely human has a significant role in our interpretation of various events. Additionally we must examine if placing divinity on a human being is a rational direction of thought or primarily fantasizing reality.

Yes, our *behaviors here and now* hold more importance over whether we believe in an afterlife, resurrection, other legends and myths or even a god for that matter. This is because the behavioral choices we make directly affect the outcomes of our choices regardless of our beliefs. Problems occur when we behave in hypocritical ways that defy our beliefs. A person who cheated on their spouse when asked if they believe in carrying out such behavior may well say no just as the shoplifter agrees that it is wrong to steal or the church preacher who inappropriately fondles children knowing this is wrong. We have free will to behave as we wish and often exercise it to our detriment even when we know the resulting outcome has a very high or even 100% risk factor to the negative. Our immediate need for perceived gratification overrides the more rational area of the mind that looks ahead and recognizes consequences. The need for sexual gratification, unrealistically quick short cuts to increased wealth, addictions and revenge are normally at the top of the list of troubling behaviors – those that we struggle with the most to control.

Perhaps these are the prime examples because they can easily be traced way back in an evolutionary perspective. The ultimate bodily pleasure of sexual release is deeply planted in us to ensure reproduction which when unfulfilled for an extended period of time and/or nature calling for greater variety within the human species to ensure that we survive with a more diverse gene pool calls ever harder for satisfaction. When there has been severe mental, emotional and/or psychological trauma including physical or sexual abuse or perhaps some type of in-born abnormality entering the scene, sexual behaviors can become unnaturally diverted into such behaviors as homosexuality, transgenderedness and pedophilia but the strength of the desire for release is similar, dysfunctional as it may be. Our sexuality is perhaps the most challenging aspect of life we deal with because it is a need that requests constant fulfillment – more so in men it seems – that when not routinely released leaves life duller without this great pleasure and leads some to approach others in ways they do not wish to be. I believe the sexual harassment accusations now so commonly portrayed in the media, much as some are fakes to intentionally bring down reputations, demonstrate how our biology (nature doing its job) is at the core of who and what we are. To ignore this need is clearly unhealthy to our mind and body. It is my opinion that men and women should become better educated on sexuality of both sexes and never underestimate its importance. As a man it is my rule to let women the first obvious romantic moves since doing do eliminates potential harassment accusations.

As for taking action to get rich quickly money represents security at our roots even though many of us realize that we could cut our incomes in half or more and still would survive. But regardless, that other deep area of our minds tells us that robbing that armored truck and driving home with those sacs of cash is an instant short-cut to not having to worry about survival. Of course robbers are not consciously thinking in that way during the spirit of the moment but this is what underlies the behavior. And revenge comes about from the need to "level the playing field" in order to create social justice which is essential for a human society to function within a reasonable level of calmness and peace necessary for survival of the species. Another cause simply involves the survival of the individual in self-defense though also has an effect on the society. Unfortunately our emotions can get out of hand and way overreact. Shooting my boss, should I feel poorly treated, and killing fifteen bystanders is not going to level the playing field though rationally discussing a problem with him or her may. It may not and when one's financial survival is at stake this can be a recipe for violence as the last resort, especially among those who perceive that there are no alternative solutions and are mentally unbalanced. Feeling trapped in an extremely painful situation certainly is a recipe for bringing out the worst behaviors.

For many people having a godly belief system maintains their moral status which without they would feel somewhat lost and confused since this is how they were raised. There is nothing wrong with maintaining such a belief system if it works for them but to express that others who feel differently are in some way missing something is wrong. Human beings are merely animals at the highest level of the evolutionary scale. We all are born with equal rights and the ability to be free. What religion we attach ourselves to or not is simply a result of our environment. Mormon parents are not going to raise Catholic children any more than Muslim parents would raise Hindu or Buddhist children. Yes, if we dare to step out of the box and declare ourselves free from any of these religions, we are frequently ostracized including being killed in some areas of the world.

Such irrational behaviors revolve around how religion affects our emotional and psychological brain components. This exists especially in the areas of gullibility – weakness due to societal peer pressure to fit into the group and needing an everlasting confidant (God) no matter if verifiable or not. For some knowing the god belief is a fantasy actually makes them *more* attracted to it because fantasy can be anything one wishes it to be. It can always be supportive almost like the life sized dolls that make great girlfriends who never respond negatively for some. The social aspect of church attendance has many psychological benefits; yet, many people have the fear of feeling emotionally lost should they dare to simply accept reality/nature as it is with many questions still unanswered. It is also no coincidence that religious structures are so ornate and spectacularly decorated in ways that emotionally please adherents along with soothing music to get in the mood to worship, honor and thank the deity – an activity I find to be quite unique in human behavior. All of this virtually priceless artwork and precious elements also represent the concept of selflessly honoring a deity. The argument can be made that such valuables could either be used for more practical purposes - perhaps in manufacturing machines and technology or sold to generate wealth in order to improve infrastructure and reduce poverty.

Regarding worshipping this is something to analyze as a behavior. Sure we can say that we are thankful for being alive and well but why? What am I other than another statistic of human life on the planet that is the result of a man and woman who made love, engaging in sexual reproduction as dozens of billions of people have been performing for millennia? I happen to exist just as worms, ladybugs, oak and banana trees, tigers, cows and birds do. I may feel fortunate that I happen to be born from middle class, loving parents in the freest, wealthiest country in the world and am thankful to my dear parents for raising me to become reasonably well adjusted. And certainly I feel fortunate to have good health. I think that some of the answers to why for the religious lies in the fact that we could be sick, injured or dead tomorrow and therefore, we feel humbled that we now exist alive and healthy.

However, I can also ask the question; what if the universe as we know it never came about or formed in a different manner so as not to produce the earth and humanity as we know it such as on the planet Mars. Isn't it all just random within the order of the formation of the universe? Or is there some type of consciousness involved in creation which many people give the title of god to? The truly honest answer is that nobody knows for certain though they may choose to believe based on their inconceivability of material reality being all that there is without a conscious entity. Albert Einstein once said: "Everyone who is seriously involved in pursuit of science becomes convinced that a spirit is manifest in the laws of the universe- a spirit vastly superior to that of man, and one in the face of which we with our modest powers must feel humble."

Here I must point out the difference between *fortunate and thankful*. Who should I thank if I win the lottery? The answer is nobody because I *randomly* purchased a ticket. Maybe I could thank my state government for having a lottery yet must also take into account that 99%+ of other ticket buyers are losing money to the state. But should I inherit money I have my parents to thank because they consciously lived in a manner that generated enough wealth to leave an inheritance and put me in their will. I could become ill at any time due to something I am randomly exposed to out the in world, a drunk driver crashing into me or an organ in my body that ceases functioning properly – despite my concerted effort to reduce such risks. I could have been born missing a leg, mentally handicapped in the ghetto of the Congo with hardly a drop of clean water to drink. I just happen to be me here and now and am the result of "rolling the dice" as to which sperm and egg bonded together. Incidentally well over half of the world's population is not in much of a position to feel at all thankful or fortunate as they are not far from the edge of survival.

This activity of worshipping crosses over into thankfulness, I think mistakenly at times. In addition does our deity or whatever ultimate force of the universe there may be *expect* to be worshipped? Not that I know of and in fact this is the last thing someone as humble as Jesus Christ or Mohamed demanded. I can praise a great leader such as a president for helping to create policies that positively affect our economy and well-being but I think I can question praising a deity for a couple of reasons. First of all the deity is an *unknown* possible entity and second, even if the deity is of the description most mainline religions adhere to why do we admire and offer praise to the deity considering that so much of the human race has so little to be grateful for and in fact lives in near squalor? The question of suffering has been leading theologians and philosophers to dead ends for centuries and truly does not have logical or even compassionate answers. Where religious belief or at least some sense of spirituality may come into play in a positive way is to *assist* the suffering. I certainly feel an instinctual desire to help others I observe significantly suffering as there is always a form of self-identification – the message ringing in the background that says that could be me or direct empathy to make someone else feel better.

What about a more naturalistic spirituality that gracefully accepts that we are a component of the flow of energy, time and space? I think we need to examine to what level our emotional consciousness is actually getting in the way of simply accepting reality/nature as it is. Are we permitting our consciousness to interfere with the acceptance of us being the animal that we are – being born, living, perhaps reproducing and dying? Sure we may leave a legacy behind for others to make use of and/or recall as I may do in writing this book, recording my life in a daily journal and large collection of photographs but I realize that I have no choice but to accept that at some point in the future I will no longer exist, period. Yes, as wonderful and all but miraculous that human consciousness is, it also combines with our emotional and psychological state to produce a mind that tends to stray and create possibilities and potentials for explanations of mysteries well into the fantasy world to cope such as gods, goblins, ghosts, messiahs, angels, witches, devils and demons.

Our brains naturally want to solve mysteries and find solutions to problems including the ultimate enigma of why the universe exists as well as human consciousness. Many of us will create "solutions" to these last two for our minds to feel that some level of explanation and resolution is within reach. To do so, large numbers of us jump over gaps via assumptions without complete, accurate, irrefutable understanding. Hence we end up believing in the impossible that we provide with the label "miracle". A miracle cannot occur by its very definition because every event that occurs in the world is explainable, even if not presently understood. A blue pumpkin is not a miracle because either someone painted it blue, placed a blue solution into it or if a photo used photo enhancement software to alter it. We do not have to dig deeper for an explanation.

My opinion is that Jesus Christ's birth occurred from the meeting of a sperm and egg via sexual reproduction as has every human being for hundreds of thousands of years though we are free to believe – stray from reality – as we wish. We can seek exotically obscure alternative explanations to substantiate our beliefs if we want to under pressure from many others who believe but again, *only reality* tells the truth. As for witnesses who wrote in ancient times what they believed they experienced, without the objectivity of mechanical recording devices we never will know for certainty because we cannot go back in time with such equipment. Therefore, how can we honestly believe with certainty? Without certainty we are not being true and honest with ourselves. Uncertain answers to the big questions of the universe, life, consciousness and death is not evidence for an imaginary being. There is nothing wrong with accepting uncertainty but there is plenty wrong with artificially forcing certainty on that which cannot be irrefutably verified to be certain. Certainty cannot arise from uncertainty!

Carried to the next level we have organized religions and cults around with such enticing, imaginative, idolized figures with books loaded with grandiose stories. Such stories are arranged with the intent to obtain respect from the masses that enables some leaders to gain control of and even exploit entire populations, not that these stories were intended to generate such outcomes in all cases. Are we looking for explanations for some mysteries that either have none or are not comprehendible at this time and therefore generating fantasy to fill up the gap? Worse yet are we being kept ignorant by so much acceptance of fantasy, getting reality and fantasy confused and intertwined at times and unwilling to learn real science? A mind infiltrated by religious doctrine to the point where it can no longer rationally think independently and be willing to read factual works in such topics as anthropology, astronomy, biology, psychology, earth science and philosophy books has been *conquered* emotionally (brainwashed) as with those with extreme political ideologies who flatly refuse to read views with differing opinions. Such closed mindedness breeds ignorance and slows the progress of the society.

There are many studies on the pros and cons of religious belief on our health. There are quite a number of studies showing marked improvements in health by religious devotees over those who choose to not be religious. And there are a several obvious reasons why this is the case. Engaging in spiritual thought, experiencing the communing of others with similar beliefs, surrounding oneself with soothing or inspirational music and spectacular works of art while accepting that a higher power exists over us keys into our deepest emotions which most certainly can lower blood pressure, cause positive hormonal changes and more. In addition most religions promote traditional marriage and teach restraint from excessive decadent behaviors, alcoholism and unnatural sexual expression which are values that add further to better health and longevity.

Such well-known atheists as Christopher Hitchens, Sam Harris and Richard Dawkins highly criticize religion due to its distortion of reality as well as the tendency for a relatively small minority of members to radicalize and create terror and mayhem. Unfortunately these radical minorities grab enough media attention through their heinous acts that some conclude that religions are to blame. In some cases they may be correct as when *leaders* of religions promote violence. However, leaders or not, anyone who becomes religiously radicalized is mentally unstable in some manner and often poses a significant risk to others. So perhaps we should throw the blame for radicalization more toward mental illness, lack of educational and economic infrastructure (There are a number of exceptions to this.), poor parenting and conflict of political and moral ideologies rather than religion though religion is often used as a conduit to support it. I still believe that whether officially religious or not, if one is deeply conscious of their health and lifestyle, makes appropriate time to relax, sleeps well, and is content with their social, work and marital or single life then they may receive the same benefits of the religious. What matters is how healthy the *choices* we make are over whether or not we officially join a religion though for many becoming a practicing member of a religion may influence them to make better choices which they may not make without such devotion.

# Irrefutable Facts of Knowledge VS. Beliefs

Science seeks to explore and understand reality/nature as precisely as possible via theorizing, testing, measuring and compiling information, therefore ultimately demonstrating proof so that when identical repeated actions are performed one obtains the same result with the goal of *irrefutable knowledge*. Science does not exist with the intent to marginalize religion though to some extent this has been the unavoidable result since science seeks to explain what is while religion attempts to explain *why* what is, is. I love the question why but to say "Why does the universe exist?" or "Why is there anything?", while perhaps are the ultimate questions a human being can ask, do not have answers or certainly not obvious ones. One can ask why there is a sandwich, the answer which is to be eaten but to ask why everything exists may be a nonsensical question because the sandwich has a known purpose/reason to exist – for consumption – but asking the same question about all of existence takes us off the chart! But science tries to do an honest effort at explaining *how* the universe operates. Science is not and never could be a religion nor is it something to be worshipped and in a number of respects is quite the polar opposite of religion in its approach to understanding the universe. It is however, something to be *experienced* and simply by existing we all default to science to some degree because science studies reality, not fiction.

Above I mentioned that virtually everything can be described by mathematics, perhaps even our emotional and spiritual mind because the thinking mind operates based on configurations of atoms and molecules biochemically interacting with energy that all can be described mathematically. So math is the basis of science and science simply describes reality, from every movement we make, how the blood roars through our veins, our eyes see, how our brains work, how we walk, how plants grow and bloom, how far away and hot the stars are, how old the earth and universe are, the chemistry of the oil in our cars, and endless more. Religion attempts to try to explain *why* all this grand order of precise scientific principles and life originated, certainly a venture to be greatly admired though perhaps unfortunately, leads us only down a very short road to quick dead end. It seems that our brains are lacking this capacity to comprehend such matters. This may be because the why to the question of the origin and purpose of the universe may not be the type of question that actually has an answer because the universe has always existed transforming in various ways forever.

Another possibility is that the religious are to some degree correct that there could be some "higher power" that created and manages it all. But then we run up against the inevitable question of why the higher power exists, what it is and if it is infinite in some way. As for the concept of infinity, though our brains can easily understand the concept that something may have no beginning or end we are not able to truly visualize it since everything we experience in the empirical world is quantifiable in time, distance, volume, depth, height, length, velocity, etc.

Another way to view and question the origin of reality and existence is to follow the logic of reasoning that insists that "something" - whether it is matter, energy, time or some higher power cannot originate from absolute nothing (no matter, no energy, no time, no higher powers, no vacuum). This unbreakable, foundational law of reality leads to the assumption that the universe has *always* existed in some form no matter if there is a higher power or not. Anything that one can give a name to is unable to derive itself from absolute nothing. If the universe is finite we have an extremely difficult, intellectually puzzling challenge for cosmologists, philosophers and theologians – that of asking what the universe is contained within since it obviously appears to be impossible for anything to exist without being surrounded by something else? As an old expression goes, when the spaceship reaches the brick wall at the "end of the universe" we can always ask what is behind that wall. Therefore the one self-evident fact is that infinity *must exist* by default since something exists now (us, trees, planets, stars, galaxies, quarks and god particles, empty space, time, dark matter and energy, etc.), therefore something must have always existed since something cannot derive itself from absolute nothing. Put another way, if there ever was a time when nothing existed there could not now be something! Perhaps this is where religion and science may come together since neither has certain answers – a commonality at the origin of everything.

Accepting reality as all there is rather than taking that consciousness we all have and deviating from reality and inventing fantasy is our brain operating rationally while deciding to go off on a tangent without honest, irrefutable evidence is an irrational choice. Unfortunately the brain can be relatively easily tricked by other human influences into believing that one is operating rationally when this is certainly not the case. Scientists have even discovered a "gullibility gene" in the part of the brain called the inferior supra-credulus. This may be a serious deficit among many who tend toward being more susceptible to money fraud schemes, vitamin, mineral and food supplement promotions that frequently offer little value for a high price, and most certainly cults and most organized religions.

Perhaps with our great sense of consciousness we can become more aware of this tendency and consciously counter our propensity toward such behaviors and not rationalize that because large numbers of others think and behave a certain way that it must be correct or good. It is well-known that there is a tendency for populations to vote for the more popular, higher polling candidate in political leadership races no matter who voters actually like. Unfortunately this behavior opens up the door to manipulative practices such as deliberately distorted polling to increase votes. We should be supporting the best candidate for leadership, not necessarily the most popular.

To simply summarize there are two forms of accepting. They are *belief and knowledge.* Belief is just that, only belief in something we are *uncertain* about. Many believe in the big bang theory of the development of the universe. There is reasonable evidence for it but not absolute, irrefutable proof. Though the theory of evolution is now about 98+% proven with various ape/humanoid remains being found, human DNA being almost identical to the highest ape, and the observation of human fetal growth demonstrating countless millions of years of development over its nine months of gestation but technically it is still only a theory. Beliefs in gods, resurrections, virgin births, messiahs, alien beings and ghosts are also merely beliefs with only limited evidence. The concept of divinity and miraculousness concerns something or someone that is not a part of empirical reality, therefore such ideas are in the fictional world and once fictional can have any attribute one wishes from a loving god to pink elephants dancing on the moon. Knowledge is that which is *absolute, factual and irrefutable.* I exist, the earth exists, the sun exists, plants grow via photosynthesis, various principles of chemistry and physics operate with 100% accuracy under the same conditions with irrefutable certainty every time they are demonstrated with *zero exceptions*.

So let's get it straight and clear our minds! Organized religion is based on the beliefs in a higher power which humans are attracted to for emotional and spiritual support which due to being human with our higher consciousness that we are naturally attracted to. Why? Because we want answers to why we exist and what our purpose is which many feel they can only attribute to a greater power. Christianity in particular is a religion which mimics human-like consciousness (personification) given to its god while knowledge is based on known reality of how the world is. One can never know God the way they can know that their car is parked in their driveway, *never!* This is because belief and factual knowledge are in two *different* realms. And God by definition must remain intangible and elusive for if not then God would be part of empirical reality and therefore not God. In their dire attempt to generate sensible explanation and comprehension of life and the universe human beings use their consciousness to create beliefs and the entire religious infrastructure such as churches, mosques, temples and rituals supporting the belief in a higher power. Unfortunately many devoutly religious people view their beliefs as full blown knowledge – being misguided largely due to a variety of emotional and psychological vulnerabilities.

When a religion or cult is able to convince its members that its legends, stories, myths, occurrences and messiahs stand on the same footing as irrefutable scientific knowledge then they have successfully commandeered a portion of their higher level thinking part of their brain. Again I should not have to apologize for appearing to criticize or denigrate religion and honestly this is not my intent. My true desire is to open people's minds to honest, sensible, rational thinking. I relish enormously in sharing, educating and helping others whether it be teaching them about finance, natural science, other places and cultures around the world, political issues and becoming more deeply aware of how to use our brains and minds to the absolute maximum that can be achieved.

Explaining to readers here that whatever their spiritual beliefs may be they may need further and closer examination, especially when under the influence of humanly created, organized institutions, I find extremely satisfying. This is because many years ago when I arrived at these conclusions the intellectual and motivational quality of my life grew exponentially. My mind became much less cluttered and I was able to focus on goals more clearly such as making certain priorities in my life. Examples are making my marriage better, staying meticulously on top of my financial goals, making time for being a decent father and fulfilling my great desires to more deeply absorb myself with nature and place ever more passion into my need to travel the world, record, learn, teach, share and assist others. And interestingly enough I feel more spiritual than ever while even being supportive of some religious teachings though I am not particularly ritualistic.

Also, a substantial portion of the population is more attracted to fiction and fantasy than the challenges that reality places in front of them on a constant basis. Reality is far more stressful to deal with than fantasy because it forces itself upon us on a continual basis regardless of our desires. With fantasy we have choices since we create it within our comfort zone. And what could be a better fitting and a more outlandish fantasy than the belief in a virgin birth, physical resurrection and the ability to instantly heel to support human divinity? Therefore this could be the ideal belief platform upon which to spread a religion – especially when the person being so idolized was also so well known to promote charity, compassion, humility and morality, state that he could forgive sins committed by those with the most evil of intentions and was the son of the almighty power of the *entire universe*?

Combined with the fact that the vast majority of people at the time of Christ and after for hundreds of years were poorly educated and gullible, very desperate for something to brighten their lives and believe in, and no objective recording instruments existed such as cameras and the answer becomes obvious. Supposed "miracles" are great magnets for religions, being ideal tools for indoctrination. As stated in different words above the word miracle is truly an oxymoron because the natural laws that govern all occurrences are unbreakable while the definition of a miracle involves the breaking of such laws, placing this word firmly into the realm of fiction. Religion thrives on mystery and fantasy, the first being that which we are not able to understand and the second being what we invent and decorate to enhance our beliefs. Now that we know that the whole earth with every human and all thoughts and knowledge to date is an infinitesimally tiny dot that sits in a dauntingly delicate balance that could be wiped out in an instant by a random astronomical event and inevitably will be at some point in time, such belief systems face the challenge of unstoppable reality.

Am I now supposed to apologize to the religious for indicating that they are weak, vulnerable, and gullible and merely believe instead of live by the irrefutability of reality and knowledge of scientific principles? Am I being arrogant for simply choosing to live by reality/nature as I experience it over consciously choosing to deviate out on a tangent of humanly created belief systems because I am mystified by suffering, death, the beauty and order of the natural world, life and the origin and evolution of the universe? Frankly I am well aware that for the religious their beliefs actually provide them with joy, excitement for life, drive, strength and energy no matter whether they are based on irrefutable knowledge or not. I have written this section to simply point out the clear differences between *believing and knowing* which I consider crucial in this discussion just as a meteorologist defines the difference between a cloudy, rainy day and a clear, sunny day. I find it particularly amusing how the religious often say to the free thinker, "Seek God and you shall find Him." when the whole god concept is tenuous at best and the more realistic expression should be "Find and you shall know." I like this quote from Jim Walker. "The power of faith has so forcefully driven the minds of most believers, and even apologetic scholars, that the question of reliable evidence gets obscured by tradition, religious subterfuge, and outrageous claims."

Let's make it very clear that arrogance is a feeling of superiority over others and it is often the religious who promote that their belief systems are superior, not only over each other's belief systems but over those who prefer to live via the experience of reality/nature rather than being part of a humanly created belief system on this infinitesimal speck in time and space of the universe. And there are extreme atheists who believe they are superior because they do not need religion. We have a choice to live rationally via the experience of reality/nature or more irrationally via belief systems we have consciously and artificially created as humans to attempt to explain mysteries. Let's also note that while mentioning the infinitesimal speck called earth that should there be advanced life forms elsewhere which I believe there is a very high chance of, we can speculate on the possibility of such civilizations ever knowing about any of our religions – almost certainly an extremely remote chance – reinforcing the near certainty that our religions are self-created on our speck with no relevance billions of light years away. Believe me; I obtain no thrill from criticizing religion except in the cases of radical extremism that leads to terrorism. I feel well-grounded on my views here and no apology is needed, for I want readers and all people to live their lives to their *full potential*.

Do I believe the world would be a better place without religion? No, because the majority of the human population either benefits from religion or at least believe that they do which makes them feel better about their lives. A number of atheists as alluded to above say that most or all of the greatest wars and killings have occurred due to religious differences, therefore concluding that if religion was exterminated the world would be much more peaceful. In theory perhaps but in actuality most conflict around the world involves struggles for power, resources and political ideologies more than religion itself. Iran wants nuclear weapons for power and deterrence over spreading their form of Islam and World War II was about imperialism rather than religion. On a smaller scale certainly there are religious wars or at least under the guise of "religion" as with the various skirmishes involving Muslims and Christians, Sunnis vs. Shiites, etc. though much of this is territorial and involves the ownership of resources, wealth distribution and ideologies. Some of the most extreme terrorist groups such as ISIS just seem to kill most anyone including their own with no resemblance of any level of sense, order or humility toward anyone – true savages at the bottom of humanity.

## Morality, Indoctrination & Radicalization

The *good side* of religion and godly beliefs is the moral guidance it provides to large numbers of people and the charitable giving around the world to the disadvantaged. As already discussed in different words there are many who maintain their moral compass based on their religious beliefs which keep them at a further distance from decadent, deviant and immoral behaviors and if this helps them retain a more ordered life so be it. The moral benchmarks of right and wrong are reinforced by most mainline religions along with a sense of reverence and respect for life and the universe. It is such benchmarks that provide for an ordered society which without we decay into a society of relativism in which right and wrong lose their intended meaning and can be redefined depending on circumstances. Healthy, useful religion is not about scientifically attempting to prove or disprove Biblical stories or even whether or not there is a god but to help provide *moral order* to the world. As true as it is that a secular society can operate relatively peacefully I ask how such a society defines moral benchmarks of our behaviors since many are not understood as self-evident.

When the religious simply use the word "God" largely as a way of expressing the ultimate order of life, nature and the universe there is really nothing for atheists and free thinkers to feel uncomfortable with. It is when the god concept is personified and used to segregate and control people via conversion to a particular religion that trouble often arises. And let us not forget that living a satisfying, balanced, moral life can be accomplished whether religious or not and that study after study shows that one's happiness/satisfaction level does not vary significantly based on one's religiousness. In fact a number of people view religion as a hindrance on people's freedom to think objectively. Indeed this is most certainly true among certain groups that not only take their religious beliefs literally but also become emotionally bonded in ways that create a whole new set of problems, some of which are very dangerous for societies. I could not get out of the box and produce this work here if I was overly attached to a religious or atheistic point of view. *Balance is the key.* Indoctrination however, can be very troubling; especially in parts of the world where theocratic governments encourage or worse yet, require specific religious beliefs.

In the worst case scenarios look at strict fundamentalist Muslim women in certain countries who are not permitted to drive a car (Saudi Arabia recently gave permission to women to obtain driver's licenses.), work, divorce no matter how often their husbands beat and rape them, cannot come within a few feet of any man other than their husband, father or brother, cannot show almost any part of their bare skin in public, are deterred from becoming educated, must pray several times a day and may be *legally murdered* under Sharia Law. In addition there are some people that refuse lifesaving medical treatments for family members strictly based on their religious beliefs which is ethically very questionable. The most troubling aspect of organized religion is when it takes on more of the attributes of a cult which can exploit emotionally susceptible people toward negative behaviors and even terrorism. Through such activities as long hours of chanting, beating drums, repetitive praying, and being exposed to antagonistic literature and videos may appear relatively benign to some people these activities are often the first steps in radicalizing minds so should be a warning sign to others. Should friends and relatives of such victims not be able to help someone appearing to be falling into radicalism it is their moral obligation to seek out law enforcement.

Virtually all religions in the world have sects and splinter groups with radicalization potential. For various complex reasons including theocracy style governments Islam tends to have more problems with radicalization and perhaps more violent expressions in the Koran that can easily be taken out of context. Traditional theory has suggested that large numbers of disenfranchised young people in poverty with minimal positive futures to anticipate may be susceptible. Just imagine oneself in desperate poverty with an anti-western upbringing living out in the desert and then some young guys come up and make an offer of $600 a month, shelter, food, water and a shining, new assault rifle. No wonder it is relatively easy for terrorists to recruit.

Interestingly this is not necessarily the case as first glance or assumption about this topic may suggest. Doug Saunders explores the reasons behind how and why people become susceptible to becoming terrorists in his excellent book titled, The Myth of the Muslim Tide. These quotes from Saunders introduce quite a different view that contradicts most public assumptions on the topic. "The image of the self-ghettoized Muslim living in a parallel society dissolves once you encounter the actual terrorists." And "A number of major studies of the demographics and psychology of terrorist recruits have shown that adversity, including poverty and violence, is rarely a significant factor in radicalization or terrorist recruitment. If anything, it is the opposite, as middle-class, well-educated Muslims are drawn into jihad." Additionally many Muslims and those of other very traditional cultures tend to resent Western values being all but forced up on them. Yet, regardless it is not the fundamentalist Muslims – again – as many westerners have been led to believe, that are more susceptible to radicalization but those who have been influenced to believe the West is out to destroy Muslim culture and to relish in the glory of martyrdom. Another possibility is for the Muslim culture to come together, disregard what sect they are such as Sunni or Shiite which clearly is extremely challenging, perhaps create a leader as Christians have the Pope and maybe even look at revising the Koran. After all the Bible went through a major revision from the Old Testament to the New Testament which promotes considerably higher levels of social order, civility and morality than the old.

## Extreme Anger Due to Unjust Treatment Is Dangerous

True fundamentalist Muslims adhere very closely to strict, traditional ways of life including strong restrictions on women which go well beyond reason in the eye of most other cultures, praying five times a day at the Mosque and strong family values and generally do not (with some exceptions) promote Jihad. Nobody has the intent to destroy traditional cultures (again with some exceptions such as women's and gay/transgendered rights) and martyrdom is never something to glorify! Unfortunately quite a number who would not commit a terrorist act themselves are in support of some of these very dangerous movements throughout the world. And though violence and terrorism most certainly do not resolve the emotions of anger and revenge many simply do not know of or have access to any other manner in which to express their extreme frustration. I think that in a more general sense it truly is the perception of an issue or law being unjust that causes some of the deepest anger in humans which may bring out the worst reactions.

Haven't most of us experienced thoughts of revenge toward others who we perceived have severely mistreated us? Bullying and mocking repeatedly or jealousy can cause anger to quietly grow and fester to a very dangerous boiling point leaving someone with the belief that violence is the only possible response. There are people who have had to leave their positions due to jealous managers because their work was *too good!* It is not difficult to understand why employees occasionally return to work places with a weapon after being unfairly fired from a job. There is not much that creates as much anger as the perception of extreme injustice on oneself, especially if it directly impacts one's finances and the ability to support oneself or a family. If combined with mocking one enters the danger zone!

Receiving traffic tickets by the police is largely also nothing more than a way to basically steel money from motorists, some of which goes to the state for road maintenance and some toward police departments – a billion dollar industry of legal theft that has minimal effect on highway safety. Surely it is not uncommon for motorists stopped by the police while driving plenty safely to wish they could take out some form of revenge on the police because they feel so unfairly invaded. Worse yet I know a friend who had a police motorcyclist accidentally drive into his van with multiple witnesses observing the event, lied about it, got away with the lie and even walked away with $50,000 by suing my friend's insurance company while needlessly causing my friend lost work time and over a year of stress because the cop tried to sue him as well.

Another great example is the police traffic camera installed at an intersection near a school that increased ticket revenue from a couple of thousand dollars a month to half a $million over less than three months. Though the accident and injury record for that area was flawless we all know that this camera will remain a permanent "cash cow" just stealing from the public under the guise of child safety. And people wonder why motorists become so angry that they become violent when the answer is obvious and perhaps even deserving (not toward a particular officer but the system). On the other hand police have a very difficult job, belligerency is in the minority and only in the rarest of cases do they deserve to be arrested or shot at. As for race related issues among the police of all races it is not surprising that they tend to profile and be more suspicious of young black men since in percentage terms this segment of the population has by far the highest crime rate. Unfortunately the media thrives on racism as another avenue to increase ratings so they pound to death the news of police shootings, especially if a white officer kills a black person, which only makes this problem worse. This problem would be solved simply if only people would obey the police! When a police officer says to freeze, drop a gun or whatever one is holding *don't argue!* Not following orders by police is a fast way to die.

If some Muslims perceive that the West is wrong to promote freedom for women to merely uncover their face, drive a car, chat with a male friend who is not their husband and work and earn money or for two people of the same sex to share their life together, this is their problem, not ours, because all human beings are born free with equal rights. But let's also understand that for the West to intervene in countries that legally suppress people from freedoms we take for granted is highly questionable no matter how harsh their laws appear to us. And for these media cartoonists to repeatedly and purposefully test the boundaries of freedom of speech by mocking and depicting Muslims as terrorists, though legal and in a sense good to set the example of one's rights, is offensive to many Muslims. Certainly deliberately inciting possible violence as has happened several times is something we as a society need to examine and consider the ramifications of. Yet clamping down on free speech and in particular defining exactly where we draw the line of what jeopardizes public safety over the right to speak freely is a most delicate issue to say the least. Sadly as we become more polarized with small groups consistently testing the boundaries of civility unlike ever before, we are moving away from understood common sense tolerance to ever more discord.

Suppressing any people merely because of their genetically inherited appearance or sex is universally wrong, not merely a Western concept, because it is simply ignorant. And other laws that restrict certain types of choices and behaviors also can bring out the very defiance and anger they are trying to stop. For example, placing someone in jail for years simply because they are legally carrying a gun in their car and merely drive a few feet over a border into another state within the same country which has different gun laws because they happen to receive a traffic citation and police search of their car would nearly make me want to commit violence. And what about the teacher who permanently lost his job because the school does not permit guns on the property because someone happen to notice he had his hunting rifle in his trunk intended for shooting practice after work one day? I will bet he thought about going right back into that school with the gun fully loaded with his finger right on the trigger! We have the capacity and ability to make the world a fairer place for everyone but make the choices not to. We must also realize that this may be something we all may never be able to agree on since what one believes is fair another may not. But at minimum many state laws could be universalized.

While I obviously do not believe we deserve to be terrorized I do believe that in a number of cases the United States and other westernized cultures need to stop interfering with the values of other cultures being expressed in their own countries unless clearly heinous and abusive. Though I believe that our system of constitutionality promoting "The Rule of Law", democracy, individual freedom and capitalism generally does lead to a better quality of life when ethically and morally managed well, I have reservations about pushing it around the world. And more than ever our culture is polluted with not so wonderful values in my opinion so I have greater doubts that "our way is always the better way". I was enormously pleased to see President Trump be so respectful to other cultures on his May and November 2017 international trips while also making it clear that those who want our protection must pay their fair share. Additionally he has increased pressure on China to get tough on North Korea and China is more than listening.

When I travel internationally I want to experience the culture and values of the country I am in – *not* American music, movies, excessive emphasis on diversity, promotion of the LGBTQ agenda, endless spending and borrowing, etc. Why else I am traveling out of the country? Americans should realize that we are not always the best and only a comparatively small part of the world population. I have seen simple forms of resourcefulness applied in innovation and adaptation involving various forms of infrastructure and how it is utilized in other countries that I never have observed here. This observation is largely a result of necessity of conservation to survive.

No matter our religious beliefs *we must survive* and how we mingle with and put to use reality/nature itself is *only* what is going to actually make a difference in our lives. Good, kind, loving, compassionate, creative and productive behavior is rewarded rationally with positive feelings and experiences it produces, as are negative behaviors that bring on destructive feelings of conflict, anger, regret, depression and revenge no matter if there is a god or not. To obtain the most from life we must be well disciplined and focused, be able to exercise self-restraint despite the appearance of immediate enormous reward, realize the rewards of delayed gratification, develop a kind and decent personality and hopefully read this book. Though under some circumstances extreme religious devotion can be similar in intent and outcome to the use of artificial substances, to attempt to leave reality using such substances as drugs and alcohol is real cop out behavior and does not belong in anyone's life.

With regard to our spiritual outlook on life I hope I have clarified how to think more objectively – to be able to stand back and distance ourselves and then decide what avenue we feel most comfortable taking. I sincerely hope that after reading these last few pages readers can more rationally and independently decide what type of spiritual path to take. This is whether through the rules of a god centered organized religion or just by living via the continual experience of life itself in reality with nature, simply nudging fate and randomness to one's benefit while gracefully accepting events when they occur beyond one's control and feeling comfortable that mysteries beyond our present understanding remain unanswered. Spiritual and emotional health can contribute to our physical health whether we obtain comfort and peace within from a belief in a god or simply carry a more optimistic attitude toward life by interpreting our circumstances more positively.

# CHAPTER 5

# Fast Guide to the Best Financial Management

A S WE KNOW all too well money is practically our conduit for survival in these modern times. Even for our most basic survival needs *we need money* and there is no avoiding or denying it if we should honestly want a prosperous life. Comfortable housing, food, water, electricity, gas, transportation, clothing, telephone and internet, entertainment, health care, insurance, credit, raising children, travel – you name it and there is almost always a monetary cost. This is just a simple fact of life of modern societies and need not always be one of grim frustration as it appears to be with most people, municipalities and governments. It is my firm belief that we as individuals and the society at large can learn to deal with finances in ways that are more ethical and moral, friendly and useful to all. However, due to our varying emotional make ups and personality dispositions, talents and skills money will always be problematic at some level to handle. There will always be tendencies toward greed among some, money avoidance behaviors among others, luck, materialistic insatiableness behaviors (the failed belief that one never has enough), corruption and fraud, and other psychological entanglements involving money. Money arguments are the number one cause of marital conflict and divorce and frequently a direct or indirect cause of war. But money can also be nearly our best friend once we know how to deal with it most effectively.

Unlike in my last book, I am trying here to provide readers quality information and opinions more at the individual level for direct usage than hoping to solve the world's problems. And at the individual level one can learn to make money a very positive force in life. The first issue surrounding money that always comes to mind is this problem involving our nature that we all think we don't have enough – a distorted emotional characteristic that may be traced back to our survival instincts to have more than we need in the present should necessary resources become scarce in the future. Back in the first chapter I already mentioned the study which demonstrated that more money beyond a certain point does not add to happiness or satisfaction in life.

I will mention one more perfect example that I literally just experienced on the job as I am writing this book. I assisted with a delivery of a new stove and refrigerator. As we arrived in the truck it immediately became clear to me that the neighborhood in this area was one of relatively low income since it was in a rundown mobile home park with mostly very old appearing vehicles parked in driveways. We walked in to the customer's home, removed the old appliances and replaced them with new ones. The wife was nearly in ecstasy looking at her new stove as she contemplated cooking with it and the husband delighted that they would not keep hearing an annoying screeching sound coming from the old fridge. The thrill was exactly the same as other customers receiving a whole house load of new cabinets, countertops and carpeting for over $35,000. Certainly a young person who wins $25,000 in the lottery and pays off their student loans in one lump is equally as excited as the older person who wins $250,000 and pays off their home mortgage in one lump – different amounts but the same principle.

I was motivated to write my first book on money in the mid-1990s when after spending almost fifteen years with my wife as we both struggled after college earning between $3.00 and about $8.00 an hour yet without government or significant family help bought cars in cash, purchased our first home, began raising a child, took family vacations most every year, and built up over a quarter of a million dollars in net worth. Meanwhile we observed friends, neighbors and coworkers who continually complained about their financial struggles, were buried in debt and could hardly even dream about taking vacations – yet most earned double to triple what we did. Naturally I had the huge desire to explore what we were doing differently that led us to enter into the middle class on near poverty wages.

I will now offer an updated, scaled down version of how we accomplished this and how readers here may do the same – even in today's higher cost of living and more competitive job market.

First let's ask you readers some basic questions of desire. Do you want to own comfortable, dependable transportation paid for in cash in a very short time? Do you want to own a comfortable home also paid for in cash or in a shorter time than the standard 30 year mortgage? Do you want to travel or have other avocations and hobbies to enjoy? Do you want to become debt free around age 40-50 or sooner? Do you want to be financially independent and perhaps retire from your work well before the standard age of 65? Do you want to avoid most medical care costs? If your answer is yes to the above questions then read the following. These strategies *do work* along with focus and discipline.

It is clearer than ever to me how we accomplished our goal of becoming fully middle class, being free of all debt by the age of forty and closer than ever to enjoying life to its fullest. After some discouragement over the minimal value of our college degrees and our good work ethics we relocated to a much more affordable area of the country, Texas, where despite low wage jobs we could still pack away from 20-50% of our take home wages. We regularly set goals of finding better work, saving for things we needed and achieving ever higher levels of savings in the bank. We were willing to live in a very simple apartment for several years in a mediocre area, delayed starting a family for a few years, bought most household items and clothing for practically nothing at garage/yard sales, were perfectly at peace never buying health and life insurance and had cheap, high mileage cars that we kept for many years.

Thrift and frugality became a deeply entrenched way of life, much of which we still are in the habit of. When a child arrived we simply maintained the same lifestyle with him. And frankly with the exception of areas of significant sacrifice why not continue the habit of thrift? Just because we become wealthier does not mean we should now spend more on things because that which costs more beyond the basic level of contentment does not bring on more satisfaction except for *experiences*. That wonderful weekend out of state with the grandchildren, Hawaiian vacation, or simply an evening with one's best friends certainly means more than the "latest and greatest" smart phone or Ipad! Much of the concept of thrift involves disposing of or not acquiring that which does not reap value and further contentment in life and targeting worthy resources more directly is precisely what does. Here is one way to view my life strategy regarding spending. If one spends money on a "better" phone, hotel room, car or whatever and receives a perceived value of 20% improvement but the cost is 50-100% more, then one is needlessly spending and better off saving this extra cost. A family can have a great time together eating lunch out of an ice chest at a park, a fancy restaurant or a fast food restaurant.

I have great memories of buying $200 worth of baby clothes and toys for $15 early Saturday mornings at garage sales while stashing the extra $185.00 into the stock market. We had free rabbit ear TV, paid $9.00 a month for a landline phone, less than $200 a month for groceries, under $25 a month for electricity, had no internet and gasoline ran around 90 cents a gallon. Life truly was simple! We did finally buy a house. It was small but plenty adequate and in a decent neighborhood with a mortgage of $530 a month. In addition to our low paying jobs we were willing to work at extra jobs as well. I took my frustration of not finding more professional level work and instead of going back to school and getting in debt while losing wages and further ability to save and invest, taught myself all about the stock market, mutual funds, IRAs, taxes, compounding interest and other investing strategies in my spare time and wrote my first book while my wife worked, obtained a teaching certificate and began teaching school.

We kept working hard and investing in the stock market plus we sold our house at a decent gain. We moved to Pennsylvania with enough cash to buy a comfortable house in cash in 1998, struggled again to find decent work for several years while the cost of living in Pennsylvania was higher than in Texas. And now the electric bill runs around $150 a month, the groceries at over $350, three cell phones at nearly $200, cable TV and internet at $90, much higher gas prices and horrible property taxes than run almost as much as our entire mortgage and taxes combined on our Texas house – yes at times it feels like we are still renting even with no mortgage. A point can be made that in theory people here never really own their own houses because of mandatory annual property taxes – mostly to pay for the operation of public schools no matter if one has children or not.

## We Can Do More Than Live
## Paycheck to Paycheck

Yes, despite the much higher cost of living now and unemployment problems in the economy I firmly believe that *anyone* with the right attitude and determination along with willingness to learn the basics of personal finance which I present here, and take reasonable risks can accomplish the goal of being middle class and having a financially good, satisfying life. Numbers have changed since my first book but the principles remain exactly the same. One must set goals, live with sensible thrift in all areas, take on some reasonable risks, be organized, and learn how money actually works. The thrifty lifestyle is especially important when young but is always a healthy, common sense practice even if rich for there is *never* an excuse to waste money. For those who are not willing to take on the commitment to improve their finances and instead make up excuses why they cannot set solid goals there is little purpose in reading this chapter. A poor outlook toward money is destined to keep one in mode of experiencing struggle rather than prosperity. Remember, the purpose of money is first to pay our essential bills but second to improve our lives over time – being free of debt and enjoying the freedom that money can provide *beyond* merely bill payments. Our potential is to go way beyond merely putting a roof over our heads, keeping the lights on, the car running, being fed and clothed!

Most everyone knows that they can combine car trips and drive a more economical car to save gas money, wear double layers of sweaters in the winter to save money on heat, insulate their homes more to save money on energy, buy stuff on sale – particularly close outs, shop at garage/yard sales, use coupons, shop around for car insurance, etc. But how many of us know *what to do* with the money we save by engaging in such thrift? Where does it go? Do we just have the attitude that "It's only $5, $20, or $50 so it doesn't matter?" Or do we realize that an extra $30 a month can make a difference over time and an extra $130 a big difference? Do we understand where to invest extra savings into places where it will grow safely? Do we buy lots of insurance because we have those around us and the media hounding down our throat telling us how we could go bankrupt without so much insurance in our lives, that buying it keeps our paycheck so low that we can never get ahead? Well, it's time overdue to place *ourselves* at the highest priority over the insurance companies, grocery stores, big box stores, gas stations, pharmacies, the electric, cable, phone, water and gas companies! Sure, we must spend to survive but in all of these areas we can cut and save and with that savings we can pay down debt, increase our savings and therefore build our wealth. Our *attitude* toward money and willingness to get organized and set goals is over 80% of what will create financial success and the other 20% or less for learning financial basics. The combination of thrift and wise investing is a powerhouse for wealth creation!

When one makes this critical decision to truly be passionate about financially arriving at where one wants to be, yet without being insatiable for more things that cost money, one is on the road to prosperity. Of course depending on many factors such as age, debt load, income, family size, cost of living, and perhaps an unfortunate mishap, becoming more comfortable with one's finances and actually achieving greater financial independence is possible sooner or later – hopefully sooner! One major mistake many younger people make is to live way beyond their means. Many buy costlier houses and cars than they really need, for example. Others blow through $hundreds extra each month on eating out and buying expensive drinks and clothing they do not need. Then they wonder why their payments are ruining their ability to save and get ahead. Just because one lands a good paying job and can make student loan, car and house payments does not mean this is how they should live – especially if they would like to become debt free ASAP, a huge start toward financial independence, which should be a goal. Here is a quote I happen to see posted on the side of someone's garage that sums up one key to life success so well.

"The reason most people fail instead of succeed, is that they trade what they want *most* for what they want at the *moment*" How could I say this any better than Napoleon Bonaparte? Everyone wants more financial independence, being free of debt, having more choices in life to pursue and engage themselves in their dreams. But most people either never achieve their dreams or only partially so – not because they do not earn enough money, not because they do not have enough education or are of a certain race or sex. People achieve their dreams because they want them badly enough to exert self-restraint in the present while also knowing that what they want most – what truly generates satisfaction and happiness – is not the next $50 dinner out, not unlimited comforts with their corresponding $300+ electric bills, not the cool sports car, but that which brings about a *permanent relief of anxiety about money* with the comforts, nice meals out and a nice car and home, vacations, etc. Yes we can nearly have it all!

It usually makes more sense to live simpler and thriftier and pay far more than the minimum on loans while getting rid of them at a much faster rate. Remember, we only have just so much time alive and time is a huge player in how money works. There is the principle of "less is more" which applies so well much of the time because less clutter means less stress and less or at least lower bills without significant sacrifice means more money for oneself to enrich one's life, while the use of less time to complete tasks without compromising quality opens up more time for what we cherish. I believe such ideas should become common sense to all as we age but oddly this is not the case with many people who continue to live far too much in the present with minimal regard for their future. The future becomes the present on a continual basis!

Unfortunately many choose to be their own worst enemy causing an *enormous price* to be paid later which may not be correctable since we have only so much time here. What we must all understand is that every moment we spend unproductive and/or unhappy is one less moment remaining in the "jar of life". There are only so many beans in the jar with each one representing a unit of time because life is finite. Of course the same principle applies to money. Every dollar spent now on anything including potential growth of that dollar invested is one less we will *ever* have access to no matter how much we earn because the instant that dollar leaves our hands and becomes someone else's it is gone from our repertoire. *Money spent is money gone!* I have created a comfortable, debt-free life and am able to fulfill my dreams mostly by spending less rather than earning more though I don't deny that earning more and spending less may well be the best combination.

Obtaining a high quality profession anywhere is no simple task. The traditional path, usually very taxing in energy, time and money, of studying to receive a university degree if in a subject area in demand in the work world, even after taking into account all of the resources placed into it, often does pay off. I really must emphasize how critical it is to only attend school if a degree honestly is going to lead to an interesting, decent paying occupation, for if not, then it largely can be little more than a big setback in moving one's life forward. If one is not going to work in a field which requires the degree then naturally I ask why they obtained the degree, spent four years generally not working and probably accumulated a pile of debt making saving for the future ever more difficult. Yes, if we are not careful attending college might be a black hole to our life. And who is to say that we must spend 4 years to acquire a good skill? There are many trades that earn good money with 1-2 years of schooling.

Employers pay people to get a job done well – degree or not though many do expect the degree. They also expect employees to carry themselves appropriately, be timely, have confidence, carry the knowledge to get the work done properly, get along well with others and are comfortable taking orders from above. The big first step is the interview. We are judged by others often within less than ten seconds odd as this may sound and five seconds may well be more accurate. And once an image and reputation is set in the mind of an employer changing it can be all but impossible. It is truly amazing how fast our brains interpret and gather an impression and opinion about someone else merely by a combination of how they are dressed and groomed, their style of eye contact and smile, tone of voice and mannerisms – and more often than not we are correct.

## Become Debt-Free, Stay Debt-Free, Pay Oneself Forever

Paying extra payments on a home mortgage can literally save tens of thousands of dollars over the life of the mortgage – especially if done within the first five years, after which the rate of return drops but still may be worth doing though with very low interest rates it could be to one's benefit to keep the tax deductibility of mortgage interest, and invest this money for greater returns depending on one's tax bracket. Then once one becomes debt free one can improve their lifestyle some and save more without those burdensome payments. But no matter what, even if one must work an extra job to do so, one must *always pay oneself first* every month regardless. This is the first law of personal finance – making absolutely certain that money goes toward savings (If the benefit is greater to put more at a rather high interest loan such as credit card debt then this can go there since this is a guaranteed tax-free rate of return.) consistently. According to CreditLoan.com. over the course of a lifetime, the average American today will pay more than $600,000 in interest on all the money he or she borrows. For those who prefer to not be average, *don't be average!* Become debt free as soon as possible, stop being a slave to payments, and earn interest instead of paying it, a guaranteed winning strategy.

A big part also is the ability to say no to the constant temptations to spend on non-essentials. There are households now spending upwards of $4,000 a year simply on smart phone service and cable channels – costs that did *not exist at all* twenty years ago. This is $40,000 over ten years or a solid year's income for many; funds that if well invested could easily grow to over $200,000 in another 20 years and generate $1,300 a month in income. Anything that carries a monthly charge is a *real killer* to the family budget.

## Start & Meet Financial Goals Now, Not Later!

Everyone needs to create some type of budgeting system because we must know how much we earn, what our bills are and what is left over. This is very simple to do. Simply create a couple of columns on paper or computer and write down the in and out figures to understand the flow of money in the household. Then examine where reasonable cuts can be made. If dealing with someone else that shares finances this can be challenging but must be dealt with honestly and agreeably reaching a point of mutual agreed enthusiasm. As stated earlier a major cause of divorce are bitter disagreements over finances since our brains view money as the key to survival on a more primitive level which triggers heavy emotions. Because the roots of our spending and saving habits vary considerably we all view money differently. Some are more naturally prone toward thrift and foresight into the future while others tend to spend more in the present for immediate gratification despite the fact that delayed gratification is most often the key to a much better life down the road of time.

Being at either extreme is not good, though on a temporary basis to reach a goal frugality is usually worth the sacrifice. After becoming more organized people usually realize that they can be the master of money rather than money being the ruler. Another great rule to stand by is "No matter how little my income is it will *always* be greater than my expenses." This is called living below one's means and should be a lifelong habit. By living more resourcefully one will always be better prepared for the day that fridge, computer or hot water heater dies, the car needs repairing, a funeral, medical occurrence, a wedding, new baby appears on the scene and college tuition. And better yet we will finally take those great vacations we have dreamed about as well. We may have to kick ourselves into high gear to create solid change and guess what? *Now is the time, <u>not</u> later!*

## Yes There Can Be Enough & More Is Not Always Better

As I have said in my other books, we must all reach an understanding of what it honestly means to have *enough* stuff in our lives that consumes our money, time and energy that all work together. This is what I call the "peak of fulfillment curve" which demonstrates close to where we have just enough material goods that provide us with the greatest return. Remember, life is precious. What is the purpose of life if we are wasting it instead of enjoying it? Almost none in my opinion! Just the way garages and basements full of junk we never will use need to be cleaned out (Ideally don't overload them with junk to begin with!) so do other things in our lives that consume our resources. Remember, we only have a limited supply of all resources to make use of while we are alive so let's get the most from them. Excess crap in our lives only is a drag so it is best to not create it and rid ourselves of it as soon as we can. We most certainly would not choose to tow a trailer around with our car if we don't need the trailer, right?

If we are paying for 250 cable channels but only watch less than twenty certainly there is room for cutting. Can our mortgage insurance be cut by eliminating mortgage insurance? There is always room for trimming energy and water bills. Can we benefit by moving closer to our workplace as gas prices rise? How about bagging our lunch at least three times a week which at a savings of at least $20 a week equals over $1,000 a year, equaling at least an entire year's pay during a working lifetime? Are we still writing paper checks, placing stamps that cost half a dollar each on envelopes, walking to a mailbox and waiting days for a bill to be paid or clicking a mouse a couple of times over a few seconds and being done with it or better yet on auto pay? Are we shedding our use of old incandescent light bulbs and now using mostly led bulbs which use a fraction of the power of these old ones? Are we considering buying a larger house for our expanding family or to retire in when what we have is actually just fine or could be modified for much less? When older and retired it should make more sense to want to size down in a one story house, have less to maintain, pay less in property taxes, have less to insure and secure along with a smaller yard to tend to – *not bring on more cost and stress*. I have seen many regrets in this area.

I will repeat myself one more time that obtaining the most from life relates more to how *we consciously manage our lives* than what we earn. So many people have this wrong who simply think that once they finally earn a certain figure, be it $25,000, $50,000 or over $100,000 per year that their lives will fall right into place and practically be perfect. Yes, a good paying, interesting job is a great addition to one's finances as well but real financial satisfaction arrives from the security, freedom and wider variety of choices that money may bring no matter the income and of course the quality of how our money is earned and moreover, our relationships to others in this world.

Choosing to major in a particular field of study primarily for the money will never be a winning strategy. Sadly so many people are misguided in this area as money is perceived as the ultimate goal in life while it is far from it. Money causes as many problems as it solves. The perception by most people is that more money will bring about greater personal freedom of choice in life. Indeed this is correct but only when managed appropriately. Someone earning $150,000 a year has more choices than another earning $25,000. But one's life stress levels remain about the same no matter the dollar differences. The stress of paying $2,500 a month for a mortgage for the higher wage person is no different than the $700 payment for the lower wage person. In my opinion the real key to greater financial satisfaction and avoidance of the greed trap of endlessly thinking that more is always better is to live well below one's means. The $150,000 income earner could pretend they are earning $100,000 and the $25,000 earner might to pretend they are only living on $20,000. This way the higher earner would save $500,000 in ten years and the lower earner $50,000 not including taxes or investment growth of the money. Instead most people spend most of what they make or even more than they earn which only brings about all kinds of problems of course.

Should our income honestly not be enough to have the lifestyle we had expected by this time in our lives even after implementing numerous strategies of thrift, there are other solutions. Obviously one possibility is to obtain further credentials needed to move up. Another is to find better paying employment and the third is to find a second, probably part-time job. None of the alternatives are ideal and they all require effort, sacrifice, and time but this is how the world works – the more one puts in the more one receives back. We must weigh and balance such options and seek the most appealing one to ultimately improve our lives. Perhaps it may be worth working a second job for a period of time to pay off a debt and then either continue working the part-time job to pack more money away or terminating it to have more spare time in the present. Going back to school to obtain more credentials is very costly and exhausting while also working though may be well worth it if doing so truly leads to higher income and more interesting work. Other possibilities include starting one's own small business, babysitting or at least exchanging babysitting hours with friends and neighbors to save on childcare, renting a room out in one's home, being a paid volunteer in a drug or college nutrition study, donating blood plasma for over $3,000 a year, buying and selling things on E-Bay, doing temp work or giving out food samples in grocery stores.

## The Insurance Mess (Or Scam?)

We also need to examine our employee benefits and fully understand exactly how much our paycheck shrinks from such deductions. Employers love to boast about their benefits such as health, vision and dental insurance, long-term care insurance, short-term care insurance, life insurance, 401k plans, legal plans, etc. We have been trained to buy all types of insurance to feel more secure in the case of the occurrence of some catastrophe in our lives. And yes, this is comforting for many. However, the principle of how insurance works which is to spread out risk among a large group to pay for the small minority who enter into unforeseen, unfortunate circumstances does indeed only help the small minority. This of course means that the vast majority are paying and paying for very few who need to use it, most of whom may never use it or most certainly will pay many times more for their insurance premiums than the actual cost of their usage if paid for in cash over time.

For example I have been fortunate to probably inherit good genes and also practice considerable preventive health and I estimate I have spent around $800 on all of my medical care and drugs over my 60 years while I know many who are constantly running to their doctor for something and taking various costly medications. Additionally, numerous people are paying more for their health insurance than this in just one month. With life insurance one can usually pay oneself the premiums, invest them and come out way ahead of the insurance pay out upon death unless one dies unexpectedly early which of course is much of the purpose of life insurance.

The whole health care and insurance issue is a terrible mess and grossly overpriced to the point of being an *outright scam* on the public. I reached the conclusion many years ago that buying health insurance would have reduced my pay so much that I never would have the lifestyle I have now so I chose to "take the risk" and not purchase it. But the real issue goes far deeper. The absurd cost of medical care will never come down to affordability in cash for those with an average income as long as there are third party payers (insurance companies and the government) to pay because there will be no incentive for the medical industry to be more cost conscious as long as it is assured of being paid by insurance companies and government programs. As a result I firmly believe that we need far less insurance around and that we mostly should be paying in cash *reasonably* for medical care. Additionally if people would save even half of what they pay for insurance each month they would have plenty of cash to pay directly for their medical needs in nearly every case.

As it is insurance usually reimburses little over half of the asking price which irrefutably demonstrates that those who pay cash should obviously not be paying close to the full cost. I reiterate that we need to pull the carpet from under the health care system which is insurance money to flush out the greed and fraud. Health care services should simply be based on supply and demand as is food, building materials, energy, household needs and clothing. Having the insurance component artificially sets the bar of what the medical industry can charge for its services and products at totally unrealistically high prices. The same principle applies for government and unionized wages and benefits being unrealistically high – because they have access to what they perceive as a bottomless checking account from tax payers rather than more directly what the market will bear. The third party payer system simply creates an environment ripe for non-competitive predatory pricing in which each individual is analyzed in order to shrink their wallet the most, the *absolute worst case scenario for the consumer.* Some alternative hospitals that take cash only for a much lower price are beginning to operate – so far mostly in the state of Oklahoma.

Florida attorney and ex-hospital administrator, Steven I. Weissman has blown the whistle on the health care industry, making it ever clearer that the industry is truly a scam of the greatest proportions starting with the most powerful Washington lobbyists. I wonder how we as consumers have remained so ignorant over the last five decades while tolerating astronomical cost increases in medical care and ever more complex insurance plans with ever higher deductibles, co-payments and exceptions. When one needs lifesaving surgery for a heart attack by the best, most conveniently located heart surgeon, why should we have to care if that surgeon is "in network" or not, after which when the bill arrives one just might have another heart attack? And why do we tolerate paying $400 for a blood test at one lab with a $40 co-pay with our insurance when we could pay $40 in cash at another lab for the same? Yes, there are now people who literally pretend they have no insurance because paying cash is less than using their insurance! Most everyone I know thinks I am crazy for going without health insurance but I have learned that those who run the industry's finances obviously have no ethics or mercy – caring about nothing other than endless profits, and that other than generating major changes in Washington, boycotting, staying healthy, and protecting ones assets are the only methods to fight back.

As another example I recently got an estimate for doing some body work on my car to fill and paint a rust hole. The body shop wanted $350 – of course assuming insurance would pay even though their actual cost of materials and labor were perhaps $60. I hired someone on my own who knew how to do this job and they only charged me $65. It used to be common practice for auto body shops to offer a much higher price if one had insurance to cover the cost, this of course being blatant exploitation of insurance companies. They soon caught up with this, lobbied to change the law which happened but now we all pay the higher price no matter.

## Insurance Defies Common Sense & Compromises Lifestyles

Another sickening example of how insurance interferes with the natural and moral manner in which people respond to situations is this real life example I experienced recently. I was assisting a group of people in cleaning a part of a housing complex, part of which had suffered fire damage. The building was insured. The insurance adjuster came out to this place and generated a report explaining what the insurance would pay for to replace. In the area of the building where I was working (largely cleaning things that did not need cleaning due to fire or smoke damage) there was no noticeable damage or even the smell of smoke. However, a large high quality couch, matching chair, a brand new treadmill in perfect condition, many other things and at least $300 worth of perfectly good, sealed food containers with quality food all well within the expiration date was *required* to be thrown away. Yes, *required!*

I asked the supervisor why I could not simply take home some of the food or even give it to a food bank for the poor and I certainly would like the $500 treadmill and others would have taken the couch and chair, etc. He informed me that if anyone of these items are placed anywhere other than in the trash, that doing so is considered "insurance fraud" which of course is punishable by law. So I estimated that at least $3,000 of perfectly good merchandise and food went right into the dumpster because "insurance paid" to replace it. A security camera is even placed over the dumpster to keep people out! Let's multiply this example times hundreds of thousands of similar circumstances and imagine the horrendous waste and environmental hazard being created. The insurance industry has created an attitude of "the cost does not matter, it's insured", certainly a morally bankrupt scenario that plays out constantly. There are solutions to this dilemma but as always, we must care enough to create them. Again, the insurance industry creates economic anomaly going against the natural flow of money toward the better good. In many other countries this example does not occur because waste is not tolerated nor should it be anywhere!

Similarly the hotel industry naturally promotes its "rack rates" first which are the highest prices for rooms yet if the traveler inquires they will find discounts for early booking, AAA members, various business rates and perhaps other types of discounts. Hospitals should be in the *competitive market* just like retail stores but having the third party payer stifles competition and worse yet allows them to be secretive about their prices. This same principle applies to subsidizing anything from college tuition to housing. When colleges and universities know more federal funds are coming into student's pockets via grants and loans they up the price accordingly. Meanwhile the higher costs fall on families and taxpayers struggling ever more to pay. Subsidizing almost anything is rarely a good thing, especially an entire sector of the economy, because doing so only maintains inflated prices based on the subsidy rather than the free market of supply and demand. Insurance also has pretty much the same effect on any market – guaranteeing payment of a service or product.

If I purchased every type of insurance – health, life, full car coverage (I most certainly do buy at least the liability as I realize I am driving a potential weapon and state law requires it.), long-term disability, short-term disability, home owners, personal liability, travel, etc. I might as well not bother to have *any* financial goals since so much of my paycheck would be gone well before being able to save anything extra. Insurance is really something to think long and hard about. If I were to tell everyone here never to buy any insurance, sure, most would prosper well from this decision but a small percentage would have hospitals suing them and ruining their credit, some might lose their home in a fire or total their brand new car with no recourse, have family life ruined from lost income due to the death of the primary earner, be sued by the neighbor who hurt themselves helping cut down a tree, become brain injured from falling off a ladder or have the once in 5,000 year tornado destroy everything. Insurance is a great concept theoretically in that with all participating all are covered for major mishaps.

The problem that arises is when those with modest incomes struggling to become middle class are paying insurance premiums at the same rate as the middle and upper income people, therefore a considerably greater share of their incomes which makes getting ahead that much more difficult. Yet those with lower incomes and usually lower levels of education tend to use most of these insurances more frequently than those in higher income brackets. I must then ask: Would it be fair to offer policies for those who earn less at lower rates than those who earn more? Perhaps not but then many should not be surprised at those who have not obtained high income that expect to reach middle class status who choose not to buy much insurance and instead take on greater risk for greater reward. Medical insurance in particular has become so expensive that young and healthy people more and more feel that they are throwing huge amounts of cash out the window every month which could otherwise vastly improve their quality of life. Life is about choices and risks that we must seriously contemplate.

The concept of everyone sharing in the costs of the very few is not new. Insurance has been around a long time and in some cultures they simply take up a cash collection from those who are less in need. However, in very recent times of the last few decades advertising and psychological fear tactics have become far more creative in insurance marketing, aggressive and manipulative of our minds, especially as money has become ever more a substance viewed as the solution to practically everything. And with the outrageous costs of medical care way outpacing the average inflation rate, the marketing of health insurance has been an easy score for the industry. In addition the legal industry has taken full advantage of more and more deep pockets with the growth of wealth during this period which has created an environment far rifer for suing.

So out go merry-go-rounds, jungle gyms, high tree climbing, giving away of tons of "old" but safe food by restaurants and grocery stores, going to school in -15 degree temperatures with eight inches of snow on the ground, etc. in fear of liability suits. Are we going to let our emotions be manipulated or enjoy the simple, common sense, reasonably calculated risks we always have lived with? It is a pathetic world if we can't let kids play on jungle gyms, climb forty feet up a tree or simply dress appropriately for below zero temperatures! We learn as children by exposing ourselves to the natural forces of reality and yes, occasionally we will get banged up, cut, bruised or even break a bone in very rare cases. Regardless I think it is healthier to get out and climb a tree rather than merely look at pictures of them on a computer or phone. Parents now even walk to and sometimes stay at the school bus stop until their child is picked up – never seen just thirty years ago. Perhaps the continuous news channels have made us fear that there is a pedophile hiding behind every hedgerow or tree which is absurd. This "helicopter parenting" that really got off the ground around 1990 and remains pervasive in the society has generally been a detriment to the emotional growth of children, not permitting them to properly mature.

So now practically everything operates in overkill mode out of fear of law suits costing us all a fortune while bank rolling the lawyers. I doubt I will ever fully understand what makes lawyers worth hundreds of dollars per hour when the rest of the population generally earn between $10 and about $40. And in comes ever more insurance and supposedly safer lives yet at what cost are we honestly safer? The cost is not only financial. It is emotional and psychological. We all have become much less aware of nature and the environment and how to become responsible for managing basic risks on our own than in the past. And almost everyone has reached the point of practically not being able to sleep well if they are not "covered" by shelling out ever greater portions of their paychecks for insuring nearly everything in their lives. Oddly, they seem to be nearly immune to cost increases no matter the sacrifice since not being insured is perceived as not being in step with nearly everyone else and placing one at a very high risk to the downside. We desperately need a revolution with the public finally saying they have had enough and just will not pay costs this high. We the consumers will hold the purse strings if we take more personal responsibility for our health and absolutely refuse to grossly overpay for medical services. Truly the goal for doctors should to become unemployed.

The health care and legal industries in particular, also fueled to some degree by the technology sector, have very cleverly and aggressively used fear tactics to tap into our emotions of insecurity. In addition such sectors of the economy are protected somewhat by their corresponding associations such as the American Medical Association with their disgusting lobbyists. We frequently hear spokes people from these industries via the media telling us that "we could lose everything", "damage our credit scores", "have liens placed on our property", etc. basically communicating the message that our lives could be ruined should we happen to become seriously ill, injured or sued without their costly insurance. Indeed for those who do not plan their finances properly, know their rights, understand how to negotiate, and generally make an extra effort to use common sense judgment in various circumstances there are very rare situations in which one may be up the creek without a paddle as the old expression goes. If one has significant wealth to protect it may well be worth the time and money for an asset protection attorney as there are trusts than cannot be accessed by the medical industry. We work hard most of our lives for our money so we must protect it.

## Children and Money

The sooner children can be taught appropriate money values and resourcefulness, the better. They most certainly need to know that water, food, housing, energy, internet, cable, phone, and money itself has value and is to be treated in a highly responsible manner. They should be given some modest amount of allowance to use, spend and save as they grow. Having a lemonade stand or assisting in a family business is a great experience to demonstrate how money flows. As they grow into their teens, they should get part-time jobs perhaps mowing the neighbor's lawn, babysitting, entering art, music, science, writing or spelling contests, house painting, etc. And should they take finance more seriously perhaps they could buy a few shares of some stock and watch how it performs or create a mock portfolio of real stocks. As clearly stated here earlier experiences and relationships mean more than money but money is an essential ingredient for comfort, security and when managed properly may also add potential for more great experiences. The experiences of operating lemonade stands, collecting cans and bottles for recycling money and selling my photographs set the stage for me to become acutely aware of the relevance of money and how to generate the most useful outcomes from it.

If a personal finance class is offered in high school insist that your children take it and otherwise the basics can be taught at home. Once they start working probably the smartest thing parents can do is match some or all of their children's earnings by opening and depositing money into a Roth IRA account in the child's name. An eighteen-year-old would have over forty years for it to grow tax free with no taxes owed from it upon withdrawal or investment returns which over this amount of time would most assuredly increase in value many fold tax free. When the child's income one day is much higher the traditional IRA and/or employer 401k might be a better choice depending on income levels. Also tax-free contributions by employees to 401ks are often matched to a point by employers which is extra tax-free cash in one's pocket, a very smart choice for employees.

## A Quick Primer On Personal Finance

So once one has some extra money left over each month by learning to always pay oneself first over all other obligations where should it be invested to grow in value? This is probably the area where most people make the biggest mistakes which even I did once many years ago. In addition to reading this one can read magazines such as Money and Kiplinger's along with trolling around many websites that discuss everything from basic investing to the more advanced. It honestly is rather easy to learn this stuff. I taught myself all I know now and regularly obtain returns that equal or exceed that of professional investors. Taking a personal finance class through a continuing education or extension service at a local college can also help.

First of all extra cash beyond having an emergency fund of a couple of months pay (Some emergency fund money can be in the form of a credit card assuming one has a reasonable amount of cash left over each month as this reduces cash having to be tied up.) in a local bank or place where it can be obtained fast for that unexpected new washing machine or car repair, money needs to be invested where it will grow over time at a rate that will *exceed* the rate of inflation which tends to average around 3% per year. Since banks at this time in 2017 offer interest lower than this one is losing money leaving their money in a bank which is why placing most it where it will grow faster than this is a wise decision. Never forget that most of our assets such as our house, our cash and most of our possessions should be either *appreciating in value or not depreciating* significantly or be of sentimental value. One cannot avoid this in all areas such as cars, appliances, furniture and some other household things but even many of these items can be purchased lightly used in good condition in which case the immediate loss from paying new is skimmed off upon purchase, therefore retaining a higher percentage of the real value and reduces the percentage of depreciation.

While mentioning credit cards lets briefly explore this topic. As most all of us know we can obtain a credit card which then permits us to purchase now and pay later, normally around a month later. Should we not pay off our credit card in full, interest will be charged which usually runs in some cases from under 10% to typically around 12-18% of the remaining balance due. And should we not pay on time usually a late fee will be charged which may be from $15.00-35.00. When we sign up for a credit card the rules are stated very clearly in the brochure that arrives with the card so if we are not responsible there should be no surprises. All credit card banks are set up for online payment that with our permission permit the card bank to withdraw funds for payment from our bank account electronically at no cost which is very convenient. After a period of time of using the card as well as making car and/or house payments, student loans, utility bill payments, etc. the credit system assigns us a credit score which is based on our payment history. The score called FICO runs from 300 to 850 with the higher number being the best. A new scoring system called Vantage is also in place with a range of 501-900.

There honestly is a best way to make credit cards work for us rather than against us. In addition to obviously not paying late fees or interest it is simple to find a card bank that offers cash back on purchases of at least 1%. Well, this adds up over time. I have received cash back of around $2,500 over my many years of having my card – funds that I simply would not have otherwise! Usually I just have that cash added right back into whatever I owe on the card a few times a year which allows me to lower my bills and have more money to save, invest or enjoy. Therefore, if one wisely uses their credit card and pays for most every purchase they make on it in full, the card actually *makes one money instead of costs*. Therefore, the more one uses their card *only* for what they would normally purchase with cash or debit, the more one receives back in cash. And there are also many card banks that offer airplane tickets and other bonuses. Check out nerdwallet.com/the-best-credit-cards to compare deals. The only drawback of credit cards is fraudulent use by criminals which unfortunately happens too frequently so one must always watch for charges that are not theirs which the bank will delete.

We must not fall into the trap of spending more merely because we have that large line of credit in our pocket however, which is why I emphasize only for that which we must spend on no matter. In addition often utility and insurance companies such as cable TV, internet and phone providers and auto insurance will charge their bills to one's credit card. Of course if a provider charges extra fees above the percent of what the credit card offers back it is clearly wiser to pay in cash, check or debit. Some people like to use cash or debit for everything knowing that purchases are fully paid instantly avoiding the dread of seeing a huge credit card bill at the month's end, a feeling I understand well, but as stated above, if a credit card actually pays one back cash, not using it as much as possible for expenses one incurs every month regardless, is *your money gone*. Engaging in that which is most practical and reaps the greatest rewards over our psychological and emotional entanglements is often what must be addressed in life.

Scoring is used to calculate the risk involved by institutions that provide loans to estimate the risk involved in lending money. The higher the risk the more interest is charged. When one applies for a credit card they will be provided with a credit limit, the maximum allowed to be charged on the card. This limit will be raised periodically with timely paying by the creditor. For a young person with limited experience using credit it is far better to have limited or no credit than bad credit. Though most places charge for one's credit score I did find one site, creditkarma.com, where I instantly obtained my credit score for free without having to more than sign up for some advertising which I had sent to a non - personal e-mail account. It is easy to obtain one's credit report for free at annualcreditreport.com which is a good thing to do since one may view all outstanding loan accounts and any possible errors which can be corrected by calling. If one suspects any errors they should contact any or all of the three credit reporting agencies; Experian-1-888-397-3742, TransUnion-1-800-916-8800, Equifax-1-800-685-1111 or their corresponding websites. Once a dispute letter is written and the agency(s) investigate, errors can be deleted from one's credit report.

Over the long-term it is not hard to beat the inflation rate which tends to average around 3% a year. There are financial planners who only receive commissions on one's invested money or accept cash for advising time, many who are very good at what they do, though it is not hard to research companies called mutual funds that one can invest in directly. Mutual funds accept investors' money, pool it together and invest in groups of various stocks and bonds which in theory reduce the investor's risk by spreading out the risk over many companies though investors can buy such equities themselves if they wish. While they all have some sales charges to fund their operations some such as the Vanguard Funds have very modest expenses yet fine returns as a whole. One can research the many mutual funds at morningstar.com as well as individual stocks and bonds. Yahoo Finance is another great site as well as MSN Money. Should one wish to carry their investing a step further they may open a trading account online with such companies as Scottrade and E-trade and buy and sell stocks, bonds and mutual funds. Another option is to invest in real estate though the costs and responsibilities of maintenance, property taxes, insurance and dealing with tenants comes into play which must be considered. Also for beginners and those with little cash to invest real estate is generally not an option as one cannot buy a $200,000 piece of property at $50 a month the way they may be able to purchase mutual fund shares.

We need to invest with time horizons. There are usually three – one for short-term time limits of up to about three years at which time one may need to use the money, one for medium term of around 5-10 years and one for over ten years to retirement. The shorter amount of time one may need to use their savings the less risk one should place into their investing since risk goes hand in hand with volatility as stocks never always move in the same direction day by day predictably. So with a longer time horizon higher risk in one's portfolio is more advisable since over the long-term the average annual rate of return for stocks increases due to the good years when the market rises significantly.

When one buys mutual funds that purchase big lots of stocks, bonds, real estate investment trusts, precious metal mining companies, foreign stocks, etc. they are buying pretty well diversified portfolios which keeps the individual from having to research specific stocks, bonds or whatever investments to buy. For the novice the mutual funds are great and simple to invest with and most all retirement plans and pensions are invested in them. One generally has been able to invest in good quality well managed mutual funds over the years and come out quite satisfied though more recently the economy and financial markets have been somewhat more volatile. Unless one has spent a fair amount of time studying these investments and feels comfortable it could be wise to consult with a financial planner.

Certainly one rule of thumb is to never invest in anything not properly licensed through the Securities and Exchange Commission, to buy some stock based on a rumor from a friend or coworker or play with penny stocks that trade for under a dollar a share with money one cannot afford to lose. Even with the best of intentions often by the time novice investors hear about a stock to invest in that stock may well have already appreciated substantially, making most of its short-term gains. In fact there are many "pump and jump" schemes in which several thousand people are sent postal mail or e-mail with overly sensational literature claiming that a stock will move up hundreds of percent in a very short time. The insiders who publish this jump in and buy the stock making the price go up and by the time the mail reaches others who start buying they take their profits causing the stock to go right back down just as some buyers come in causing many to lose money. We all work too hard for our money to gamble it away. This goes for wasting money on lottery tickets also.

## The Amazing Power of Compound Interest

Let's now discuss my favorite compound interest chart: We have two people who are each 22 years old and both of them have an extra $2,000 a year to invest as they choose. One begins depositing $2,000 into a traditional tax deferred IRA which averages 12% annual return and continues doing so for six years at which time he or she never contributes another penny for 37 years. The other 22-year-old does exactly the opposite – spending the $2,000 a year on him or herself for the same first six years and then begins investing the $2,000 a year for the next 37 years in precisely the same investment also in a tax deferred traditional IRA.

So the first person invested $12,000 while the second person invested $74,000 to achieve the same goal. The "magic" here is that both of them ended up at the age of 65 with very close to the same amount of money in their IRAs! The first person had $1,074,968 and the second person ended up with $1,087, 185. Does this drive home the cost of procrastination or what? *Wow!!*

The manner in which compounding works is so simple yet so incredible! If people read nothing else about money but this they may become inspired to be good money managers. $1,000 can accumulate to nearly a $million by age 65 if placed in a growth investment at birth without having to add any more to it! Let's glance at a few other examples to really make my point even clearer.

Saving merely $1.00 a day Monday through Friday - $20.00 a month or $260.00 a year - will accumulate to $3,433.76 at 5% compounded annually or $4558.10 at 10% over a ten year period. In 20 years such growth will come to $9,027.01 and $16,380.65 respectively. Over 30 years we are talking $18,137.81 and $47,045.29!

If one bags their lunch three days a week, thereby saving an extra $18.00 a week over buying it we are now looking at a savings of over $150,000 during a 30 year period compounded annually at 10%. Even math majors I know are skeptical but it's true!

What about that despicable habit of smoking cigarettes? At a nearly a pack a day this comes to at least $100 a month, not including the health problems associated with smoking which statistically is even more than this. $100 a month invested at 5% grows to $15,499 in 10 years, $81,870 in 30 years and $257,971 in 50 years. At 10% annual return this calculates to $20,146 in 10 years, $207,870 in 30 years and $1,471,243 in 50 years and at 12% annual return arrives at $22,404 in ten years, $308,097 in 30 years and $3,063, 983 in 50 years!

By having one less simple cell phone in the family at a savings of just $12.00 a month if invested at 10% equals $8,688.14 compounded annually over 20 years. Eliminating family cell phone service at $100 a month over a landline would reap a return of $207,870 at 10% over 30 years but now the cell has pretty well taken over though one can reap considerable savings by shopping around and using free Wi-Fi more than data.

Turning down the temperature on our hot water heater to a comfortable

115-120 degrees from 130-140 for a savings of $10 a month would grow into $21,713.21 at 10% over 30 years.

Spending $6,000 on our wedding instead of $25,000 will have netted us $49,281.15 after 10 years at 10%, $127,822.58 after 20 years and $331,538.80 after 30 years. If we are still holding on together after 50 years the savings arrives at $2,230,427.15! Remember; money does *not* buy love.

A $1,000 deposit will grow at a 10% annual return to $17,448.63 in 30 years but at $12% return it will grow to $29,960.46.

Sharing $1,000 a month rent with a roommate for *just two years* which saves $12,000 in rent at age 22 is worth $173,051.86 at the age of 50 assuming 10% annual compounding.

Obtaining 11% average annual return on our investment portfolio instead of letting our $150 a month deposit sit in a bank savings account at 2% annual return, assuming we begin with zero is a difference of $305.431.14 over 30 years.

Avoiding the use of ATM bank card use fees four times a week at other banks than our own at $1.50 each time 52 weeks a year turns into $32,223.77 over 35 years at 10% annual return.

Wearing glasses instead of contact lenses at a cost of $200 every five years for replacement glasses averaging $3.33 per month over $15.00 per month for replacement contacts will net us over $20,000 in 25 years assuming a 10% annual return.

These figures are approximated using annualized compounding before any taxes paid courtesy of www.dinkytown.net. Yes, this is *amazing* stuff to say the least! And it proves that even many who claim to be poor and indeed are in the poverty bracket according to government guidelines have the potential to leave poverty behind them. Getting at our inner psychology of why we will not engage ourselves in such relatively simple tactics since we all want to have greater financial means is the tough part but so incredibly rewarding. Perhaps my *favorite example* is one personal to me. Approximately twenty five years ago I purchased a hair cutting kit for $45. I calculated not long ago that the amount of money saved over visits to the barbershop for me and my son (I will never attempt cutting my wife's hair ever again!) if placed in a growth investment returning around 10% per year would now have added up to well over $35,000 – in a few more years to reach 1,000 times its value! And this only keeps growing in more than one way since the $4.00 haircuts from when I was younger are now between $12.00 and $20.00 while free is free so each time I spend a half hour cutting my own hair I am paying myself up to $20.00 tax free. Another real life example I love is buying a $110 wool sweater at a thrift store for $5.00 which has saved my household nearly $500 in electric heating per year, year after year and continues to.

One final example so clearly shows the enormous cost of waiting to start saving and investing. Suppose one saves one dollar a day and receives 12% compounded annually on it. For the person who starts at age 25 they will have $296,515 at age 65. But if this person delays beginning *just one year* and starts at age 26 they will end up at age 65 with $264,402 so that *one year delay will cost them $32,114*. If they wait until age 30 to begin they will have $116,858 at age 65, a cost of $179,658! $1,000 invested into a newborn baby's investment account by Social Security would be worth a staggering $883,000 if averaging 11% return for 65 years – obviously something the Federal Government could consider but when has Washington ever acquired such common sense? Truly incredible isn't it?

As one ages and begins working they could slowly pay the government back and the account could gradually move from aggressive investments to more conservative ones. So one has three choices; to become completely financially independent and fulfill the dreams that primarily money buys at a reasonably young age, eventually achieve the same goal by retirement age of about 65-70 or perhaps the third though I ask why such a person choosing the third option would be reading this book. The first choice is to *start now*; the second is to *start later* and the third choice is to *do nothing*. Of course all this wonder of compounding needs time so the younger one is, the more effectively time will work its wonders. The older one is the more they will have to save and the more aggressively they will have to invest which puts one at risk later in life that in itself is a highly questionable risk to take. And certainly nobody can guarantee the percentage of return.

I realize that not every dollar one saves in one area of life automatically will be put in a high returning investment but a very clear point is made. Being frugal early on, being disciplined to invest every month no matter what (first debt pay off and then wealth building), and learning the basics of how and where to invest can only make one's financial life a lot more prosperous. Another very important point to make regarding this compound interest stuff is not to become overly addicted in the sense that one walks around essentially being a calculator every time the in-laws arrive and the two families go out for ice cream cones – the ones I so clearly recall for 5, 10 and15 cents depending on whether for one, two or three scoops – now over $3.00 each bringing the total for the perhaps nine people in the two families to about $27! Yes, I know that $20 could be worth $271.19 in 25 years or $3,692.02 in 50 years and that we could buy a half a gallon for $3.79 but, as much as I hate this expression, at times like this we had better "get a life". I doubt we wish to be remembered by our in-laws or grandchildren as being a calculator all the time yet numbers do *always* dictate the truth!

Another neat and simple concept is called *dollar cost averaging*. For those who commit to an automatic investment plan and have a set dollar amount withheld from their paycheck or withdrawn from their bank account each month dollar cost averaging mathematically assists in one's total return. For example, if one invests $100 into a mutual fund each month, some months he or she will receive more shares for their money and some months less due to normal market fluctuation but in the long run as the market rises overall, one may receive more shares total than only investing their tax refund once a year or stashing savings into a money market account all year and then dumping $10,000 into a couple's IRAs. This happens as the price fluctuation permits the purchasing of more shares when the markets dips, gaining some market timing effect. Of course the theoretical ideal is to place that IRA maximum in right at the lowest point of the year. Being able to successfully time the market to this extent is truly guesswork even among the top professionals so I don't recommend putting much effort into it.

We must never forget tax strategies as they relate to investing. Of course all gains and dividends in *retirement* accounts go tax free until one begins withdrawing money from such accounts but most investment gains from *regular* taxable accounts, including interest, dividends and capital gains if a security is sold are taxable to some degree depending on one's income. Investors can sell shares of a stock, bond or mutual fund investing in them at losses and gains with them canceling each other out to some level in terms of taxes owed.

If we lose $200 on a stock or mutual fund we sell but gain $200 on another one we sold we pay nothing in taxes. And we can place funds (up to $2,000 a year as of 2010) into Coverdell child custodial education accounts for minor children in which gains are not taxed up to a point for individuals with adjusted gross incomes of under around $100,000 or married couples with adjusted gross incomes of under around $200,000. Cash gifts of up to $12,000 a year as of 2014 can be given directly with no tax consequences, a tax law that I wonder how is enforced. For example, suppose a parent writes a check to a car dealership for $30,000 for a new car for their son or daughter and the child drives off. If such gifts are for college costs and may exceed the gift limits of non-taxability some of the gift can be sent directly to the college in which case such funds will not be taxed. But the giver cannot claim their gift as a deduction unless their money is a *donation* in which case it will not help with tuition. And the American Opportunity Credit is an improvement over the older Hope Scholarship Credit. This Opportunity Credit covers the first $2,000 spent on tuition, fees, books and required materials and 25% of the next $2,000 in expenses. Tax laws are regularly changing so going to www.irs.gov will net us all the up to date information we need and where we can download forms as well.

## Understanding The Basics of Dividends

There are dividends (extra profits) which a number of companies give out to shareholders. I firmly recommend that one *always choose to have dividends reinvested* when using mutual funds since doing so will create growth in more than strictly share price increase. When share prices increase obviously the value of each share is worth more dollars and cents. When the shares produce dividends and/or a capital gain distribution which is money skimmed off the net profits of a corporation being distributed to shareholders, this money may be taken by the shareholder either in cash which the investor can reinvest in additional shares or use for whatever purpose. And sometimes companies offer a stock dividend instead of cash – the most obvious benefit being that taxes are generally not owed on this type unless it has a cash option.

If we choose to take the dividend in additional shares we will have more shares invested which means as the price moves up more money will be made by the shareholders at a faster rate than before. For example, if we own 100 shares of a company which trade at $10.00 per share ($1,000 value) on the day dividends are distributed and the company declares a dividend of $1.00 per share we will now have 110 shares priced at $9.09 per share. In other words we will still have the same total dollar value but the share price will drop proportionately to the dividend being paid whether in cash or additional shares. So there is no immediate result to the shareholder monetarily but now 110 shares will be available to grow in price instead of 100 which will provide greater growth potential in the long run. If 110 ten shares rise by 10% we see more actual dollar growth than 100 shares rising by 10%. In other words more shares are now working to complete our financial goal.

## Protecting Assets And Privacy

Last but certainly not least is the necessary protection of our assets and privacy. As already stated earlier, assets held in retirement plans are generally protected from most creditors though some may be able to garnish some of the income from them though rarely will. Money can also be placed in trust fund accounts which also are usually creditor proof though one will need a lawyer to set them up which may well be worth the fees involved if protecting a substantial amount of assets. Then there is what we can do ourselves such as being aware of whom we give out our personal information to. We all should have one file where we keep all of our passwords, user names, security questions, financial account numbers, Social Security numbers, etc. With our computer and the file itself password protected, and properly internet secured we should be fine though it is always wise to print out a paper copy with all this critical information and lock it in a file cabinet as well. I don't recommend keeping such valuable, personal information in highly portable electronic devices that can more easily be misplaced or stolen. Another option could be to keep such information in a secured personal website such as Drop Box yet I always question just how secure anything is online. While we are implementing such security we should also go to www.dmachoice.org/dma/member/regist.action and get ourselves removed from junk mail lists to further reduce our lives from clutter. Unfortunately we are all being tracked and watched through various systems by the government and some private enterprises as well so truly hiding is virtually impossible now except for the most technological savvy.

Junk mail just clogs up the post office and wastes paper. Of course all unsolicited e-mail should normally not be responded to and never open attachments from such mail as often they have malicious computer spy ware and viruses that deliberately ruin computers and/or steal the very information we are trying to protect. And we have the choice to unsubscribe to e-mail we don't want to hear from again. There are also "phishing" scams in which operators send e-mails that look very much like the real thing from financial institutions hoping to get our personal information. Some are a bit hard to recognize but most are not and when in doubt we must contact the real company we deal with to find out. And obviously the endless "lottery winnings" and flashing pop-up windows telling us we have won an Ipad or smart phone, etc. or a large inheritance should be immediately deleted along with ones that state that we must "click here" to stop some virus which probably is a virus.

We also must beware of our charitable giving since there are scammers waiting here as well. Go to www.charitynavigator.org to check them out before giving. The one entity that can pretty much get what it wants is the IRS so it is not worth cheating on one's taxes. Be honest, save all documentation for at least seven years and there will be little to nothing to worry about. And when filing taxes feels overwhelming get help from a professional or better yet use VITA (Volunteers for Tax Assistance) which can be found by calling your local government offices and online. It is free for most people. As for enforcing Obamacare's mandate to purchase health insurance enforcement was cancelled by President Trump so there is no more concern about being penalized for not having health insurance.

Note that being forced to buy health insurance from the government is only the beginning as long as the democrats are in charge. There is already discussion of keeping track of what foods people buy, how much they eat, how much time is spent exercising or watching TV as a way to be able to exert further control over people. Public schools have already been starting to send students home because their lunches are not up to standard! In theory some of these tactics have good intentions to improve health yet restricting freedom is quite another problem. If I want to stuff my kid's lunch box with nothing more than cookies and soda I should have that right! Parents are in charge of their children, *not schools*.

To briefly summarize, money plays a very pivotal role in our lives. How we learn to view money, learn how it grows, manage it and otherwise deal with it can place us most anywhere on the financial happiness scale from absolute misery to nearly flawless contentment in financial terms. Once we learn that continuously engaging in "if only" behaviors meaning if only I had this or that all would be fine and settled and therefore I will be happy, is not the true answer to contentment, we will have solved a major hurdle. However, there is always a feeling of accomplishment that a certain hurdle has been reached. And then gathering the full understanding of what it means to us to have enough will really top it off. Yes, the "if only" thinking drives us somewhat to complete financial matters and it is a relief to be finished with a financial challenge but there is never endless smooth sailing since sooner or later the boat will encounter some rough water again. We must understand that this is how life is and that there is no utopia. If we had everything we want from perfect health, perfect marriages, perfect finances and a perfect workplace we might actually begin to atrophy somewhat. Some conflict, stress and unpredictability is necessary though we can learn to contain much of it to within reasonable and tolerable limits.

## Being Practical, Sensible and Moral With Money

Let us not forget the Biblical quote from 1 Timothy: 10, "For the love of money is the root of all evil: which while some coveted after, they have erred from the faith, and pierced themselves through with many sorrows." Money does not corrupt people but the *excessive love* of it does which is also called greed. Media news is a great example. Whoever thinks we get honest, objective news coverage from most media sources is fooling themselves. Media outlets from TV to radio, newspapers and many internet sites cover the most sensational news that people want to hear to receive the most listeners and readers to be able to charge the highest they can for their advertising sponsors – Yes it is all about money, not news and often not honest news and even false news to keep up ratings for money. Why are drug prices double in the United States over other countries for the same drugs? It is because of corruption in the industry which again, all boils down to money. Until the human race can get grasp on its basic selfish desires and truly know what it means to have enough the advancement of civilization may continue to be threatened.

If our families have been smart with their money, planned and invested well we may inherit a sum which if rather large could significantly affect our future. At some point this topic will have to come up, hopefully in a practical manner. Certainly our parents and we should always have a basic legal will describing our desires of how we want our assets distributed to our children, charities or whoever. Wise families who have healthy relationships and wish to pass on wealth to the benefit of the next generation have several choices. They can gift away assets to help children and grandchildren with major expenses such as college, perhaps buying their first car or a down-payment on a house. As long as there is plenty of money for retirement years extra can be given away well before death which permits the giver to share in the satisfaction of the receiver. I believe it is sad to observe wealthy elderly people hold onto all of their assets until their death and never see the joy money can bring to those who honestly can responsibly benefit from it whether it is their children, friends or charities.

Also, to avoid seeing most or all of one's whole life savings vanish into the hands of the medical system and nursing homes which charge over $10,000 a month it is best to give a lot of it away early on. Early planning with a financial advisor on such issues is also highly recommended. Some say concealing assets to keep wealth preserved within the family may be adding to the government going bankrupt since Medicare/Medicaid will have to pay what one cannot pay privately. While this argument has some validity what is really needed in addition to aggressive self-preventive care is enormous pressure on the health care and long-term care system to charge far less for its services and it seems that the only way to accomplish this is to simply *make less money available* to the medical schools, providers, suppliers, equipment manufacturers and drug companies. There are requirements regarding downing one's assets which change too frequently to cover here but must be looked into. Generally appropriate planning and implementation of such strategies must take place several years in advance of one needing long-term care.

# CHAPTER 6

# Healthy Behaviors and the Family

T HE MAJORITY OF human beings are gregarious creatures; they enjoy and significantly benefit from interaction with each other. Numerous studies have shown that generally people are healthier and live longer if they have regular contact with others in a mutually positive relationship. However, some spend far more time alone than others or choose a life of singlehood coping better than others would under the same conditions. And now with the various forms of communication technology available more are physically alone but in regular communication with whoever they wish. Facebook is a fabulous invention permitting me to share whatever I wish with whomever I choose anywhere allowing an incredible exchange of information permitting me to enrich my life ever more! I have now reconnected with people from over fifty years ago, old friends I never dreamed I would meet again and fascinating people from cultures all over the world.

Skype is free chat and video and is the next best thing to having someone right in the room with us! I ask what several of my interests and passions would mean to me if I could not share them with others. My beautiful butterfly collection, over 60,000 photographs, my writings, and opinions on various social, moral and political issues, my love of travel, watching and attending sports games, concerts and movies and more would retain considerably less meaning to me if I did not have others to share such interests with. For most people life is simply richer and more stimulating when *shared*. Feeling needed and appreciated by others is important to our well-being. Touching also has clear health benefits under various circumstances.

Carried to a much deeper level of friendship, the relationship between two people who experience sexual attraction toward each other, usually male and female, which is the biological design for perpetuation of the species, is quite another aspect of life. A permanent, intimate, committed, loving relationship is a positive addition to life and includes numerous health benefits. To recognize and celebrate such a union of a man and woman who have the potential to create offspring most all societies title it with the word *marriage* as they have for thousands of years.

In recent times in the United States and some other countries LGBTQ relationships are being given the marriage title which for numerous reasons I do not agree with. This is because I believe without animosity toward anyone in retaining the standard definition of marriage based on the irrefutable fact that male and female sexual organs are designed to come together like pieces in a puzzle, have the potential to create offspring and that same sex marriage opens the door for marriage to have practically any definition one wants. Already in California courts have been looking at having more than two people being married. One man even tried in court to marry his computer expressing that he received so much sexual satisfaction from viewing pornography on it. Are dogs next? A woman tried to marry a train station as well. And who knows where this movement may lead us as we endorse conscious forms of sexual expression that deviate from how our bodies are obviously designed for male/female copulation. Another offshoot of the acceptability of more varieties of sexual expression is the reduction in interest in traditional marriage by young people. And add in the availability of choosing mates by merely touching a tiny photo on a phone app now often reduces romance within people dating to little more than sex hook up appointments only killing the beauty and sacredness of intimacy so longed for in marriage.

Such behaviors which are naturally tempting with the ease of access to such technology may supply people "the frosting on the cake" without the cake leaving a real sense of emptiness without the fulfillment of a real relationship and lowered interest in marriage. Such hooking up fulfills the most basic biological need but does virtually nothing for the need for deep, compatible friendship and emotional support which is essential in marriage. In the past most people delayed sexual intimacy until marriage but now this is comparatively rare only bringing down the excitement and anticipation of marriage itself, almost certainly one cause of why young people are delaying marital commitment more now.

Additionally parents of the 1980s and '90s children have raised these millennials with more freedoms and perhaps placed more emphasis on school performance, finding work and money than dating and marriage. Now we have a set of young people who often view marriage as an old and less appealing way of life with commitment being viewed more as a hassle perhaps in part due to the increased divorce rate and something that can wait much longer. And having children is also frequently viewed as a big responsibility and expense over the joy of having a family in part due to a rather sluggish economy during the first 10-15 years of the 21st century though I think more due to increased selfish attitudes, high housing and medical costs and student loans. A lifelong marital commitment that works, however, is still usually viewed as the most ideal with its feelings of security. Humans naturally gravitate toward that which is perceived as easier while not having to be forced to mature and marriage and parenting most certainly do place us into a necessary higher level of maturity. It is no coincidence that our birth rate is down considerably and the rate of pet ownership is way up which many choose now over having children. And obviously the gay movement does not encourage baby making! The constant appeal of social networking has also had a negative effect on dating and marriage with more young people connecting online than in person.

This quote from the Heritage Foundation website defines marriage so well. "Marriage is based on the anthropological truth that men and women are different and complementary, the biological fact that reproduction depends on a man and a woman, and the social reality that each child needs both a mother and a father." There most certainly is something very dysfunctional about denying the self-evident differences between men and women which exist for a variety of reasons from the essential need to reproduce to emotional and psychological characteristics needed for the most ideal parenting.

Study after study confirms that children perform best and statistically become more well-adjusted adults due to the complimentary influence of a *mother and father*, ideally the biological parents but many do fine adopted as well. Frankly it seems peculiar to me that studies on this topic even need to be performed because this fact is so obviously self-evident. And though most mainstream religions from around the world affirm this biological and traditional relationship to be the healthiest, this model of the family goes back well before the firm establishment of such religions. As children mature their behaviors which are largely developed via their relationships with adults most close to them, namely their parents, assist them in one day being able to better relate to the opposite sex.

## Let's Stick To Common Sense

Sons and daughters who regularly observe their mother spending more time in front of the mirror and packing more cosmetics in her suitcase in preparation of trips and seeing their father shaving his face and more engaged with his tools is being prepared for his future. This not to say that women do not become adept at using tools but let's face it; How often do we see female diesel mechanics and heavy equipment operators or male manicurists and childcare workers? What is the point of denying our natural tendencies, desires, talents and abilities? To prove that two men or two women can raise a child successfully, that we can function with both sexes in public restrooms, that women can perform well on the front lines of battlefields carrying 80 pound backpacks and men can be good stay at home fathers?

We all know there are examples of well-functioning exceptions to these stereotypes in our culture and some other cultures have other norms in which women actually do at least an equal amount the hard physical labor. But when it comes to mothering biology divides the sexes by default. Men cannot breastfeed. Men's muscular skeletal system is more designed for heavy lifting. I could learn to become adept at driving my car backwards to work, use a brick to shave with or a leaf rake to shovel snow but what is the point in doing so when the risk for a negative result is obvious? I could also set my dinner plate on a chair and sit on a table but again, to do so is not natural since a chair is clearly designed to sit on while the table is designed to place objects on such as my dinner plate.

As discussed earlier when we make the conscious choice to go further and further against the laws of nature/god (reality itself) we enter a *danger zone* where the human society becomes less prosperous in every way. The scary part is that we now have a significant part of the human society that is endorsing more of these unnatural and risky behaviors whether it is sexual deviance, placing ourselves in wild, dangerous motions and positions or the consumption of broken glass and highly toxic substances to create the latest internet video. When we cater to the whim of every minority's ideas and what they perceive as rights in the society we become ever more chaotic, unnecessarily complex and therefore less productive, efficient and orderly causing further social decay. This occurs because the mainstream majority of a civilized population must carry the weight of everyone who deviates from the norm in ways that generate a cost that we must all inclusively incur. Freedom without responsibility is not freedom at all because freedom beyond certain boundaries infringes on others freedom often created by these boundaries. I have the freedom to safely drive but if someone else obtains the freedom to drive through red lights and stop signs I lose my freedom to be safe on the road.

At what point do we take action to change or create laws? Generally speaking laws are created to protect the safety and well-being of a society along with living within "reasonable boundaries" of morality. Defining the boundaries of morality is where it becomes dicey for many in present day society, though interestingly used to be self-evident and not something to question. I have neighbors who leave their outdoor Christmas lights turned on close to twelve months a year. I could complain to my municipal authority but choose not to. Should a neighbor's dog regularly defecate in my yard or keep digging holes in my gardens I would probably take some level of action – initially attempting to communicate with the owners of the dog. Should this not bring about desired outcomes I could contact my appropriate local government authority to deal with them or sue them. If I should poison or shoot their dog then I most likely should suffer an appropriate consequence. When too many people "take the law into their own hand" society can degenerate into a danger zone as we see in many parts of the world where law enforcement is minimal at best and corrupt at the worst. Questioning norms is harmless but acting on them is quite another story.

## The Law Is The Law Whether You like It Or Not

Worse yet, is when what have been standard offices of authority such as local, state and federal governments not merely loosen laws but intentionally ignore them as has happened numerous times with our federal attorney generals under Barrack Obama. While laws banning the recreational use of marijuana and same sex marriage were still on the books in various places attorney general Eric Holder deliberately ignored enforcing such laws simply due to his own personal opinion! And President Obama also ignored what he did when he could have stopped this or even fired him. This type of behavior by a person in such a position of authority is a classic example of societal breakdown, especially when nobody seems concerned other than a few conservative news reporters. We don't violate a law because we do not like it and perhaps think we are above it. We vote and legislatively change it.

One can view pornography online in the privacy of their home if they wish but should one get involved in *child* pornography they receive a penalty for this as they would if they walked down a public street naked. Patronizing such sites is equated with child abuse or purchasing illegal drugs. One may be using their own earned money to buy and perhaps use the child porn or drugs in the privacy of their own property but by doing so is supporting child sexual abuse and drug trafficking which the law states is wrong – I should hope everyone reading this agrees. Laws are laws and must be enforced as they are written or simply taken off the books by a legislature of politicians voted in by the public, *not* by individual court judges.

Following through with the rule of law has become less fashionable which is only softening the social/moral structure of the society. And when laws can be changed by a single judge's decision – legislating from the bench – the majority is being forced against their will to comply as has occurred in the gay marriage issue in various states before the Supreme Court legalized it everywhere. Bypassing or turning over public referendums is almost never a good thing. Why should 75% of a population who disagree with a proposal with 25% who either don't care or are supportive of the issue for only about 1% who actually may make use of a potential law?

## Minorities Can Not Rule Majorities

I understand that even that 1% must be treated with dignity and respect but do not believe it to be a good thing for a majority to have to be forced into not merely treating a minority politely but *endorsing* a dysfunctional sexual behavior with the same label that nature placed in our bodies for normal sexual functioning. And please do not tell me that homosexuality is in any way normal or natural because it cannot be, or try to make the argument that normal is different to the individual so it can be whatever one believes it is. I can't say that it is normal for everyone to love chocolate but I can say it is normal for everyone to enjoy eating because our bodies are designed to acquire pleasure from food in general. Normal sexual functioning is the act of copulation between a man and a woman with a small percentage who vary from this model who are not normal, not very complicated at all and almost never questioned in all of human history until the past decade or so. The standard definition of normal is "the usual, average, or typical state or condition". Abnormal does not necessarily have a negative connotation.

Liberalism is steadily lowering the thresholds of what has been considered to be understood common sense decency for many centuries, undermining our moral foundation. The limits are now being tested on a regular basis unlike in the past. Many questions are being regularly asked by sociologists and political theorists in this regard. Though the classic example may be ancient Rome numerous civilizations have been through cycles where liberal policies break down a civilization at its maximum or peak where the largest percentage of its citizens are adequately provided for, crime and decadence are comparatively low along with unemployment and families reproducing at a bit more than replacement rates.

Then the stage arrives where greed at both the individual and governmental levels starts to become out of balance as corruption also increases. Class envy increases and jobs decrease in certain sectors of the economy due to improved technology and/or outsourcing. The government goes deeper into perhaps unsustainable debt due to corruption, unwise spending, poor policy making and covering the increasing amount of poor and illegal immigrants. Progressive ideas come along such as the celebration of LGBTQ lifestyles, abortion on demand for all nine months of pregnancy, polygamous marriage, legalization of mind altering substances, support of labor unions that overly burden or bankrupt cities, states, corporations and tax payers, freedom for some criminals and illegal immigrants, a weaker police force and military, concerns about the rights of terrorists who have no purpose other than to destroy civilization, ever more entitlements such as food stamps, welfare and Medicaid, increased government subsidies for things such as health care and insurance and college tuition, income equality at any price, and the limitless printing of money.

Finally the crushing national debt causes catastrophe in the financial markets until the citizens pull out their guns and revolt. Perhaps civil war breaks out to some degree and then the country turns to tyranny and perhaps a dictatorship. There are clear signs that our great country may be headed for very challenging times. The saddest part of this is that we have the knowledge, ability and intelligence to change the course yet are choosing a potential path to destruction instead. President Trump is trying to put the brakes on this destructive economic path that President Obama accelerated, yet our country remains so politically divided.

This path toward breakdown permeates most everywhere even in seemingly insignificant areas as we accept and tolerate ever more behaviors that were simply understood as something either one does not perform or certainly not in public in the relatively recent past. Here are some examples. Not long ago all public school children placed their hand over their heart and recited the pledge of allegiance to the flag to help reinforce patriotism and love of our great country. Now schools and teachers make the *choice* to engage or not engage in this activity along with the National Football League Not enforcing its policy to stand during the national anthem in honor of those who have served the nation. The great classic works of literature are rarely taught anymore while social studies textbooks have been interpolated toward the left along with corresponding class discussions that often denigrate our country. The list of recommended books to read for one school district not long ago included a novel on how to murder your teacher. Have we become so afraid of "stepping on someone's toes" that we are permitting political correctness to seriously divide us? To accept, include and pay for every behavior and belief outside of the norm with virtually no limits will inevitably create ever more complexity, chaos and cost to all. Is this really what we want in the name of political correctness? The majority will only tolerate so much inconvenience, cost and morally questionable behaviors before they revolt. And now more public schools are being pressured to teach children why it is perfectly acceptable to have two moms or dads as part of the indoctrination process to be inclusive through diversity training while we do not dare place judgment or boundaries on practically any behavior other than being judgmental itself. At the worst extreme some schools are even teaching that we can *defy reality* and encourage children to act, dress and use the bathroom of the opposite sex that they are, if they *feel* like it.

Due to the diversity movement toward boundlessness and extreme political correctness we are supposed to accept a wider and wider variety of behaviors that until very recently were all but unacceptable or tolerated but not endorsed and celebrated. Unnatural behaviors that are not of immediate danger or harm, while tolerated, are *not* to be encouraged. During 2013 in California governor Jerry Brown signed bill AB 1266 into law, commonly known as the "Co-ed Bathroom Bill" which permits children of any age in the public schools to use either sex bathroom depending on which sex the child self-identifies with no matter what sex they actually are. Since when do young children have gender confusion? If so it must be an *extreme* minority. But apparently if .00000000001% of any group does not fit in, the other 99.9999999999...% must accept, be inconvenienced, embarrassed, harassed and pay. Are we honestly going to expect hormone driven teenage boys to politely ignore naked girls in high school locker rooms and showers? Or instead are we going to suspend them or worse from snickering as schools now foolishly do for five-year-olds who aim their finger or a banana at someone pretending they have a gun, let alone creating inappropriate sexual arousal? Or can we not even define the word inappropriate anymore?

In my home state of Pennsylvania our legislature is debating the

"Fairness Act" which also will legalize public and school restrooms, showers and locker rooms to anyone of the opposite sex that identify otherwise. Yes, this insane law will actually permit physical males into female restrooms, dressing rooms, school locker rooms and showers and into any public facility where one would obviously expect privacy. Additionally all private and religiously based schools would no longer be permitted to only hire staff that support and live by biblical teaching on human sexuality. The standard model of behavior for children will be thrown in the trash. Religious business owners will also be forced to market and promote that which violates their own faith. As usual the democrats cleverly name the bill with the word fairness rather than calling it the privacy destruction bill which is what it is. After obtaining gay marriage and now this type of thing I have gone from being a quiet conservative to a fighter because tampering with the healthy norms our sexuality and giving such mixed messages to children is where I draw the line in the sand!

Celebrating and promoting dysfunctional sexual behaviors such as being gay, bisexual and transgendered is hardly something to celebrate. Do we celebrate other unnatural or unhealthy lifestyles? Homosexuality has to be unnatural because of how our genital organs are designed to come together for both pleasure and procreation. Do we celebrate being handicapped? No, we accept, and offer help and compassion trying to enable the handicapped to function as closely as possible to those who are not handicapped.

I don't care if someone is gay any more than I care what race or sex someone is but I do care about what they stand for. And I see no need to "come out" and celebrate with pride marches and rainbow colored balloons in my face. There is nothing proud about engaging in sexual dysfunction while also not publicly condemning those who do so as mature, consenting adults. For those who feel offended by my analysis and opinion here no apology is needed because I am only in support of using our bodies as they are clearly intended to be used. If I come upon a tree that appears to keep facing away from the sun it is an anomaly, not normal and most certainly a path toward illness for this tree since plants all require sunlight for their health and survival.

Dr. Neil Whitehead, PhD believes he has confirmed in extensive studies that homosexuality is not genetic, that is there is not a specific gene that expresses sexual orientation the way others express hair color, height, eye color, etc. I quote him here. "Because they have identical DNA, it ought to be 100%. If an identical twin has same-sex attraction the chances the co-twin has it are only about 11% for men and 14% for women. Because identical twins are always genetically identical, homosexuality cannot be genetically dictated. No-one is born gay. The predominant things that create homosexuality in one identical twin and not in the other have to be post-birth factors." Additionally a 143 page paper published in the National Atlantic Journal by Drs. Lawrence Mayer and Paul McHugh of John Hopkins University researched hundreds of studies and could not find a biological explanation of sexual orientation and gender identity.

There are a variety of other studies, some of which conflict some with others – some indicating hormonal issues, some conclusions from epigenetics and social factors as one develops. I do not deny that there are people in relatively rare cases who claim to always have felt same sex attraction since they reached puberty for reasons much further research is needed on. Some even have gay tendencies beginning early in childhood when they desire to dress in opposite sex clothing and other opposite behavior's, the origin of which remains a mystery to those who study such behaviors though a number of psychologists point toward abusive and neglectful parental environments.

I suppose we could also celebrate those who feel more comfortable driving their cars in reverse to work, designate special driving lanes for them at everyone else's expense or slow down the other traffic. It may only be one of 100,000 vehicles on the road but, my gosh we cannot discriminate. Being born without legs is not normal though a percent of people are born this way that we accommodate with wheel chairs and artificial legs yet we must accept that they will not play contact sports.

By celebrating such sexual behaviors more and more people, especially teenagers who already have a hard enough time transitioning from child to adult with rare, short periods of some mild natural gender attraction confusion now feel free to experiment more. Unfortunately, more parents also are accepting their children's varied behaviors rather than discouraging them because liberal experts tell them it is wrong to do so. I will add that discouraging does not mean beating them into submission but simply some compassionate redirecting which for centuries has worked to set them on a normal course of healthy sexual functioning for the vast majority. We direct our children away from crime, drug use, bullying, excessive internet use, poor eating habits, taking various questionable risks, etc. Why shouldn't we question and discourage sexual behaviors that are out of the norm with increased risk for disease, suicide and emotional disengagement? According to the Pediatric Journal of the American Medical Association suicide in teens is up by around four fold over the last 60 years and though not totally due to relaxed sexual standards this is certainly a contributing risk factor. And unfortunately the gay rights movement has banned gender confusion reparative therapy which has had a modest success rate in bringing young people back to the natural form of heterosexual expression.

Also let us not forget that the more gay rights activists can recruit people that will declare themselves to be gay despite the fact that many may not have gone this way with an appropriately supportive environment, the more votes they will gather to further expand the gay and open sexual agenda over time. They do not simply want dignity and respect from society which I am happy to give them; they want *full marriage rights* for all government, Social Security, employer, health, inheritance and tax deductions identically to heterosexual married couples along with multiple forms of marriage, full parental rights no matter how their children are acquired, varied public restroom rights and the right to engage in intimate affection in public to the level that heterosexuals are accepted.

Meanwhile what about the rights of the religious and those of other cultures who firmly do not believe in rights being carried to this level to support a dysfunctional lifestyle? Why should they have to tolerate paying for and publically experiencing the exhibition of this lifestyle? The argument can be made that we all pay extra for handicapped ramps and adaptive equipment and supplies for those who need it while only being a minority and by placing homosexuality in a similar category we should respond in kind. But there really is a difference because a significant majority if not all homosexuals and others of varying types of sexual identity are this way due to the interplay of *environmental, psychological and biological factors*. As shown above in Dr. Whitehead's studies it is well confirmed that a specific gene does not play a direct role in homosexuality. In support of celebrating the union of love between anyone certainly homosexuals do deserve a level of recognition with appropriate, respectful vocabulary but marriage is not it.

## Placing Judgement Does Have
## Its Time and Place

Of course we do not get near values clarification or civics anymore either as we all but walk on eggshells in fear that some child from another culture or with differing beliefs or ideas, no matter how outlandish, could be even the slightest bit offended. Only a few years ago nobody would dare to bring their dogs into retail stores yet now this is a nearly daily sight despite signs in some that say no pets allowed. When I was growing up church was always a place of near silence as the minister spoke and music was played while parents naturally understood that bringing in children under the age of five or so was obviously inappropriate. Now I often miss much of the church service due to babies and toddlers whining, crying and fussing even though the church has separate quarters available for such young children.

Will people soon be bringing their dogs to church? And we have moved from the healthy formality of dressing up for school and church to people wearing jeans, sneakers, shorts and junky t-shirts with advertising and political slogans printed on them and not even tucked in in such places. Out of wedlock pregnancy and divorce were comparatively rare only a generation ago and now accepted as common place – again because we are told that is *wrong to judge* most any different behaviors no matter how irresponsible they may be. Well, guess what? There are times when placing judgment on other's behaviors and opinions is the *right* thing to do and certainly within our rights of free speech. It is easy to point out that the left's agenda firmly includes discrimination against those who give traditional opinions on a variety of issues despite their near obsession with discrimination and rights.

We must acknowledge that we are all equal in terms of the dignity of every human being and realize that some human behaviors must be treated and judged differently than others. And it needs to be understood that placing judgment, even negative judgment on some, is acceptable under particular circumstances and that rights only extend just so far. What is wrong with judging those who engage in clearly unnatural and unhealthy behaviors – whether it is illegal drug use, homosexuality, prostitution, excessive alcohol and/or junk food consumption and weigh nearly 400 pounds or more? Feeling ostracized by those who make better choices in life may be an incentive for some to improve their circumstances while remaining silent or out rightly accepting poor behaviors can encourage such dysfunctionality. Poor behaviors *should be negatively judged* by the majority though certainly bullying, name calling and hate crimes are wrong. And negative judgment should not have a price to pay. Learning politeness and appropriate respect is an art that parents should be teaching. Good etiquette can go a long way in preventing extreme discourse and fighting.

It seems that most every behavior imaginable other than murder or intentional immediate extreme danger to other's safety is now "a right" that all must tolerate. Yet should I attempt to exercise my right to free speech and express such opinions on these topics publically boy am I ostracized, perhaps to the extent of jeopardizing my personal safety. I can just imagine if I attempted to get involved in political leadership how the media would trash me if they got ahold of this book no matter the irrefutable common sense logic I use to justify my opinions! The progressive liberal establishment has almost literally stolen our sense of reverence and respect for traditional, solid common sense values and reasonable boundaries to our social well-being.

## Free Speech Is The Law So Do Not Be Silenced

The left is even engaging in the firing of conservative employees, having school assignment grades lowered when conservative opinions are expressed, excessive income tax scrutiny and intentional use of conservatively run businesses to force their radical agendas on them and other related forms of harassment. This is very wrong and should have strong legal support for suing. This is *silencing*, a clever tactic to get what they want but blatantly against our first amendment of free speech. Conservatives have less leverage because they base living more on self-evident, common sense reality while the progressives are creating and promoting ideas that defy the natural and healthier flow of living. The very serious danger is when progressives significantly alter the balance of the Supreme Court because the Court can put more of a squeeze on free speech and religious liberty. Hopefully Donald Trump will significantly turn things around to a more responsible, accountable level of normalcy though the media is inventing and distorting everything they can to bring him down.

## Behavioral Boundaries Are Essential To A Prosperous Society

There is a very severe price we all are paying for such loosening of standards with few analyzing, understanding or taking the long-term ramifications of such change seriously. Meanwhile the liberal establishment keeps encroaching on society analogous to cancer taking over an organ and eventually the whole body. Now what would have been considered obscene only a few years ago is being accepted like apple pie yet the very people who are pushing for a nearly boundless society without discrimination *are discriminating* against those who prefer to hold onto the more traditional social/cultural boundaries. I quote Cal Thomas in his book What Works, Common Sense Solutions for a Stronger America (2014) – "What we tolerate and promote we get more of, and what we discourage and don't promote we get less of."

It is most unfortunate that as each younger generation takes the place of the eldest generation the moral bar drops another notch. We see less formality in how we dress, more sexual overtones and innuendos in every form of entertainment and commercials, increased acceptance of dysfunctional sexual behaviors, the perpetuation of sexual enhancement drugs with TV commercials pushing it during prime time, the definition of marriage and family being ever more open to opinion rather than being held to a standard (Governor Jerry Brown signed Bill SB 274 into law in 2013 permitting triple parenting.), less respect for religion, spirituality and nature, less concern about fiscal responsibility, over use of technology reducing important interpersonal communication, permitting the greed machine to keep permeating health care, less interest in taking on the essential responsibility of parenting, the legalization of marijuana for recreational purposes, increased apathy regarding politics and ever greater levels of narcissism. I ask how such destabilizing ingredients can be a healthy recipe for a continuing future society. Yet this appears to be exactly what liberal progressives want in order to experience their version of utopia.

Living by the natural rules of nature does not mean we must negatively discriminate against minority groups, especially if their behaviors do not negatively affect the majority. Having ramps, walkers and wheelchairs for the disabled and elderly to ambulate themselves is a plus to the society since such devices and infrastructure permit them to integrate and perform the same functions in the world as the non-disabled and young. Having equal access to education, pay and benefits for men, women, people of all ages and races accomplishes the same. Laws that support such ideas are based on natural law and the promotion of people to reach their maximum potential. If a special education student can honestly reach significantly improved academic performance through the use of adaptive equipment and therefore become more self-sufficient and productive in the society our goal is again achieved and tax money is well spent.

Generally what type of sexual behaviors people choose to engage in within the privacy of their homes is nobody's business as long as it is consenting adults except that certain behaviors and high levels of promiscuity increase the risk for illness which everyone ends up paying for in higher health care costs. We must all recognize that how we behave outside of accepted healthy boundaries has an effect on the rest of the population because we are a society on only *one small planet*. So we only have individual freedom up to a point where it forces others to compromise. Those who waste excessive amounts of energy warm the world for the remainder of us. Those who commit crime force the remainder of us to pay more for all types of products and services from the judicial system to higher prices in the supermarket due to shoplifting. And for those of us who choose to smoke, drink excessively, drive too fast and engage in risky sexual behaviors, they raise health care costs for the remainder of us because everyone pays for everyone else – whether via higher insurance costs and/or taxes.

Gay marriage significantly interferes with how we define the bedrock of society, the family. Study after study supports traditional marriage for the purpose of the family consisting of biological parents and children being of the highest standards of integrity – obviously with some individual exceptions. And I prefer not to hear about gay marriage being about equal rights – equating it to racism and equal rights for women. Being female, of a particular skin color, blind or missing an arm or leg is a physical attribute one is born with. However, being gay is a *behavior*. Normally behaviors do not qualify as immutable characteristics which are what discrimination is normally based on. But it must be acknowledged that for the vast majority of homosexuals they insist that this is honestly how they feel and very unlikely to change. The issue is complex.

## Traditional Marriage and Family Remain the Foundation of Social Order No Matter the Challenges

Marriage and families are the foundation of human society which provides order, responsibility, maturity and discipline to humanity and have been around for thousands of years. Religions have promoted and established marriage as the standard order of civilization which has worked quite well for many centuries. The Hammurabi Laws in 1760 BC were among the first to *define* marriage along with the Levitical marriage codes in the Bible. In nearly every human culture marriage has followed such rules as fathers "giving away" daughters, the bride in particular being a virgin and there being strong penalties against adultery. Movement toward monogamy began strengthening during times before Christ though Christianity firmly reinforced this ideal.

Romantic love as we presently know it with friendship, dating and courtship, though obviously sexual attraction occurred in ancient times, was not an established foundation for marriage until comparatively recent times of around 500-700 years ago. I firmly believe it is this romantic love that blossoms from a solid friendship over about one to two years that is the most ideal foundation for marriage. A couple should be in "cloud nine" madly in love upon marriage and if not something is not right at all. Marriage has had the effect of tempering our often overpowering sex drives as well which studies have shown over and over offer greater sanity and order to the society.

However, as true as this may be, from the research I have read monogamy may not be what our biology intends so there is some conflict with marriage structuring our sexuality. The level of sexual infidelity in marriage around the world is far too high, yet most all of us know all too well what we feel when an exceptionally attractive person of the opposite sex or same if gay enters the area where we are or how our eyes always make an instant bee line for the most sexually appealing person in a crowd *no matter* how deep our love is for our spouse or dating partner. This fact has me wondering if we are kidding ourselves into fully believing that monogamy really works satisfactorily for our entire adult lives, especially if one spouse significantly loses interest in intimacy leaving the other to live in quiet desperation as temptation keeps growing. This quiet desperation can lead people toward depression and various potentially regrettable actions. Regular sexual release is deeply tied to our sense of well-being in all areas of our health, recently even being shown to reduce prostate cancer in men.

Such emotions so clearly demonstrate the more primitive, animal side to us with the never ending assurance that reproduction will occur but for the betterment of social order we use the higher, conscious parts of our brains to turn down desire or fulfill it with our spouse. It is this higher part of our brains that accepts *moral structure* to life and is able to look to the future being better for some sacrifice in the present. It is when we attempt to "burn the candle at both ends" or "have our cake and eat it too" by engaging in immoral, excessive and decadent behaviors in the present while also believing we can have a brighter future, that places us in an emotional quandary. This is because of that basic law of human operations, "easy now, hard later" or "hard now, easy later". Generally one cannot take the easy way out and have all the spontaneous, unrestricted behaviors they wish early on in their lives for very long and then have wonderfully prosperous, healthy and fulfilled lives later on since obviously hard work, delayed gratification, staying morally grounded and setting goals is what brings about a better life in the future.

# Delayed Gratification is Critical

Having to *wait* for things – opening Christmas presents, having one's first bicycle, receiving an A in a hard class, waiting for the delicious grabbing taste of sweets until the end of the meal, graduating, taking a spectacular vacation, buying one's first car and yes, ultimately one's first sexual experience are not only *maturing* experiences but *far more rewarding* due to the waiting period of anticipation. With sex the reward goes far deeper than the receiving of material goods or school grades since delaying sexual intimacy until being with a most special person enormously enhances the experience. And sex has a far more serious level to it – the ability to produce another human being and on the downside the possibility of catching a dreaded disease and perhaps emotional regret. Those who don't learn to delay gratification lose their sense of self-discipline and even purpose in life as having most anything one wants anytime one wants it *reduces* meaning, value and pleasure. Most mature adults, especially those who have managed to happily remain married for the long-term, are well aware that delaying sex until or very close to marriage has *enormous benefits* for the mind and body. Many people regret early premarital sexual encounters they had before being in a deeply committed relationship shortly headed for marriage or marriage itself.

There is something *invaluable* in having that *one special person* who is or will be one's *husband or wife* very shortly, be the *first* person to share sexual intimacy with. I am not sure if this is a perfect analogy but consider the rush of pleasure most of us immediately receive upon eating a delicious piece of chocolate cake or ice cream for dessert and why traditionally this part of a dinner is consumed after the main meal of meat, beans, fish, rice, potatoes, noodles, vegetables, etc. The main part of the meal may be equated with the importance of the deep friendship so essential in a relationship which needs to be created over time before physical/sexual passion commences. I have compared Christian, Islamic, Hindu and Chinese marriage traditions and most as expected consider marriage to be a deep and highly regarded lifelong commitment between man and woman. Except for Islam and occasional offshoots of mainline religions such as the Fundamentalist Church of Latter Day Saints group in the Southwest US and a few obscure tribes in remote areas of the world, marriage is strictly between one man and one woman – Islam differing in that men can have multiple wives though most choose monogamy.

While most desserts are unnecessary and often downright unhealthy to eat sexual passion is an essential ingredient to a happy, healthy relationship and marriage when properly timed. I knew I was falling in love with my wife before I so much as held her hand or kissed her! When the friendship did become physically romantic I was in great ecstasy – as I believe love should be. Having many sexual partners before marriage typically *decreases* the level of enjoyment with one's spouse due to the comparison of such experiences which can be confusing to deal with, in some cases leaving one to view their spouse as merely another in the line of many partners. Numerous studies confirm that *faithfully married* sex has the *highest ratings* for emotional and physical satisfaction with this bond and trust adding to the sense of security with one's partner which brings on another dimension well beyond merely the few minutes act.

It is clearly not good that some polls as recent as 2016 are coming up with results that show as much as 44% of people under the age of 30 believe that marriage is headed for extinction and 39% for all ages while being about a third less from similar surveys done in the late 1970s. Studies done by such well-known figures as Joseph Daniel Unwin and Carl Wilson have clearly shown that societies in which sexual frequency and expression of most any sort becomes more and more accepted the society as a whole develops more disorder and chaos. I also believe that when one had to make more effort to communicate with their boyfriends and girlfriends in person rather than this constant, instant electronic communication we now have, there was more expectation of this effort and cost to pay off with greater commitment to the relationship. And more in person contact was necessary and expected that naturally provided stronger input by the closest of relatives and friends whose wisdom helped maintain or separate the relationship before marital commitment. On the other hand video Skype for free from anywhere sure beats being billed upwards of a dollar a minute for landline long distance calling as we did in the past!

Abstaining for that special person is surely worthwhile since having that one person we can *trust* is such a big stress reliever since now the relationship has unlimited potential to grow. And our resources of money, housing, effort, time and energy become shared which reduces the individual burden to each spouse, leaving more resources to use for our enjoyment. If I did not have the hard working wife I have I probably would not have time to write this book since I would have to take on her portion of essential family and household duties and in reverse if I vanished she would feel equally as overwhelmed and frustrated that she had less resources to spend on things that have personal meaning to her. Living life to its maximum is about *more* than going to work, grocery shopping, cleaning the house, paying boring bills, mowing the lawn, shoveling snow, cooking, eating, washing dishes, and sleeping! We can accomplish most anything we wish should we just focus on goals.

## Marriage Remains the Ideal

Rates of divorce, unmarried cohabitation and illegitimate births have all risen considerably over the last few decades as standards have gradually deteriorated with the acceptance of greater varieties of lifestyles. In Europe cohabiters often receive most or all of the same benefits of marriage so there is even less incentive to marry. Caitlin Flanagan writing for Time Magazine is quoted saying, "There is no other single force causing as much measurable hardship and human misery in this country as the collapse of marriage. It hurts children, it reduces mothers' financial security, and it has landed with particular devastation on those who can bear it the least: the nation's underclass." Cohabitation in theory is "practice" for marriage – being able to live together and test it out on a trial basis. This sounds sensible on the surface but over and over research demonstrates that while well intended, those who cohabitate before marriage actually have a significantly *higher* chance of divorce once married with the exception of those who only live together briefly and have a traditional engagement.

Marriage provides a stronger sense of commitment to the relationship which presents a greater incentive to work things out between couples and raise children to adulthood. Also, once married, there are extended family members on both sides that normally help provide support to stay married. Cohabiting in a sense is a form of cop out or unwillingness to take the risk of the commitment for the "easy life" of childlessness, perhaps a pet and materialism over parenting. Yes, lifelong traditional marriage, parenting, and becoming grandparents are certainly hard work at times but again I must emphasize that it is the hard work that reaps the treasures in life. A life of avoiding responsibility, commitment, some risk taking and hard work will not result in obtaining the great maturity, richness and wisdom of middle age and beyond that brings us to the highest level of being human we can reach.

The broader acceptance of cohabitation, out of wedlock births and now President Obama's health care law pushing forth unlimited "free" birth control translates into further social decay. Girls are able to obtain birth control in their teens for free without parental consent meaning that parents may have no idea they are sexually involved with whomever – *not* something I believe most any parent I know feels comfortable with. Hopefully Donald Trump's changes in healthcare will be for the better. And more than ever the rather sacred act of human reproduction (sacred in the sense that the sex act can produce a new human being, the highest life form and greatest responsibility) can be brought down to the basic, practical level of brushing one's teeth or wearing a coat in the winter reducing the act of intimacy to be more closely in line with that of the squirrels, cows and dogs. Sexual intimacy without deep loving friendship and commitment brings us down to a lower, more spontaneous way of life and if done repeatedly reduces our chances of one day finding that possible lifelong lover and spouse – let alone increasing the chance of acquiring sexually transmitted diseases which are costing our country over $5billion annually in health care costs.

And we cannot avoid the emotional entanglements of sexual involvement with others because we are human, not animals. Should we arrive at the point where we view the sexual act as little more than the high and stress relief the orgasm supplies it becomes similar in nature and pattern to the use of illegal pleasure centered drugs and alcoholism which leads us down a very difficult, addictive, lonely road and often to a dead end. Worse yet, statistics show that the rate of unintended pregnancies, abortions, STD transmission and male abuse of women increased as birth control has become more available. Additionally hormone based birth control places women at increased risk of ovarian, uterine and vaginal cancer. The bottom line is that we simply cannot avoid personal responsibility for our behaviors much as we try. Freedom has consequences. More and more we hear young people talk about having friends of the opposite sex "with benefits" – referring to friends that mutually relieve themselves sexually with minimal emotional feelings just to take care of their physical needs while avoiding the responsibility of a committed relationship. This lifestyle permits people to grab their dessert without eating their dinner – getting their sexual desires relieved without the harder work of maintaining a mature love relationship. Delaying maturity delays contentment, not something rewarding over time.

In Glenn Stanton's great book, "Why Marriage Matters" the thesis of his book is solid and straight forward as follows, "First-time, lifelong, monogamous marriage is the relationship that best provides for the most favorable exercise of human sexuality, the overall well-being of adults, and the proper socialization of children. Marriage has no close rival. It stands independently above any other option: singleness, cohabitation, divorce, and remarriage." If I could say this any better I would! This is also stated similarly well in "Marriage and the Public Good: Ten Principles" put out by the Witherspoon Institute which states as follows: "Marriage binds two individuals together for life, and binds them jointly to the next generation that will follow in their footsteps. Marriage elevates, orders, and at times constrains our natural desires to the higher moral end of fidelity and care."

As always there are exceptions with the other options that live balanced, satisfying lives but lifelong marriage statistically scores higher on the happiness charts on average. And as much as I advocate marriage with its benefits of providing long-term security for the family and order for the society I certainly acknowledge that some marriages are not meant to be with divorce being the best option for all parties. But I insist that the present high divorce rate is *horrendously unnecessary*. The black divorce rate has reached to as high as 70% which obviously is a significant component of why such a large percentage of the black population in the United States remains impoverished and crime ridden though according to Nisa Muhammad of the Wedded Bliss Foundation the rate is down to 48% overall. The illegitimate birth rate in this population is totally out of hand now at 72% according to the most recent research by Centers for Disease Control and Prevention, National Center for Health Statistics.

Over and over it has been demonstrated that children reared in intact married homes have significantly higher academic scores, are about 30%

less likely to cut class or miss school, have around a 50% lower rate of alcohol and drug abuse, have a strengthened ability to use self-restraint and delay responding to sexual invitation, are statistically less prone to be involved with crime, and have twice the high school graduation rate of others. Also preliminary data from a University of Arizona study suggests that pheromones, the biochemicals that transmit sexual information between people, present in men other than their fathers such as step fathers and boyfriends may awaken puberty earlier in girls since the biological father's pheromones are not patterned to do this. So marriage may help delay the onset of sexual activity for more reasons than one. This may be part of the reason that sexual molestation of daughters is more prevalent among step fathers than biological fathers though by all means never justifies acting out such behavior. This scientific fact of pheromone mismatching further supports not promoting gay parenting as well.

And now we have legalized same sex marriage, only further weakening the rock solid definition of marriage that has been with us for millennia. I ask if our religious institutions, courts, universities, and governmental legislatures don't continue to uphold natural marriage, how will our young people learn and understand what it means to marry, stay married, be faithful, and remain loyal to their commitment of parenting? Do we want society to remain and grow with higher quality, more orderly lives via the commitment of marriage or keep moving down the road of excessive freedom, hedonism, anarchy and chaos? We have a choice and at heart I think nearly all of us know what the *right choice* is for humanity to keep prospering and that is to maintain order, discipline, humility and stability. In redefining marriage legally we are also redefining what a family is and acknowledging no special arrangements or needs must be met for the health, development and adjustment of children.

There are even health benefits of marriage with studies having shown that married people have less cancer, colds, heart attacks, lower blood pressure and dementia as they age. To reiterate the happily married also statistically live longer and generally have children who are more well-adjusted, achieve higher academic grades, and have lower rates of teen pregnancy, depression and suicide which also saves $billions in social services, criminal justice and health care costs. Having children also usually provides significant levels of support and companionship to parents as they age into their elder years though I would not always bank on this. Marriage also reduces the probability of poverty in children by up to 82%. I quote Robert Rector, Senior Research Fellow at the Heritage Foundation, "Marriage remains America's strongest anti-poverty weapon, yet it continues to decline." Rather than wasting so much money our government should be investing in the promoting of traditional marriage as a method of fixing many of our social ills.

Should a couple who have dated a year or two and very honestly feel deeply in love and wish to marry little should get in the way though some premarital counseling is always a good idea. Such counseling has the purpose of placing some objectivity on the decision to marry since when under the influence of the high of raging love hormones most of us are anything but objective. A healthy variety of compatibilities must be well discussed – things in common and complimentary from political opinions to health habits, household chore designees, expectations of having children and the most difficult marital issue of money and resource utilization and how to spend, save and invest. Whole sessions on proper communication, conflict resolution and trust are essential as well. The idea that opposites attract is really not very true – physically perhaps but not in most other areas. Having agreement on core social, religious and political values and just what trust really means are the ingredients for a life-long marriage in addition to understanding each other's practical goals in life.

As with everything in life we must become *solution-oriented* or we will not find solutions! Two methods of finding resolution to disagreement are to finally break into mutual humor and better yet, to sincerely apologize. Apologizing can work miracles in many circumstances in life! Additionally just talking a lot about everything from settling conflicts to politics is a great indicator of a healthy marriage while regular silence is quite the opposite. As marriages progress further occasional counseling can be very beneficial as well. Ideally premarital counseling should be easily available and affordable to all engaged couples. Once married however, follow-up counseling and support also needs to be widely affordable and available as married couples learn to live together, communicate better, learn the art of compromise and bridge differences that may be holding them back from achieving longevity and joy in marriage. Often religious and other charitable organizations have affordable sliding scale fees.

# Being Selfless, Not Selfish

Dealing with work and career related problems, finances, raising and disciplining children, sexual expression and frequency and dealing with aging parents are almost always challenging at some point. Oddly often the most petty annoyances can cause some of the worst conflicts such as merely commenting that someone forgot to place small amount of food back in the refrigerator, purchased vanilla instead of chocolate ice cream, did not use a coupon to buy something, left hair remains from shaving in the sink, dressed the baby in blue instead of tan colored pants or forgot the sunglasses for a short walk outside. Often there are underlying marital communication problems which make these seemingly minor issues to come to the surface. If one spouse, for example, resents the other for not being around more, not pitching in with essential household chores more, disciplining the child differently, spending on frivolous things, or having less interest in intimacy minor annoyances may be intensified. It is really crucial that we understand each other's personalities and eccentricities that we all have and learn to tolerate them.

It honestly is not easy to adjust to living with another person, no matter how much you may be in love with that person. Sooner or later dirty socks left on the floor, dishes not washed or put away, bad smelling breath, questionable table manners, "backseat" driving, procrastinating habits, certain types of verbal expressions, etc. will generate conflict in *every* marriage. And I don't just mean trivial conflict. These seemingly petty issues over extended amounts of time and regular repetition build with greater annoyance, cause anger and resentment to grow which is very corrosive to love and romance. As with all conflict there are solutions! First every married couple should read Willard F. Harley Jr's excellent book, "Love Busters, Protecting your Marriage from Habits that Destroy Romantic Love" which covers marital issues in wonderful detail along with over a dozen other great books at the Marriage Builders website. He has a great understanding of the fact that all of us at heart are quite selfish and naturally put up resistance to change our habits we have taken for granted for 20-30 years or more. We often react to our spouse by justifying them as trivial – essentially saying to our spouse that they are so minor that the complaining spouse should "just deal with it". Trust me, this is the wrong way to behave if you love your husband or wife and want a permanent, loving marriage.

We must take into account our spouse's feelings and put our own down the ladder of priority. Sure it is easy to think ourselves into believing that our spouse should not care about a few dirty socks tossed on the floor or if the cat litter box is cleaned out until the next day but *get into how your spouse feels, not just you!* That little extra effort to place the dirty socks into a laundry bag or washing machine and to clean out the cat litter box every day could make the difference between a happy spouse or an angry one. Showing such compassion in a marriage on a regular basis is a huge component of long-term loving marriages. Once one is married life is not only about oneself but both spouses. When spouses make this effort to listen to each other's feelings and take such action that makes each other happier love will bloom regularly! Even carried one step further, taking the action to surprise each other in small ways and ask each other how the other can be helped routinely works wonders for happiness and love.

Some people say that when you marry you are marrying a family, not only the man or woman. Dealing with a family of in-laws can be anything from wonderful to agony. However, each spouse must realize that their spouse has parents and usually siblings who cannot be ignored and in fact must be acknowledged. Yet we must also realize that it is our spouse who we have probably dated a couple of years and married who we are best friends with and know well while his or her family are pretty much strangers or at least not the person we married. Being forced into a relationship with an entire family can be complicated for a number of reasons from obvious differences in interests, social and political opinions and distance from each other. Creating a line of demarcation as to how many resources are allocated to dealing with family and in-laws is not always simple though a comfort zone should be established, understood and agreed upon by both spouses. Much of this book is about having boundaries of all types because knowing one's boundaries in all areas creates a known working area the brain can adjust to and become comfortable with which without causes anxiety, worry and stress.

This consideration of how our spouse feels is also very important in the sexual area of marriage. Though certainly not a sex therapist my research and personal experience brings me to the clear conclusion that we normally know our bodies well and what we enjoy. Without going into clinical detail my message is to very intimately know our spouse and learn to please them even when not always comfortable with particular activities. Once couples have healthy sexual technique down and regularly enjoy this normal, ecstatic pleasure marriage can be truly incredible! However, after many years several aspects of marriage including sex can become a bit too predictable. In this case be more adventuresome in several areas of marriage from sex to small or big trips, new little gifts for each other that demonstrate thoughtfulness, cooking up your spouse's favorite meal or going to a restaurant of choice, hiking a new trail or taking up a new form of recreation together. Like anything else in life, a happy marriage requires effort which is well worth the rewards.

## Monthly Mood Changes

Also all couples need to be aware of women's monthly cycles and some clear mood changes. Some women become defensive if I bring up premenstrual syndrome but PMS as it is called is simply a scientific fact. During a few days prior to menstruation and sometimes during it many women feel more irritable, anxious, perhaps insecure and may wish to spend more time alone due to major hormonal changes. Couples, particularly boyfriends and husbands, should key into this with more patience as these monthly mood changes which can be very significant, if not self-managed with attention to lowering stress levels, achieving better sleep, nutrition and regular exercise can be very problematic. Not being argumentative or combative could have the most significant moderating effect and certainly stepping in and cooking a favorite meal or taking the kid(s) out for a few hours is not a bad idea. When possible husbands might want to plan to have less stresses around the house at this time and ask how they may help around the home and family more – real team work. I generally also think that women simply need more space around them both physically and emotionally during this time unless they want closeness.

Trivial issues that do not irritate them normally may become intensified and distorted at this time leaving objectivity out the door. For example the husband maybe chastised for "not cleaning the house enough" when in actual time and energy expended he may well have used far more than the wife in household chores from cooking to changing diapers, mowing the lawn, shoveling snow, trimming trees, gardening, managing household finances, keeping up the cars, repairing stuff, etc. But attempting to defend oneself can be like driving a car with no brakes - don't do it. Sometimes one simply cannot fight irrationality with rationality since one side will be unrelenting to "win" regardless. It may be best to give a firm warning that "I will walk away if you continue in this unfair attack if you do not quit" and then do so if it does not stop. It must also be noted that there is a wide range of symptoms of PMS from almost zero to rare cases of women that have very painful cramping and even vomit sometimes each month, depending on body type.

Put down, insulting comments are terrible fire starters such as "You always are running late", "You constantly waste money", "Can't you finally give Susie a bath? I have done it for the last two weeks!" "The light is green. Why are we standing still?" "Put your damn phone down for once and look at me!" etc. If such comments become routine marriages are in serious trouble and need help. Romantic passion naturally dies off under such conditions as well which obviously exacerbates the problem. Low libido and routine conflict between couples are signs that there are serious problems underlying in the marriage that must be addressed to bring back joy, love and friendship.

## Men and Women are Different

It is critical that we more clearly understand the emotional *differences* between men and women, which if we understood them better, couples in particular would be considerably happier. There are reasons why a man can go into a store, quickly grab what is on the list and purchase a week's groceries in not much over twenty minutes while his wife may well take nearly an hour or more to do the same. Men tend to think more in linier terms – grab the bananas, lettuce, onions, strawberries, bread, potatoes, meat, cereal, ice cream, milk, paper towels, etc. and make a beeline for the cash register. Women are more likely to examine the products they purchase in greater detail, read the ingredients, get sidetracked some, are more social should they run into someone they know, and browse at other products not on the list and perhaps purchase some of them as well. This is partly why women may tend to spend more money shopping. Of course there are exceptions to this stereotype and note that if some men are browsing in electronics, sporting or outdoor camping stores things may be reversed. Some men will gravitate toward more interest in sports cars and hanging out at bars with their buddies than women. Though there are plenty of women now who actively participate in and watch sports and play video games such activities are still far more male dominated – a trait women must accept within reason. However, when spouses begin to spend more time with their friends than their other halves this can be an indication of trouble as it may be a sign that the love has begun to dry up.

Additionally, women perceive money and their interaction with the material world differently. Women tend to be more self-conscious of their physical appearance in part due to how men treat them in terms of desirability or lack thereof as well as other women and are more likely to shop and spend money to feel better when frustrated or down. A man may well be perfectly content with the paint on the walls, the flooring and carpeting, appliances, furniture and décor in their house as it is for decades while his wife is more likely to demand change of such items more frequently. Men tend to be content for the most part wearing pretty much the same clothes for years until they wear out only very occasionally treating themselves to a new shirt, pants or shoes while women may have over fifteen pairs of shoes and often have a large closet full of clothing but also are regularly found at the department store looking to buy more. And of course there is no end to the variety of jewelry most women like along with multiple times the cost of cosmetics that men use. Men are more tolerant of eating the same old peanut butter or baloney and cheese sandwich every day for lunch but less so for women, of course with exceptions.

Women are far more sensitive to differences in temperature and humidity than men so adjust clothing, air conditioning, heat, fans, opening and closing windows, etc. more frequently. This is due to women having blood vessels closer to the surface of their skin than men and they may have a lower tolerance threshold of discomfort at the conscious level. Conflict over indoor climate control can be a significant issue for couples to deal with. Women and men perceive money differently in that one may tend toward spending more in the present or being frugal and saving for the future in different areas. We all prioritize differently regardless of sex which can lead to money conflicts. One might spend six figures over their lifetime on cigarettes and hair styling while only carrying a $20 a month flip phone while another might spend over $1,000 a year on their phone while not smoking but cutting their own hair.

## Empathize Not Minimize

The most basic issue many couples deal with is one tending to minimize the other's concerns. If someone says they are too cold, too hot, tired, stressed, frustrated, can't sleep, can't settle a problem with a child or wants help with chores, the other spouse ignoring, minimizing or comparing the feelings to others and how they deal with them is a very conflict inducing response. I doubt there is anything that has made me angrier in my life than someone saying to me that I could be living on the North Pole when I complain about winter being too long or that I could be a paraplegic in a wheelchair upon feeling some pain in my leg! People express themselves to others with the hope and expectation that they will offer them some level of compassion and understanding in the present. If I am suffering I do not want those around me to tell me I could be suffering more, rationalizing that my level of suffering is comparatively minor. Yes I may know that I only broke my hand in the car accident while my friend died in the seat next to me but damn it all, I am minus a thumb and in excruciating pain!

We all interpret and respond to stimuli differently so comparing to someone else and how they may deal with an issue is very unfair reasoning. Negative feedback such as "Bob next door easily completed a certain task." or "Your sister got As in graduate school so why can't you?" or "You are a smart, able bodied person so why can't you finish it like the others did?" or "Why don't you get a real job instead of trying to sell your art?" is a great way to *start a war!* We need patience, compassion, respect and trust to be implemented regularly which without we will not have a happy marriage. And these four attributes or behaviors should be demonstrated through daily communication. Couples should *talk a lot* including talking out disagreements which should be resolved since letting anger fester is truly a recipe for disaster down the road. And nobody should ever refuse to seek counseling when a serious conflict or problem seemingly is not able to be resolved.

Another commonly expressed opinion among young couples is that they need to wait for marriage until they have more money. While financial security is never a bad thing getting married itself does *not* require money. Fancy, costly weddings and diamonds do not demonstrate love any more than going to a church minister or county courthouse and paying $50 for a marriage license. A celebration and/or honeymoon can come later. In fact sharing expenses and joint tax filing *save* a considerable amount of money so if truly ready for marriage money does not have to delay it. However, children do cost money and can wait when not financially prepared. And the fact that children arrive unplanned at least 50% of the time even among the most progressive, industrialized and well educated groups with the most knowledge and availability of contraceptive techniques does make one have some reservations. Being responsible for the life of a child involves far more than digging deeper into one's wallet!

As is the theme throughout this book self-discipline, a major hallmark of being human is the answer. It is my opinion that if we honestly do not want to become pregnant then we will not as there are obvious and multiple solutions to this problem while still fully enjoying passion. And remember, self-discipline does not have to equate with misery and sacrifice, especially when we have goals. In fact one's perception of sacrifice actually reverses to some degree when one is aware of the future reward. Think of it this way. When we take one marble of sacrifice from a jar knowing that it will produce two or three marbles of freedom and prosperity in the empty jar we may well view the sacrifice as worth the effort.

## Growing Older

As we age we continue to need our spouses and friendships as much as ever. If we grow old enough some of our friends and perhaps our spouse may pass away or we may be divorced, only increasing the need to be social with those we still have remaining. If we have children certainly having them regularly accessible can be highly beneficial along with old friends. Social networking technology can be helpful as well. Even remarrying is a viable possibility. If we become a care giver we must realize where our boundaries are and know where to set them since we also have a full life to live with the right to not be overly burdened in time, energy or money. We live in a society in which we have paid into a system that will take care of our most basic needs when we are old and/or disabled. As always there is a balance in life where we remain decently moral and compassionate toward others while still being able to give to ourselves. In other words we have responsibility for treating others and the world well, yet not excessively at the expense of our own satisfaction because we are also important.

Aging and losing our physical and mental capacities is perhaps the greatest challenge of life. This is when we may need others whom we can trust to assist us with a variety of important areas of our lives from money management to medical concerns, housing arrangements and more. However, as our faculties fail we become vulnerable to exploitation by potentially anyone who may want a piece of what we have worked hard for during the last 80+ years. If it is not the medical system often prescribing far more medications and procedures than we need or retirement centers charging us 3-4 times as much as a standard apartment the same size with a set number of "free" meals or nursing homes taking perhaps our entire life savings away in just months, it could even be a care giver pilfering from us. If our spouse is unable to properly handle such issues often we resort to our children who may be far away and at the peak of working and raising their own children so we may have to pay for a properly bonded caretaker or depend on a trustworthy friend. Perhaps we could bring in a local nursing student from a nearby college or university offering free room and board plus compensation.

# CHAPTER 7

## Going For it

**T**HIS IS A fun chapter to write and hopefully to read as well but especially to do because it is mostly about accomplishing what we want to do over merely what we have to do. This is about really fulfilling dreams *beyond* the usual aspects of life such as falling in love (though without love one's dreams may be significantly duller) and marriage, raising a family, having a decent occupation and income and stashing away cash for retirement. I deeply believe in life not merely being good and satisfying but truly being *incredible* because that is what the ultimate potential of human life is. Our only limitation other than our health and time is that which we consciously place upon ourselves though a good environment cannot hurt.

Many would immediately say that I omitted money in the last sentence but obtaining money to fulfill dreams is also about our choices we make – how we manage our lives. If we have followed the formulas presented here and stayed on top of our desires, hopes and expectations as we age we should now be able to take our lives to what we only thought were only dreams and make it reality. There is no rule written in stone that we must work 40+ hours a week until the age of 65 or more and if we have played our cards right we could be a good bit younger than this with a variety of possible choices at hand. I am of the belief that having more choices is more fun than having less! Fulfilling dreams and choices is much of what true contentment is about.

So life is going real well. We have stuck with our goals over a number

151

of years, are healthy, debt-free or very close to it, have money in the bank and perhaps inherited some as well. Maybe our children are nearly grown up, reasonably independent or have left the nest to start building their own lives. Perhaps we may only have to work part-time. Or we may like our work so much that we now wish to advance our skills further in our field. For some obtaining a graduate degree may be just what they want to complete what they need in their field to fill the gap in order to move deeper into precisely what they wish to work on. More and more colleges and universities are offering course work online so one can take a class from anywhere in the world which of course is very convenient.

Another endeavor might be to start one's own business. This could entail practically anything from developing software, repairing computers, appliances or lawn mowers to selling one's art online or opening up a gallery and framing shop, fishing and bait supply store, launderette, landscaping business, printing/publishing shop, summer camp for kids, pet store, fast food franchise, seamstress shop, running a music and instrument store, teaching how to play an instrument, organic farming, homework tutoring business, locksmith service, disabled and elder ride operation, financial planning office, being a day trader, travel agency, weight loss clinic, physical conditioning trainer, health food store, salvage/recycling operator, teach photography classes at home, bike shop, build furniture at home, wedding photography, real estate or stock investing and plenty more. I am choosing to write this book, travel and pursue my natural science interests, photography and stock investing which has me busier than working a regular job.

Now just imagine if one has reached the point in life where one does not need to get in the car, drive to and from work or use public transportation, often not particularly like the work and feel few alternatives are accessible. Yes, we have become wealthy enough to comfortably support ourselves merely from investment income and can in effect retire with more choices. To do so does not require one to truly be rich and worth $millions. A portfolio of just one $million can safely provide an income of over $50,000 a year. For many who engage in proper planning over the years having enough money to not require a paycheck from someone else by one's 50s is not totally out of the question and even more likely by one's sixties. I even know some who have accomplished this before the age of forty. Only comparatively very recently have people at any time in history been able to have this luxury, especially at a young enough age to fully enjoy it.

While practically anyone when asked would say that they desire being at such a point in life not everyone actually benefits as much as they believe. There are people who really feel better when they are working despite what contrary remarks they may make. Many people simply don't know themselves when it comes to this aspect of life. There are young people who have come into large inheritances, lottery winnings and insurance or law suit pay outs that end up living quite a dysfunctional lifestyle so wealth, as much as everyone says they want it, is not always a good thing though certainly we all want to be comfortable. As is always true throughout life, having a solid foundation of *values* that one lives by is what permits one to be able to set goals, remain healthy in every way, manage their freedom appropriately and ultimately be content.

## Volunteering

Now, for the creative, educated and curious who have a healthy variety of interests, passions and hobbies being financially independent can provide perhaps the greatest time of one's life. One can volunteer their time and skills to help the less fortunate most anywhere in the world. Millions of people need improved health, sanitation, cleaner food and water, better housing, and education in countless areas of the world. From the Peace Corps to many non-profit organizations and churches there is always a need to help others. This is a way to feel productive, perhaps learn about the culture and language of another country and use one's skills while also making the world a better place.

However, one need not necessarily go far to find worthwhile places to volunteer. Most every place in the country has opportunities of some type. The elderly and disabled need companionship and to be driven to medical appointments, the poor need improvements to their homes and many non-profit organizations need various types of help. Such people could even be our own neighbors. Schools and summer camps can use volunteers to add variety and quality to their agendas. There is nothing as great as exposing young children to great works of art, manufacturing and engineering, technology, the wonders of nature and the fantastic sciences of biology, astronomy, geology, evolution, physiology, foreign languages, culture and geography. Doing so creates enormous amounts of brain stimulation and often inspires our young to become passionate over some area of study later in life. What we learn in the formal classroom setting is only a part of our education in life. Broader exposure to ever greater variety in life only expands our brain's bank of knowledge and experience.

There are also many science expeditions sponsored by various colleges, universities and organizations such as the National Geographic Society. To some it is fascinating to spend a period of time in a very primitive part of the world, document and record animal and plant life, human tribes, discover unknown languages which may vanish if not recorded, observe totally new species of life, and get involved in an environmental and conservation effort to protect certain areas being devastated by human destruction. For some there is an enormous thrill and satisfaction in stepping where no human has ever been, capturing and/or photographing a life form never observed before or video filming some natives speaking a language that is totally unintelligible requiring considerable study to comprehend. One may also wish to be ever more charitable. Perhaps they would like to help assist a bright, motivated child succeed in high school and/or college or spend a summer giving their time and effort to bring clean drinking water to a poor village. Or perhaps one would like to work to change various policies being legislated here or in other places.

## Touristing

While being productive in some way is most admirable there most certainly is nothing wrong with simply taking grand vacations, hike and bike rides, time on the beach, exploring caves and rock castles, touring the Amazon Jungle, taking a cruise, driving all over New Zealand, China, parts of Africa, Antarctica, India or wherever. Simply taking in the very different sights, scenes, sounds, wildlife, people and culture is *enormously educational* and stimulating. Traveling greatly widens one's horizons and creates major great memories. With enough time one can take great driving trips around the United States to many wonderful national parks, various cities with much to experience, beautiful beaches, deserts, spectacular mountains and rock formations, forests and more.

I once, along with my brother and friends, converted a school bus into a camper and we drove all over the country for an entire summer which is a lifelong memory. I have recently fulfilled a childhood dream of going to the tropics and wondering around the rain forests, beaches and mountains of Central and South America, eight countries in Africa, parts of Asia, Indonesia, Nepal, Antarctica and Europe for several weeks and am making plans to check out other parts of the world. Sure such trips require money but acquiring money and spending it wisely is honestly not all that difficult if one follows much of what I have discussed here in life management.

## Take on a Hobby & Keep Abreast of the World

If one does not care to travel and is not the type loaded with adventuresome wonder-lust spirit there are countless other interests and hobbies to consider. Maybe it is time to take up painting, drawing, crocheting, learning to play a musical instrument, creating the dreamed of garden, designing an invention, treating oneself to a recumbent bicycle, buying, fixing up and reselling an old house, getting a basic pilots license or writing a book. We may very well discover a talent we have always had but never were at a point where we had the resources to explore such possibilities. Perhaps we never learned much about American or world history and we finally have the time to read a series of books on such topics or take classes.

One of my hobbies is amateur astronomy which has me attending the Stellafane telescope maker's convention and camp out in Vermont most summers. Another is keeping a daily journal which I have done for over fifty years and photography which has me with over 60,000 photos in my collection from family pictures to trips, wildlife, culture, landscapes and more. As a child I seriously collected butterflies and moths and other insects, built a moth trap and then got into telescope making and studying the wonders of astronomy. Perhaps we always wanted to learn French,

Spanish or some other language. For sports fans how about attending a Super Bowl game or at least getting to one's favorite team games a few times in whatever sport one likes? And don't forget politics because, even as frustrating as it is to hear about Congress and the president often making highly questionable decisions and not getting much done, we all should keep abreast of issues so that we can make informed decisions when we enter the voting booth. We may even decide to volunteer or work part-time for an organization that promotes an agenda we support.

## Get More Technically Competent

In the present world another critical area to be comfortable with is *technology*. I find it difficult sometimes to keep up with change when during most of my life the gadgets I used stayed comparatively simple, predictable and lasted for decades. A television had nothing more than a power knob, channel changer and volume control and received less than ten channels paid for by advertisers while we pay over $90 a month now for an endless list, most of which we never watch but are forced to pay for and *still must tolerate* the commercials. Being able to record and replay a TV show or movie was unimaginable. Now my family fiddles around with three remote controls and trolls through menus for a number of minutes to get things going. If we let a couple of months pass by sometimes we all forget and it takes a half hour or more to remember exactly which settings allows us to watch a movie. Then we put the DVD in the machine and the player does not accept this particular type of disk as we all wonder why all DVDs don't simply play the way the on and off knob always worked on our old TVs.

The TV we had in 1964 still works while the one we buy now won't come close to lasting that long despite paying plenty for it. The rotary dial landline phone we had in 1958 still works like new, the service it provided which cost about $8-15 a month for the last 50 years, could probably be dropped from the second story onto cement and would not die is now replaced by a pocket sized phone that costs over $200 a month for a family since each person has their own and the phones only last a couple of years. Put in another perspective this family will spend about $65,000 on phone service over thirty years compared to around $4,000 for the landline! Do note that this a rough estimate of $200 for a family, if one does their research; one may find more competitive rates by other companies such as Consumer Cellular, than the larger ones such as Verizon and AT&T offer.

Instead of a typewriter the books for Microsoft Office pile nearly a foot thick – great stuff but obviously overkill. My digital cameras are daunting to learn how to fully use with all of their menus and screens compared to simply picking up the camera, doing a bit of mechanical zooming, focusing, setting the depth of field and clicking the picture. And as with the TV theater system, if weeks or a couple of months pass by between uses I am nearly dumbfounded again. And should I dare to buy a different brand of camera everything is in different places with different batteries and chargers that are not compatible which I must travel with and I have to start learning new menus all over again. Meanwhile my film camera from 1972 still takes great photos and works fine though obviously antiquated from the clear convenience and quality of digital. The business with chargers is truly an *abomination* as certainly most small electronic devices from IPods to phones and cameras could be made to run on the same voltage and all have the same compatible chargers and connectors.

Though much could be done to increase compatibility and simplicity computer and digital technology is here to stay and something we all must contend with. It is the *constant changing* that is so frustrating to millions of people every day. I just need jpegs and raw for photography. I don't need how many different forms of Java software and plug ins that work on Windows XP but not on Windows 7 or 10, etc. I have a nearly $2,000 Nikon slide and negative scanner that I discovered only works on Windows XP which was replaced with Windows 7. A friend of mine must replace a $1,000 printer at her workplace because it only works on Windows Vista but not 7 – what a deplorable waste! This same friend is taking online classes and sends out an e-mail of a PowerPoint document to other classmates, some of whom can open it and others who cannot depending on what version of Microsoft Office they have causing hours of aggravation.

Unfortunately many of us are not well educated on how to use technology to its potential and often only use perhaps 20-30% of the capacity of most devices. We constantly get frustrated that certain software downloads only with Microsoft Edge but not with or Chrome or Firefox or the reverse while advertising pop up boxes become ever more annoying and aggressively target us. We are forced into buying appliances that have control panels that almost resemble the dashboard of a Boeing 767 with how many spin cycles, temperature settings, rinse cycles, various speeds of drying, load sizes, power levels, and requirements for high efficiency detergent that may cost more than the water supposedly saved.

Everyone I know simply sets their microwave oven to a couple of minutes on full power and walks. With a conventional stove what else is needed than high, medium, low and off? As for a fridge one area keeps food cold while the other area freezes food. Ice makers are forever prone to problems in a short few years, often causing a flood as happened to me – I say get out good old fashioned ice cube trays as they *can't fail*. As for the washer and dryer what do we need from them? Clean, dry clothes period! Front loaders do use less water but their extra cost will take years to break even on water savings and these days I wish everyone luck getting a solid 25+ years from such machines. The less technology minded and elderly practically need to take a class to learn how to operate their television! Now we can often teach ourselves from watching You Tube videos.

I placed these last two paragraphs here because the more comfortable and skilled we are with technology, the more effective we can be to maximize our life endeavors and curiosities. Technology allows us to *do more* with our life. Instead of handwriting letters, stamping envelopes and going to a mailbox, we write on a screen and click we go while the receiver gets it a second later. The GPS takes us exactly to the address rather than stopping along roadsides or dangerously trying to get our bearings with a paper map, getting lost and wasting time. Facebook permits us to share most everything with almost whomever we wish, from our deepest thoughts, to game playing to sharing photos of our latest vacation. The cell phone can save our life if we are in an emergency out in the mountains. The text message allows one to communicate privately and quietly. We can store as much information as it took to fill a whole basement or garage on a couple of disks with enormous paper savings. The microwave oven sure saves time. Photography is hundreds of times more convenient than it used to be when we waited a week to get film processed and needed a large storage closet for trays of slides and prints. Social media have permitted me to meet wonderful people from all over the world who have assisted me in trip planning and even been my tour guides which is far cheaper than using a travel agency – unthinkable only fifteen years ago! We might soon see mini spacecraft the size of a smart phone that can travel nearly a quarter the speed of light and reach the nearest stars in twenty years instead of 75,000 years!

All of my household bills are paid automatically and flawlessly via electronic transmission and every other financial transaction to my credit card as well as automatic deposit for paychecks virtually eliminating the need for cash and saving countless miles, fuel and time going to the bank, buying postage stamps, waiting days for bills to be paid, etc. The list goes on and on. What took weeks in some cases now takes seconds. Depending on who we are such great ways of saving time, effort and money (Money saving can seriously be challenged while most of us now pay an extra $2,500-$3,000 annually per household for internet access, cell phone service and cable television or $25,000-$30,000 over ten years – costs that did not exist twenty years ago.) can add to our enjoyment of life since by being fully engaged in the use of such conveniences provides us with more resources to pursue other activities. I sure am glad I have the time to write this book in part due to such time savers. I recall the days of my parents spending an hour or two every month carefully writing out paper checks, placing them in envelopes, hand addressing them and putting return addresses on them, buying and putting on stamps and finally getting them to a mailbox along with driving to the bank with paper paychecks – all *completely unnecessary* anymore. And publishing this book most certainly does not require proofreading of rolled up galley proofs, White Out and erasers.

Of course we can ask if or how much happier people are with more free time, if they are merely wasting more time or genuinely being more productive. There are several angles on this topic but I really think those who use the extra time to further their own goals of accomplishment are indeed emotionally benefitting. Remember that one of the major purposes of this book is to arouse people's awareness of how much more "mileage" one can receive from life by being the most efficient they can with all resources. By being highly organized and efficient with resources, especially those that are required for essential needs to live, we bring ourselves closer to being able to set aside more resources for our personal, more self-centered desires such as socializing, recreation, hobbies, travel or other interests as referred to above. Life *does not* have to merely be one obligation after another until we are practically ready to pass away! This includes dealing with family as well. Surely we have a moral obligation to assist to a degree with our nearest of family as they age and/or have various problems. But if we have planned for such possibilities the level of the burden can be managed with minimal detriment to our lives. And remember that giving of oneself *within reason* is much of what life is about and often results in similar favors returning in kind.

## Prioritize: Don't Regret

Unfortunately I see people all the time that have entered their older years and wonder where their life has gone and have many regrets that they did not operate with greater focus when younger so that they indeed could fulfill many of their dreams before being unable to. This does not have to be the case as I hope this book is making clear. If we keep waiting with an endless list of excuses such as I don't have the money, my kids are too young, I need to complete that degree, I want to finalize my divorce, I can't get enough time off work, I want to get my house cleaned out first, I have pets, I am obligated to dealing with my aging parents, I need money to move, etc. we may never take action on our dreams. The time is *now, not later* because later has unknowns. I sure know that I don't want to be in my 80s wishing I had accomplished something I could have when younger but never did!

Another area of significant regret the elderly have is not having taken better care of their health when younger. Most people under the age of about sixty figure that if they engaged in some poor health habits for many years that it may cut off a few years of their lives. Indeed this statistically is true. They believe the pleasure of all those cigarettes, alcoholic drinks, soft drinks, delicious hot dogs, fries and candy, racing down the highway well over the speed limit, weight gain, sitting endless hours with their computer or phone, not sleeping enough, having a wide variety of sex partners, etc. was worth it for that price to pay. And for some this may be the result – early and quick death. But for most which when younger many do not realize, it is the prolonged misery and cost of long-term illness as they move into their seventies and eighties. And when interviewed older people do have serious regrets in the health area because *nobody* enjoys suffering for years and years. Our last decade or two of life does not have to be one of nearly constant pain, expensive doctor visits, incapacitation and perhaps depression. I know people in their nineties living at home, walking normally, driving cars, reading, conversing well and still taking in the world – mostly because they engaged in good health habits throughout their lives.

Life can be lived in a moral and ethical manner while also placing one's personal desires and priorities high enough on the list that they do not get shoved under the rug. I could easily find excuses to not take my trip to Costa Rica with a close friend. The money spent on this might take away from cash I will need when older, my father might die in the nursing home, I could catch a tropical disease there or get mugged or murdered by drug thugs, my wife needs me home while working full-time and engaged in completing graduate school, I may not have enough vacation days left for a family trip later in the year, and more. I could do the same with trying to finish writing this book – yard work, house fix it projects, cleaning, getting the car fixed, managing money, time with friends, cooking meals can absorb all of my spare time or I can *prioritize* and still get this work done.

As I explained earlier in discussing the crucial importance of paying oneself first over all other bills we also need to put our own desires right in line with the obligations. Whether it's building that toolshed or butterfly garden, roaming around Peru, Uganda or China for a couple of weeks, networking the family computers, taking a class in Russian history, organizing a huge family reunion, sponsoring a poor child from another nation to live in, taking up painting, golf or photography, it is very important that we set aside the resources of time and money required to complete such relatively non-essential avocations. It is these special dreams and desires that we all individually have that truly make life richer, deeper, more colorful, and ultimately make us wiser and more content as we age.

Yes, fulfilling our own personal, self-centered desires should also be an obligation! I am regularly in touch with various people in my life who wonder where and how I obtain the time and money to travel around the world, write books, chat on Facebook, accumulate extra savings despite work that has and does pay comparatively little, visit friends, keep a daily journal, etc. while still maintaining a comfortable home and gardens as well as doing the essential obligations from mowing the lawn, raking leaves, shoveling snow, taking out the trash, house cleaning and fix it stuff, cooking, grocery shopping and more. And I am also a parent and a husband.

While sharing some of these duties and finances with a wonderfully cooperative, loving and hardworking wife certainly helps I lived similarly when single as well. Obtaining virtually everything one realistically wants from life is very possible barring a major accident or illness. Much of being able to do so is a *mindset mentality* involving determination and goal setting that is within reason, not overbooking and overestimating while having a clear understanding of risk tolerance vs. rewards. Setting goals that are not realistic assures failure before starting as in attempting to drive across the state on an empty gas tank. Also, back to understanding the nature of what drives contentment, it is essential that one must carefully examine through visualization and cost estimating of all resources required to reach a goal before honestly setting it so as to avoid disappointment in the future. It is also important stay within reasonable boundaries and not be excessively hard on oneself. Expecting to complete a 20 page college term paper in one or two days, going in debt for over a year to pay for a family vacation, wedding or Christmas presents, turning a few hundred dollars into many thousands in the stock market almost overnight, or cooking up a four course family dinner in less than an hour are real life examples that surely lead one to shear frustration rather than contentment.

## Don't Get Derailed From Gathering the Most Opportunity From Life

Estimating risk and understanding all potential consequences of such risks is also essential throughout life. Quite often I find that listening to myself and looking at the world around me says a lot while letting my guard down and being more vulnerable to the constant barrage of advertising and scare tactics used by those who simply would like to dig into my wallet moves me in the direction of having less choices in my life. I always adjust my lifestyle to cost me fewer resources of all types to maintain than I earn so as to have extra such resources to fulfill the *special dreams* in my life. When I earned $5.00 an hour I simply lived as if I was earning $3.00 - 4.00 an hour. When I earn more I stick to exactly the same formula and always will which all but guarantees me a huge return from working – easily twice or more of the actual wage. I simply refuse to live like a robot going to work, earning money and then spending it all to live merely for the basics until I practically fall in the grave without going way beyond just surviving as if my life is mostly an in and out box of giving away my time and energy for money and then handing back my money and to some extent, time and energy as well. I am very much convinced that there is so much more potential in life!

What I find particularly difficult to observe are certain young people who may have graduated from college, perhaps still attending school or about to graduate who already are or have offers to earn $60-$100,000 a year yet they are absolutely no happier with their lives than I was earning $3.50 an hour flipping burgers at that age. Worse yet most have zero understanding of or interest in endowing their future, no desire to invest their money and are on a constant spending binge purchasing the latest smart phones, I-pads, cars, motorcycles, high end clothes, eating out in expensive restaurants that I still don't buy to this day– living as if there is no tomorrow. The *lost opportunity cost* due to such immaturity is practically incalculable in terms of simply how much more one can obtain from life! Yes the present time is important to enjoy but it can easily be enjoyed while making the future ten times better.

The real challenge is to find ways to reach such people. Can we dare to teach "healthy values" in the public schools where there may be some hope to? Probably not, because giving opinions of such endearing traditional values would be swiftly stomped on by the liberal establishment. Regardless, communicating with young adults has always been a struggle and this will not change anytime soon. I almost feel like mandating that people under the age of thirty put away a percentage of their income but sure this could be going too far.

What prevents us from being savvier with our resources? This is where grabbing on to our own sense of our emotions enters the scene. Many of us procrastinate which is a killer to such efficiency. Delaying only pushes stuff further out into the future which wastes resources and thwarts our progress in life. Others are simply careless, sloppy and tend to misplace, lose or have their precious belongings stolen or become warn out or broken far sooner than necessary only requiring more frequent efforts and costs to repair, replace and set them up again. Being overly careless might even cost us the enormous hassle of a law suit against us as with the case of someone who left their car in drive instead of park when they parked their car on a hill, cut down a tree too close to their neighbor's house letting it smash into it or leaving a laptop or phone that is not password protected with our precious information open to others. Many will work at a second job while not seeing a significant gain from it due to increasing spending when the purpose of earning more money from that extra job is to save more, pay off debt, live with less money stress and experience the more special things in life.

Life is not about spinning our wheels riding a stationary bicycle engaging in self-defeating behaviors but going places, accomplishing things and yes, ultimately becoming *totally fulfilled*. As already said once there is no "over the hill". The hill is ongoing with life becoming better and better as time passes! Changing how we manage the resources of our lives for the better is not obvious to everyone. Science has even demonstrated that our genes play a significant role in how we make life management decisions. Genes or not *we all have control over our choices* and know good ones from the bad.

Reaching this generation that were born around the mid-1980s to 2,000s, what have been given the label "millenniums" also involves a generation gap. I grew up with that $10.00 a month landline for the family. Calling long-distance was a two or three times a year event. Far away friends and relatives corresponded by postal mail. I bought costly rolls of film for my camera, carefully calculated what pictures I took and had to wait a week for my film to be processed and printed while paying dearly for the prints. To perform research meant deeply engrossing myself in textbooks and libraries. To find one's way somewhere required the use of a paper map. Everyone received the morning newspaper and television was free with fewer than ten channels while many people dried their laundry on a clothesline.

There was a sense of waiting, delayed gratification and sort of sacredness about many activities in life though not all of it was necessarily better. The manner in which reality forced us to self-generate responsibility built integrity and character within us. However, the incredible speed at which information now travels including photos, money, legal documents and more is all but mind boggling and most certainly is a significant cause of the generation gap between boomers of the 1950s to 1960s. As has been said by others this present generation of young people born after the mid-1980s practically lives on the internet rather than merely surfs the internet. Additionally the sexual generation has come full course now with pornography available at the click of a mouse, gay marriage and acceptance of LGBTQ rights and greatly softened stance on extra marital affairs with a variety of questionable implications.

## Practical Survival Skills Are Not Irrelevant

Traveling to countries where people are up before dawn tending to chickens and cows, walking miles to get water, making sure their garden feeds their family, sharing cars, TV and telephone among a village, family are living in with in-laws in one small house without plumbing or electricity and largely being their own doctor has taught me more about life, what is truly important and survival skills. One major catastrophe and we Americans may be set right back to this level of survival, yet so many of us would be clueless as to how to cope. Detaching ourselves from the ultimate forces that dictate real world survival in the disguise of technology is only temporary. It keeps us in a bubble of ignorance which we will eventually if not sooner, pay a huge price for. Should terrorists knock out much of our electric grid for several weeks this means no chilling of food, outdoor cooking with tree branches, no phone charging or cell tower power, no gas pumps working, no water pumps working for clean water, no internet, no TV, maybe spotty radio at best until our batteries die and sleeping soon after dark. I ask how prepared we are?

How we spend our spare time has vastly changed. And with people becoming accustomed to obtaining things so fast and many earning such enormous incomes in health care, finance, technology, law, engineering, etc. taking the time to carefully be frugal, live well below one's means, and seriously delay gratification is not high on the priority list as often. I come from the days when people honestly made the effort to pick up a penny on the sidewalk but do not know most anyone who still does. TVs and appliances were repaired affordably and very rarely replaced compared to now where such items are intentionally constructed to have very limited lifespans or cost a three digit dollar amount to simply get someone to drive three miles to one's home to make repairs. Certainly there is an attitude of living more in the present in some ways among the younger generation and not taking on tedious, long-term tasks of dedication for rewards well down the road. This may be in part due to how they have grown up in a more affluent society where parents have focused their efforts on raising children to achieve in academics and sports and have neglected the need for children to work as a team, learn basic survival skills, and meet responsibilities at home. The percentage of millennials who become farmers, plumbers, home contractors and construction workers has significantly decreased yet we must have people who can properly perform these trades. Yes, there are some who literally do not know how to change a lightbulb!

Also this millennial generation generally is much less aware of the contrast between generations than 50-70 year-olds in the 2000 teens in part because they have grown up with all these enormous technological changes. Hearing about paying $10 a month for the entire family's phone service is all but meaningless since the smart phone is ubiquitous to them and perceived as their lifeline. And besides, paying over a thousand dollars a year for phone service which may also include internet is not viewed as nearly as much of a burden when one is earning $50,000-100,000 a year yet interestingly enough many in the working class earning far less have these costly phones as well. They can afford it, demand it and therefore do not honestly care. The same is true of eating out rather than preparing one's own food at home which may cost from a quarter to half as much. Sometimes I wonder where that extra $1,000+ a year these services are all costing now was going before.

# More Choices Equates to More Pleasure for Most

Is it just that I am hooked on using less money and therefore having more for myself? In part, yes, because I desire more *freedom and choices* as soon as I can obtain them in life over being dependent on an employer paycheck nearly forever. I have learned via experience that the ultimate ticket to security and financial freedom is being debt free and having enough cash to largely if not fully, replace the constant necessity of the paycheck. Note that we are giving up our life energy and time to get the paycheck so if the work we are performing to receive it is not the work we would chose to perform for free then there is an imperative to obtain a method to receive money from that which we enjoy.

If good paying work is not available then we need to generate income from living below our means and investing the difference with the goal of making money work for us rather than us working for money. And though clearly health, family and rewarding social interactions come first, financial independence is not far down the list no matter how much one may relish in their occupation. However, loving one's work may reduce the imperativeness of building finances to some extent. But I will still insist that it is *experiences and freedom to choose* that offers a special level of contentment that will forever be recalled in one's brain over most material objects. However, sometimes it is the objects that assist in providing us with experiences whether it is a ride in a high end sports car, the observation of a great work of art or the view of a galaxy of billions of stars that requires a large telescope. There is always the thrill of the first time riding a new bike, driving a new car, wearing a beautiful new dress or shirt, etc. but the thrill dies off very quickly because it does not have that longer, deeper, lasting feeling that experiences and relationships do.

When we look back with good and bad memories of our childhoods it is the *interactions* we had with parents, siblings, relatives, friends and school teachers and our personal accomplishments such as hobbies over the size of the house we grew up in, how old the family car was, how large and how many channels the television received or how fancy the furniture was. But it is noteworthy to mention that a special, limited number of material objects beyond the obvious necessities such as working plumbing we attach ourselves to with sentimental, nostalgic value. I enjoy having the wooden savings bank I placed my first ten cents into and then twenty-five cents a week allowance into along with pennies I would find on the sidewalk from over fifty years ago sitting next to me right now because of the past *experiences* it represents, not the object itself. Most all of us enjoy some nostalgic objects and most certainly music and smells which have us recalling past times in our lives which our brains tend to optimize toward the positive. It is most fascinating how our sensory receptors plant memories together in such a manner that decades later a mere sight, sound, smell or touch instantly arouses the memory of an entire cascade of feelings – almost as if one is momentarily reliving the experience which may be as close to time travel into the past as we can perceive.

So just how does one live in this manner to assure that perhaps 20-50% of extra resources of money, time and energy are available to fulfill dreams beyond the necessary essentials of living? It occurred to me when very young that essential errands that many were engaged in with enormous amounts of redundancy were wasting an amazing amount of time and money which was a signal to me not to live in this manner. Even my own father used to constantly grocery shop every one to two days rather than stock up once a week saving all of those trips, time and fuel, a habit I believe came from his younger days when stores may not have been so well stocked making such regular trips a necessity.

A friend of mine tells me about his neighbors who run their car in and out of their driveway well over ten times a day. I go in homes where there are about a dozen lights on when clearly only two or three are needed to light areas where the residents are occupied. Worse yet, I observe people leaving blinds and curtains closed on bright sunny days while turning on lights when daylight obviously avoids the need for the lights being on. I see people mowing their lawns twice a week when they could simply raise the blade setting on their mower and cut their mowing time, gas used and neighborhood noise by 50%. As cited earlier it amazes me that people are still spending upwards of an hour or two a month writing paper checks, addressing envelopes, buying stamps and mailing payments when they all can be paid automatically, instantly at no cost or not receiving automatic deposit for incoming money. Some people still call their stock broker the way they did dozens of years ago to make a trade for $50 when it can be done online for less than $10. Much of such behaviors are due to a lack of knowledge of how the internet works, how to properly secure settings and passwords and having the knowledge that the bank, credit card company and stock broker will be going online to perform the same function anyway. What about the cost of wearing a wool sweater saving upwards of a thousand dollars a year in heating costs?

Yes, it's simple. The more efficient we are with resources needed for our essentials the more additional resources we accumulate to enjoy our spare time, directly improving our lives. After all, isn't it how we spend our spare time beyond merely sleeping, routine self-care, dressing, grocery shopping, driving to work and work itself – even if we like our work – that rewards us with demonstrating our self-identity? For many if not all, *feeling unique* in the world is rewarding because it makes us feel special and it is our spare time that allows us to express our individuality. Therefore, using fewer resources on the comparatively mundane essentials of life opens up more to be available for that which we choose rather than that which is essential. I realize that having more spare time is not a direct conduit to great satisfaction for all as there are some people who do not handle large amounts of spare time well and in fact are brought down by such excess amounts of time and/or money. For them spending most of their efforts and resources on survival needs and life's essentials often keeps them in better balance. But for most people I know they would prefer to have more choices.

When casually dating it normally does not take more than one or two dates to figure out if it is worth continuing to place resources into this other person yet far too many of us continue seeing others while only receiving in return the most shallow of rewards or the relationship turns to one of merely using each other instead of building toward love. Another life observation that irks me is so often watching people in work places be wasteful with tools, chemicals, supplies of all sorts, and time while using the excuse that "I am being paid by the hour" or "The business is paying for it so it does not matter how much I use".

Being resourceful is *always* sensible and morally good as well as creating more time to accomplish other things, enabling money to be saved and spent more wisely and benefitting the environment that we all share. Briefly returning to the topic of buying insurance, for many of us the choice is to buy down risk or spend less on insurance and increase financial risk in our lives while having far more cash which may enable us to pursue those great dreams. For the wealthier both are possible but for most people certainly this is not the case. We must examine to what extent our fear emotions are being exploited by the insurance industry and just how possible the chance for catastrophe realistically is in our lives. We also should honestly understand that with or without insurance every moment is a gift we are fortunate to have and that we are vulnerable to nature's forces at any time regardless. And don't forget that most *everything in life is negotiable* regardless of having insurance.

## Maintaining Our Health is the Foundation of our Lives

Last but not least of course and stated earlier is the conscious maintenance of our physical and emotional health. The sooner in life we learn to properly manage our health the more value we will reap throughout life. Being healthy is the greatest pay off we can have for all the money in the world will be entirely meaningless if we are lying in a hospital bed seriously ill – though we just might need all the money in the world to pay our bill. In practically every direction we look we are informed that we will be healthier if we maintain our weight, exercise reasonably each day, eat generous portions of a full spectrum of colorful fresh fruits and vegetables, reduce our refined sugar and beef intake, don't smoke or drink heavily, obtain a full night's rest, reduce negative stresses that threaten our state of being by arguing with the people we depend upon most such as bosses and spouses, have happy friendships and love in our lives, know our family medical history and obtain occasional medical check-ups. Should we honestly and realistically hope to experience our greatest dreams, this previous sentence lays down the foundation for the remainder to occur hands down.

Certainly reading more in depth about health and wellness is something I highly recommend since tailoring how we treat each and every one of our own bodies and minds varies according to individual characteristics and genetic propensities. In order to obtain the maximum benefit to our specific body type this certainly is a wise action to take. In addition to the obvious reward of feeling well, being fully engaged in self-preventive health saves a *fortune* over using the traditional health care system. And best of all becoming more conscious of our own health and growing healthier does not cost much if any extra money at all and in fact most likely saves money from visiting the doctor less frequently. An extra few dollars a week for fresh fruits and vegetables may offset spending on costly processed foods.

Exercising is truly free since buying equipment and joining health clubs is totally optional because the health benefits acquired from exercise can be had simply by walking, bicycling, bending and stretching and a few other basic exercises that are done without equipment. For the middle-aged and elderly, blood pressure monitoring meters, home glucose and cholesterol tests are far cheaper than seeing a doctor for the same; however medical oversight is important once a medical condition has been diagnosed. The human mind and body is the most magnificent machine known in the universe and is set to operate almost flawlessly for 80-100 years if we give it what it needs to do so. Again, *the choice is ours*. We can use our conscious mind with our knowledge of science to live better or follow our addictive, dysfunctional desires that the junk food, alcohol and tobacco industries thrive off of, be lazy and get hooked on social networking until late hours when we must be at our work desk at 8AM.

Nothing is more important than our health because health is our state of being and feeling well is the platform from which all our potential arises from. In terms of our physical health if our emotional, psychological and spiritual health is well established and strong, staying physically healthy is a whole lot easier. This is because we are far more likely to make better choices as adults when this is the case. We are more likely to exercise regularly, eliminate the junk food from our diets, get rid of the salt shaker, avoid fattening desserts, maintain good sleep habits that fall into our natural circadian rhythms and avoid toxic habits such as excessive alcohol consumption, smoking and recreational drug use. We also are less prone to accidents and engaging in risky sexual habits as well as being more sanitary and orderly. However, there are other factors including genetic family history, the quantity and quality of our diets growing up, the occupation we work in and more. We may have a parent who died young of heart disease, had diabetes, high blood pressure, breast or prostate cancer or one who exposed us to second hand smoke for twenty plus years.

Health is also a state of being that which we become more and more conscious of as we age or at least we should. In addition we need to educate ourselves on the basics of health. Even being our own doctor up to a point in these days of such easy access to information is quite simple. I have avoided doctor visits numerous times, saving much money, by simply looking up ill symptoms online and even received feedback from some nurses and doctors on symptoms free of charge. It is not hard to determine when it is necessary to see a doctor much of the time plus we save health care dollars doing so. Also information about every medication, how they work, side effects and potential interactions with other drugs all are available online as well. In addition to WebMD, Mayo Clinic and many others I found Healthtap.com to be particularly creative and interesting to use along with being able to access more affordable medical advice directly from doctors or nurses.

When we do need to visit a doctor being educated on our symptoms and what they could be indicative of usually gains respect from doctors and even has them take our case more seriously. While unfortunately some doctors prefer passive patients who are more ignorant of their own health and therefore are easier to obtain compliance from being educated can only help and put the patient doctor relationship closer to the same level. After all it's our own health and we should know all we can about it, sometimes along with the advice and support of a medical professional. I am not saying that we should not trust the advice of doctors as they are the ones who have spent all those studious, challenging years in medical school but sometimes the patient's opinions are certainly of value. I had one doctor tell me that I most likely had prostate cancer because my PSA test result came out with such a high number of 21 instead of under about 3. I told him that I would like to retest after recovering from a mild prostate infection and when I did so the result came out at less than 1.

Countless sources of medical information continue to tell people to exercise more, eat less junk food, drink water instead of sugar loaded soft drinks, eat more fresh fruits and vegetables, not smoke, not drink alcohol excessively, trim down if obese, use sun protection, use appropriate safety equipment and precautions for certain trades and jobs, sleep 7-8 hours a night, avoid difficult stresses such as major conflicts with spouses and bosses, not being an excessive pack rat becoming overwhelmed with stuff that consumes one's space, planning one's life toward what one enjoys including work and wisely managing money. Going into detail about this type of advice would merely be redundant. We all have the potential to make good, informed, healthy choices along these lines with most of it being common sense. Keep in mind that feeling healthy and free of physical and emotional pain for the long-term is the foundation from which we all can achieve the best from life itself. After all what is the purpose of life if we feel sickly, run down, frustrated, depressed and unmotivated much of the time? Life is about not only having the best but being the best!

# CHAPTER 8

# What to Stand For & Why

THERE ARE A number of social, economic and moral/cultural and religious systems in place in our society which tend to lean one way or the other or combine somewhat though generally have a bent toward more liberal or conservative ways of operating. I will outline here what I believe how and why we should support how the society operates for the most benefit for greatest number of people. It is most unfortunate that we are so politically divided now on how to accomplish this feat with liberal ways of operating having moved further to the extreme than ever before, causing ever greater polarization toward the conservative end. Conservatives for the most part support what they always have though due to these more extreme liberal ideas and policies being put forth, some feel they must move more to the extreme to offset such policies. Unfortunately doing so only spirals polarization further. In the eyes of conservatives they literally believe they are desperately trying to save the country from falling into chaos to where freedom has no limits except the freedom to speak out against the apparent fall. Liberals silence freedom when it does not fit their agenda – perhaps the most obvious being that of religious freedom since the philosophy of most mainline religions support ideals that they firmly disagree with.

The most basic problem with liberalism is that its philosophy so often goes against order, unity, efficiency, common sense, health and wellness, financial and personal responsibility, morality, natural law and even reality itself. Fighting against reality is extremely troubling! Highly civilized societies became this way through operating under these very tenants that were lived by and understood by default. And many cultural traditions and religious ideas have re-enforced such a way of life as it was taught that significantly, consciously deviating from the norm and natural flow of how human life reaches its potential would clearly bring about a more chaotic and less secure world. Indeed this is irrefutably the case as we see very commonly now. The train cannot simply go full speed ahead gliding smoothly on one set of tracks anymore. We have to have multiple sets of tracks of varying widths and lengths, made of differing types of materials. We have lost our way while we are given the message that we can and should choose what track, which train and how many stops we wish to make along the way. Yes, if even just one person needs a ride we must now inconvenience the entire train load to pick him or her up with seemingly no bottom threshold where a boundary can be placed.

Burdening the majority for the sake of the minority is now standard practice. Operating this way does not benefit the greatest number of people which needs to be the goal. Should anyone dare to place even the slightest negative judgment on any minority group, no matter how minuscule, no matter how unnatural or bizarre their behavior except for extreme violence (Even the most violent behavior will often be rewarded with comfortable jail time with TV, internet, better health care than many good people receive, and fortunes of our tax money spent on legal defense.), regardless of how much others are inconvenienced, embarrassed or even harmed we are practically harassed and silenced. Even voter referendums winning by landslides have been court ordered as invalid such as with the gay marriage laws in California and Massachusetts with no religious exemptions or protections as required by the First Amendment of the US Constitution.

Yes, the federal and state courts are now being used by the radical left to force laws through without majority consent and legislative approval and as mentioned above without religious rights or exemptions which clearly the US constitution permits. Christians or those of other beliefs who do not believe in gay marriage who perform wedding photography, make cakes, provide flowers and clothing as well as court clerks are being forced against their religious beliefs to treat gay weddings the same as heterosexual weddings. I personally was fired from a job when a coworker asked me my view on gay marriage with me simply responding that I did not care for it and nothing more. Certainly operating in this fashion is very questionable constitutionally with regard to religious freedom and freedom of speech yet the giant snowball keeps rolling down the hill seemingly without brakes. The constitution is supposed to be the ultimate law of the land yet individual court judges are being permitted to ignore it without accountability totally defying what the founding fathers of our country intended. Even our law enforcement agencies such as the FBI who should obviously have placed Hillary Clinton in jail did not do their job lawfully due in part to a corrupt attorney general and president. Democrats who are supposedly all for equal treatment of everybody make such blatant exceptions – only supporting equality on *their* terms.

The liberal philosophy is that we members of Planet Earth are a *team* and all should support each other to bring about equality for all. On the surface this sounds ideal and downright utopian in thought but reality teaches us differently. Reality is that we get what we pay for, receive what we work for or as the old expression goes, we reap what we sow. Surely we do assist others who are in need of basic necessities of life who through no fault of their own are having trouble surviving due to natural calamities, unexpected famine, disease, disability and injury. However, for most anything beyond the necessities of survival people need to be far more self-sufficient and responsible for the outcomes of their own behaviors and choices. I must accept personal responsibility proportional to the risk that I chose to take. Unfortunately most democrats do not encourage self-reliance because it goes against their values and they need people to be dependent on the government to increase their party members, much as they may deny it. They will say that they have good intentions by "helping people" but it is the results over time that truly tells the story. And the results of liberal policies do not tell a healthy story over the last several decades – from unemployment to quality of education, inner city crime rates, healthcare, welfare and food stamp dependency, illegal immigration and more.

It is this philosophy of self-sufficiency and individual responsibility that liberals seem to so despise, yet the whole concept of being more independently responsible and self-empowered is exactly what generates character, integrity and maturity with the ability to cope with whatever adversity may be placed in one's way. If I cannot afford a new pair of shoes I do not expect the government to buy me a pair. I will go to a used clothing place or garage sale and buy them for 90% off. If I cannot afford to sign up for a cell phone plan I will buy a Walmart Track Phone and purchase minutes as needed. If my rent is too high for my budget I will find a roommate, work off my rent or a cheaper place. If my heating bills are too high I will wear more sweaters, turn down the thermostat, insulate my home more or move to a smaller place or warmer climate – not expect the government to pay my heating bill. If I need medical care and I am unable to afford at the grossly inflated asking price I will negotiate a price suitable to me and my doctor rather than endlessly purchase high cost insurance. As stated earlier many doctors and hospitals will lower their standard price for those without insurance who pay cash. What I *will not* do is ask for everyone else to help me via the government! We need less sharing of responsibility and more individual responsibility – you live a healthy, moral life of hard work and discipline and you get rewarded accordingly. The level of reward in life is based on the choices we make – not on assistance from everyone else though certainly help must be provided to those who through no fault of their own are unable to help themselves.

## True Dangers of Liberalism

Individual freedom can only successfully sustain itself based on trust, maturity largely involving self-restraint, common sense morality and attributes that our great society is now struggling to hold onto as more liberal values are being accepted. The liberal/progressive movement also wants freedom but they want it with far less responsibility and frequently to the detriment of the rest of society who is expected to pick up the broken pieces and pay to support less responsible behaviors. Freedom for illegals to enter our country, live illegally in sanctuary cities and threaten our security, freedom to abuse drugs and increase costs for all and freedom for thugs to pilfer and destroy property while police stand and watch is not freedom we need. Freedom is wonderful when expressed within sensible, responsible, moral, natural boundaries that are exhibited by the natural world. However, when the governing body of a human society permits individual freedoms to cost a significant price to others within the society which in turn limits their freedom we arrive at a crossroads with great potential for confrontation. This is occurring much in part due to the fact that the liberal end of society has become so focused on minority rights that the very essence of the meaning of morality itself, right and wrong, are now more relative than absolute. They have become subjective rather than objective which is clearly very dangerous for the order of any human society. Something is terribly disturbing when we must define common sense!

A perfect example is when punches were thrown by union protestors when the governor of Michigan signed the right to work law. Labor unions have spent decades robbing workers of mandated dues while offering very unrealistically high wages and benefits to them which only adds to the cost of living for consumers and tax payers and lowers employment rates. Another example is the Obamacare requirement that women have access to unlimited free birth control and abortifacient drugs with very limited age and parental consent requirements. The strong arguments most certainly can be made that not everyone needs or uses birth control, some of the religious don't believe in using it, it is not costly, and it is used for a behavior of choice – not an illness or injury, therefore should not be covered by health insurance which most everyone must pay for. When possible and most effective are laws that only users pay for such as motorcycle helmet laws where only those who ride motorcycles pay for the helmets. And by the way, the helmet laws are in place first of course to protect the safety of riders but secondarily save money for the rest of us who buy insurance and pay for health care.

Liberalism promotes only the liberal styles of freedom of course which in turn restricts the freedom of others. There is a potentially dangerous cycle that various other countries have experienced over the ages. A free democracy (we are technically a republic, not a full-fledge democracy) such as the United States which has been around for about 250 years – with some exceptions – will only remain free if the freedoms continue to be implemented and expressed responsibly and not in excess. Free birth control for all women paid by their health insurance translates into higher costs for everyone including old men and women past reproductive age who buy medical insurance and obviously encourages more promiscuity. Freedom to smoke marijuana legally also raises costs of auto and health insurance as well as our taxes due to increased numbers of car accidents which are usually covered by insurance plus emergency services which we all pay for in taxes. Freedom to have free or low cost medical insurance also costs the remainder of the population more without providing any incentives to take responsibility for our own health only further increasing costs for all. Offering "free" college tuition to all causes similar problems. Individual prosperity is built from determination, creativity, calculated risk taking, maturity and personal responsibility which are characteristics our country was founded upon, not socialistic policies that diminish incentivizing in two directions.

The first obviously is taxing the highly successful ever more when these are the people who deserve to be rewarded due to their personal success, often the creation of jobs for others and increased share prices of their companies which in turn generate wealth for many. The United States has the highest corporate tax rates in the world, the highest being 39.1% – hardly an incentive to start and operate businesses here, though President Trump is hopefully going to reduce these high rates. When the successful and wealthy have their rewards for their hard work taxed excessively they lose their incentive to work, continue to create and improve the world while money taken from them and handed to the less fortunate rarely has the intended effect of improving their lives and in fact is more often a disincentive.

Certainly incentives are lost or reduced when one obtains cell phones, food, housing, cash and medical care for free or nearly so (I have the basic necessities I need so why bother to get a job, better job or further training?). Something is terribly wrong when people can receive more in government handouts than a job may pay them! Usually when people are left on their own to survive within reason, their overall performance in life dramatically improves. Yes, hunger may be the best motivator! In some countries that I visited in Africa people either work to place food and water in their mouths or they die. While I don't support living at this extreme observing these cultures in action certainly impressed me and, by the way, I saw nobody who appeared malnourished. And almost all appeared to be surprisingly happy considering their apparent near desperate circumstances. Our perception of what we think creates satisfaction is all relative.

# Radicalization Is and Will Be A Failure

In recent years the Democratic Party has become radicalized in part by Obama being president which encouraged and accelerated radicalization. The Republican Party never was and is not radical since its goals have largely remained the same – that of believing in individual accountability, responsibility and compassion with less government control of the population. Those Democrats who call themselves progressives are generally the more radical members of the party. Examples of behaviors I consider radical are the lawlessness of ignoring the constitution, instituting gay marriage, lowering the authority and power of the police and military, all but hanging a welcome sign at our borders for illegal immigrants to pour in while no other countries do this, nationalizing health care while not attacking the medical industry for its blatant scamming, blaming climate change on human use of energy while not understanding the science, showing little concern about the national debt while continuing to spend excessively, declaring that one can self-identify as something other than what one naturally is and be taken seriously and violently protesting and even refusing to permit free speech by those opposed to their beliefs. Such extremism is a significant reason why Donald Trump was elected along with his opponent being a vicious woman of dishonor. The public at large for the most part do not support the extremes or the vagueness of limits liberals thrive on.

In our country in the past and presently in many other countries this is how people live. There were and are few if any safety nets such as insurance or government programs. I am not saying that we should eliminate all safety nets. I have visited countries where there are none and yes people are far more self-reliant which highly impresses me but to have *nothing* to fall back on in the worst case scenarios is not right either. I have learned to never take my American lifestyle totally for granted and now occasionally contemplate how I could cope if I had no power for a week or two in freezing weather, how I would get water if it stopped coming from the tap, or perhaps even have to grow some of my own food.

Becoming middle-class or wealthy does not come on a silver platter! It comes only from hard work, dedication, perseverance, education and setting goals along with a moral base. This again is why labor unions so unfairly cut out a segment of the population, forcing mostly those with no union wages and benefits to pay for the few that receive them only causing further economic division among the population. I find it ironic that labor unions supposedly have the intention to preserve and protect employee wages and benefits while at the same time have forced employers to outsource and many municipalities to file bankruptcy causing the loss of jobs while also pilfering the paychecks of employees for outrageous dues with questionable intentions – usually lobbying for more union rights only making things worse.

There is also something peculiarly strange about liberals supporting labor unions even though they so unfairly discriminate by offering select groups unrealistically high benefits and wages for a minority of the population. I thought liberals supported equality for *all*. I realize that the argument can be made that we all should be unionized and given "fair" wages or as the expression goes, a "living wage" and benefits. Yes, and then we could largely kill capitalism by doing so since corporate profits would sink along with their share prices due to having to compensate employees to this level. The stock market would drop in value significantly reducing retirement account values. Therefore, we would pay somewhere else if not in more modest wages. In addition unionization of all would place a crushing burden on tax payers. So clearly the result of doing so would be to reassign wealth creating mediocrity for most everyone – so typical of socialist policies.

Not everyone is willing nor has the disposition to organize their lives in such a manner that assures greater prosperity and freedom. We must face the simple fact that we are all *different* in many ways and will achieve very different outcomes in our lives. Some will struggle and be comparatively poor compared to others who come from more educated families, are more dedicated and organized and some will inherit and/or win lotteries or law suits. Some will pursue advanced degrees and some will not. Some investors will make fortunes on penny stocks while others will lose the same. It is essential that we accept that there are *winners and losers* – that not everyone can be a winner – something that most liberals refuse to accept because they tend to be stuck in believing that all have the right to economic equality. *Having* equal opportunity and *being* equal are in quite different categories. A child with an IQ of 94 and another child with an

IQ of 160 raised in the same environment with the same opportunities available to them are clearly going to have different outcomes in their lives. Another may have problems with alcohol or drugs even though they flew through advanced calculus and received honor awards. A society performs better with self-evident built-in incentives largely based on natural law because this is what reality is truly based on – not so much our conscious choices which can vary considerably from being morally good or not.

If an engineer who invents a car engine that can achieve 150 miles to the gallon of gas at an affordable price to the consumers this person most certainly deserves to increase the size of their bank account considerably. The obvious benefit to the consumer will be the gas savings but to attempt to spread the wealth by gouging the inventor with much higher taxes simply because fifty million people bought his engines goes against natural law. Why? Because *supply and demand* are rules of natural law. The person who invents a device everyone likes, wants, benefits from and is willing to pay a price for makes a lot of money. And yes, this person may have the multi-million dollar house, a yacht, travel the world, endless high tech gadgets and more. Additionally he or she most likely invests a pile of cash back into the economy directly from purchasing stocks, bonds and real estate which creates further economic activity including job creation. This inventor also pays a fair amount in taxes and if not, is using legal tactics to permit further investing in the business, hiring more employees and adding cash to the equity markets which creates jobs, let alone employing people to landscape the property, maintain the pool and yacht and manage properties.

Why should this great inventor be "punished" with excessively high taxes to artificially spread wealth in order to keep people lazy on government doles? For a society to function well its people must give energy, dedication and time to receive, not sit back and collect indirectly from those who are better off. It has been said that we do not really have the "haves and the have nots" but those who chose to produce and those that do not. Though everyone will not be a great inventor, entertainment star, or even a well-paid professional we all can achieve middle class status or arrive very close to it as I explained in the chapter on finance. How we live is a *choice*. We can accomplish most anything we want dearly enough. It is simply called hard work and focusing on goals! As for the role of the government it does have an important role and that role is to provide incentives for its citizens to prosper, behave morally and ethically and assist the destitute who are not able to provide for their own sustenance among some other things as well. Perhaps the only area where I might create an exception is in health care where large profits and greed clash with humility, compassion and the essentialness of medical attention to sustain health and life.

Playing class warfare by punishing the highly successful and wealthy excessively while giving the less fortunate not just incentives, but cash does not work. Since financial independence is achieved less by what one earns but more by one's attitude toward money, goal setting and lifestyle choices, handing out cash to most of the "less fortunate" accomplishes little and can make things even worse. Usually such cash vanishes within days and the less fortunate person is right back to ground zero again. I observe too many people who receive SNAP benefits and other handouts while still having enough money to waste on booze and cancer sticks (cigarettes). If they can waste $100+ a month on this trash it should be taken right from other assistance! Cash needs to be tied to work no matter what it is. If one must clean toilets at the local park so be it. Nobody has to make this type of work a lifetime calling. When nothing is expected in return for cash people naturally become lazy so yes, cash can be a *disincentive*. I personally know someone whose wife teaches school in inner city Philadelphia and this is what an eight-year-old third grader told her when she was attempting to help her learn to read. "I don't need to learn to read because when I get older I can get a check from the government like my mom." I hope this real life example makes this very clear!

Why find a job, plant seeds, cut down my lifestyle some, start a small business, learn to invest and otherwise structure my life toward success and prosperity when I have in effect an annuity from the government? It is not right for those who refuse to work who are able to work to exploit from those who do. This is nothing but cheating – the same principle as a school child cheating on a test who did not properly study for it. You want an A? Study your brains out like the others who get As. You want a comfortable, debt-free life, a nice home, a car, travel, etc.? Get the right credentials for a decent paying occupation and be smart with your money. Other than some occasional tax breaks we should not expect a whole lot from the government beyond basic infrastructure maintenance, policing and military security which simply means higher taxes and debt for all.

Liberals believe in *freedom at any price* which of course is an oxymoron since when a freedom for one person stomps out someone else's freedom they cancel each other out. In only the most recent decade or two we have started to question, lessen the worth and even implement changes to the most cherished deeply rooted, sacred values of human society which many now view only on the shallowest and selfishness of surfaces. This is liberalism gone awry – having mutated into progressivism which is an even more extreme, radical and dangerous version which people such as Barrack Obama and Hillary Clinton relish in. If you don't believe it look at this quoted statement from Allen West. "Barack Obama is the final piece of the map in the progressive movement's century of steady destruction of the U.S. dollar, income taxation, and massive liberal intrusion into the lives of all Americans from birth to death." These progressive ideas originated with Karl Marx and Friedrich Engels as outlined in the Communist Manifesto. Such principles were adopted and implemented by men such as Lenin, Stalin, Mao, Castro and Chavez. Is this where we really want to go? I don't think so! We should not have to be fighting for the basic freedoms our country was founded upon, yet we now are since liberal political leaders and court judges force this extremism on us.

Activities and behaviors that repulsed us only a generation ago are now literally being *celebrated* – from marijuana legalization to endorsing homosexuality and probably polygamy with the label of marriage, endless printing of money to only fix the present without seriously looking ahead, the diminished role of religion and patriotism, offering countless illegal aliens amnesty only bankrupting us further, permitting greed via mandated medical insurance in the health care industry to lower the quality of life for all, over use of technology, excessive political correctness and continuing to give organized labor the green light despite the obvious downfall it is causing for others. There are certainly consequences for such changes in social attitudes which cannot all be good.

Why should the healthy have to gracefully accept poor behaviors that increase costs for the rest of us? Again it comes back to having reasonable boundaries and benchmarks for our behaviors and ideals. Prohibition of alcohol did not and will not work. Eliminating cigarettes from the world would dramatically increase the health and lifespans of millions and save fortunes in health care costs but all we can do is promote how bad they are for our health hoping people take note and make the choice to change their behaviors. Ice cream, candy and long list of junk foods significantly contribute to why our country is well down the list in longevity, but of course we will not get near prohibiting it nor should we be this restrictive. The "war on drugs" has not had the greatest success rate and our jails are loaded with drug offenders – perhaps excessively and now the opiate and heroin problems are worse than ever. Understandably many people obtain access to marijuana regardless of the law but shall we endorse its use by legalizing it only adding another item to our repertoire of unhealthy substances? Is legalization of pot the gateway to legalization of far more dangerous drugs as it has been for some users? And what about the health consequences of its use and its legal ramifications in the cause of vehicle accidents? As for the medicinal value this is minimal and often used as an excuse for recreational use.

I view freedom very differently. Having boundaries is what provides me with freedom because it is rules that guide and set the tone to be practical and free. For example, I have the freedom to breathe smoke free air in most public places now unlike in the past because we have placed conditions on when and where people can smoke. Smokers still are free to smoke but now have conditions placed on where since their habit is irrefutably unhealthy and a potential fire hazard to others. By knowing one must follow rules they are then free because there is *certainty and security* in one's life as long as the rules are not excessively intrusive. This certainty brings about a peaceful sense of control over one's life that otherwise would not exist.

Uncertainty brings about chaos and indecisiveness which is not what I consider freedom. I may not agree with the speed limit on some roads but at least I can freely rest upon knowing the limit. When I look back on my favorite school teachers, those that immediately clarified the classroom rules the first day of school with virtually zero exceptions *always* come up first. Clarity is like a breath of fresh air. Now I can plan with a set of expectations within a set of rules which without I would not be able to complete my goals. Just imagine a football game with almost no rules. One side wears red shirts and the other side blue shirts. The ball is tossed out into the center of the field and each side can do *anything* they wish to get the ball into the end zone. No doubt players would nearly kill each other. In hockey players would be jabbing each other with their sticks while in basketball they would literally fight over the ball and pitch to kill in baseball. And it is the rules which without we could not be able to play with any sensibility.

Vagueness of boundaries is not healthy for the mind as it leaves the door open to follow through with temptation whether in school, the workplace and other aspects of life. Redefining the definition of marriage to anything but the obvious historically standing definition of monogamous male and female committing to a life-long friendship and perhaps parenting sets the stage for the word to have any number of possible meanings and arrangements. And doing so only adds further confusion to the society, especially the children. We simply cannot continue to cater to every different minority group while basically pretending they are the same as everyone else when they are not because their behaviors are different. Homosexuals simply are not the same as heterosexuals though obviously they do not deserve to be treated in some inferior manner and not being able to marry does not imply inferiority. An analogy is that there are slightly different rules of the road for large trucks and buses than cars – not because trucks and buses are inferior but different. Let's face the facts of reality rather than pretending things are the same that are not! There is already talk in California of quad marriages of two men and two women and even speculation of being able to marry one's dog.

Marriage implies the potential to produce offspring which gay relationships cannot do naturally. It really is this simple if only we would not flex the definition. Obviously the Supreme Court should have permanently defined marriage as the union of one man and one woman as it has been among all civilizations for millennia and put it to rest! But no, the radicals who many non-radicals support must keep fighting even by repulsively shoving their unnatural agenda into everyone's face. Obvious examples are two men marrying on the Rose Bowl float, President Obama intentionally sending gay athletes to the Olympics to spite President Putin in Russia who is opposed to gay marriage and wasting more time and energy in the military fussing over LGBTQ rights than addressing the needs of our allies fighting radical Islam. And deciphering family trees in future generations will be ever more complex as gay parenting becomes more prevalent. To carry this agenda even further we are now discussing denying the reality of our sex – telling even young children that if they feel like the opposite sex they can act, dress and use the opposite sex restroom (self-identification). Most such aberrant behaviors are naturally grown out of by adulthood yet by encouraging them with such rights and publicity we are only turning an insignificant issue into one with nearly priority status. Telling children to deny reality could be classified at a form of child abuse!

The debt crisis here in the United States and throughout much of the world is now here and bringing down the standard of living due to the simple facts of the natural law of mathematics that economists and government officials were aware of many years ago. We are at $20trillion of debt with far more heading into the future which will *never* be payable. This is literally insanity yet Washington apparently cannot stop excessive spending largely on stuff we don't need or paying far too much for what we do need. This boils down to the obvious common sense that *in order to acquire wealth one must produce* – one does not receive without giving first. I do not expect a paycheck from my employer unless I work to receive it, something pathetically obvious. I also do not expect a prosperous retirement unless I have saved during my younger years. Our government political leaders must wake up to reality! With a real businessman, Donald Trump in the White House I am more hopeful.

Even Social Security that is money paid into by employees over the years which is later returned to retirees – over all a good concept until the government started robbing funds from it years ago to pay for unrelated things. But when we create programs such as Medicare and Medicaid, unemployment insurance and public employee pensions with less money than they cost to pay out claims on and administer, we run up against the natural and irrefutable flow of mathematics once again. A cycle of basically irrational behavior begins. We create debt by issuing bonds as long as there are buyers of such bonds to raise funds in order to offset losses. We also just out right print money as well – literally creating money from nothing believing that it will keep having value to the people. For the time being the public continues to give it value, though like anything else, the more that is printed the less valuable it becomes. This in turn causes inflation that we all have experienced in higher costs across the board from property taxes to electric rates, gasoline, groceries, clothing, and the worst offenders of all, college tuition and health care. Note that the main reason for the last two being so out of line with the others is that they receive a nearly endless flow of subsidies and insurance money.

In the well-intended actions of liberals to equalize the population's distribution of wealth we try to tax the wealthier class who already pay way higher percentages of their income than the rest of the population with the expectation that doing so will provide the opportunity for a greater share to achieve the American dream. The dream still largely consists of having high enough income to own a home, a car, have access to affordable medical care, raise a family, take some vacations and basically have a reasonably secure lifestyle in the middle-class.

There are a couple of problems with this philosophy as much as it attempts to bring up those with less. First, again, to really thrive one must *earn* their way up just as most of the wealthy have. I have worked menial jobs paying in the single digits per hour for many years and often several at a time with the focused goal of becoming middle-class and having more choices in my life. I feel great that I worked all of those varied shifts, tolerated many difficult situations, lived well below my means and taught myself enough about the basics of investing to benefit immensely from doing so. Some are more fortunate and graduate from school with a highly marketable degree and jump right into a good paying occupation and others toil for years and pile up debt obtaining more degrees. Regardless, my point here is that time, hard work and self-discipline (the essence of self-responsibility) are what build character – giving one an ever stronger value on life itself.

The other aspect of overtaxing the wealthy including corporations is that the wealthy give a lot back to our society from large charitable donations, helping with causes around the world, technology for libraries and schools and the creation of countless jobs. It may feel "unfair" for the CEOs to make hundreds of times more in one year than others in the company will earn in their entire lives or appear to be grossly extravagant to see them stay in thousand dollar a night hotels and own $20,000,000 homes. But this excess cash is employing many people. This principle applies to investors as well. The wealthier of society who generally do not need a regular forty hour a week job invest in real estate, stocks and bonds, etc. which provides money to business in order to invest in supplies and equipment, both of which create jobs for workers to produce run.

Putting down those who legitimately have acquired substantial wealth or even capitalism itself that permits limited numbers of people to become rich is not very productive. For it is such great creative and intelligent minds who have developed products, services and marketing to create impressive corporations that provide us with secure paychecks. The rich already pay a way greater share of taxes of all types than the less well-off and should – *up to a point*. People are compensated by the *value* they bring to a company and though not always, usually they are worth what they earn. However, I do understand the seemingly obnoxious level of disparity in income some have and do not support ex-presidents and celebrities being paid more for one hour of speaking than several people may earn in an entire year of full-time work. But I do not blame them. I blame universities and other institutions that are foolish and wasteful enough to create this level of demand by offering such absurd sums.

Suppose I had blown the money I earned selling my photography way back in the late 1970s instead of investing it for my future and only been willing to work at one instead of two or three jobs over the years. Then suppose again that I gave up at finding decent work and got on food stamps, welfare, Medicaid and subsidized housing. Perhaps I would have fallen into the poverty trap and had even less incentives to work like hell and set goals. My marriage probably would have failed as my wife does not support living this way. I may have become a taker instead of a giver to the world. But the remainder of the population really has little responsibility to support me if I am not disabled and can work. Yet at this time in our history about half of our population supports a liberal democratic agenda that all but promotes government dependency over personal self-responsibility.

Americans now have many households receiving more in free government handouts than the average household income! The Senate Budget Committee said that in fiscal year 2011 between food stamps, housing support, child care, Medicaid and other benefits, the average U.S. household *below* the poverty line received $168.00 a day in government support while the median household income was $137.13 per day. This is the equivalent of a job paying around $30 an hour full-time or $10 per hour more than the average wage. Meanwhile our debt keeps growing astronomically. I could increase my net worth faster by *not working*! Surely something is very wrong with this picture.

Yes, a very large part of our population has become pathetically lazy and our government is giving into this victimhood nonsense. People in the United States at this time *choose* to be victims while they like to make excuses of being black, Hispanic, female, pregnant, gay, etc. or blame the economy. I will bet most anyone that I could parachute down nearly anywhere except extremely remote places with hardly a couple of hundred bucks in my pocket and that within a week or two I would find a way to survive without free handouts. I might not love what I am doing but whether I am having to clean out the cow poop from a barn, rake leaves, live in for an old or handicapped person in exchange for room and board, find work at a local restaurant or factory, clean toilets, hold a construction flag on the highway, work a night shift stocking the local grocery store or donate blood plasma I, *will survive*. If the hardship is too much I will relocate.

This is how Americans once lived. Now that I have lived without running water and power with hole in the ground toilets and other conveniences we take for granted along with observing everyone working just for their next meal, most anything else nearly feels luxurious. Everything is relative in this sense. While the person who is used to four star hotels complains when they must stay in a two star hotel the person staying in a one star one is delighted to be placed in a three star room. When I handed out a one dollar bill to some poor African children they literally snatched it from my hand and inadvertently tore it up fighting for it perhaps the way a similar group in America would for a $100 bill.

Another awful aspect of social change in our country's history is how we divide and treat various groups of people. Treating someone differently for such practical matters as college entrance, voting eligibility and employment merely because of the color of their skin, religion, sex or sexual orientation is nothing but just plain *ignorance*. We could just as easily divide people by hair color, height, or how long their nose is. What actually matters in this world is our *behavior*, not our physical appearance because behavior is what affects the society and the world, *not* our appearance. Ignorance and racism isolated various minority groups during our history which to a partial extent caused some negative behaviors to be more prevalent in certain populations. Now we often associate poor behaviors with ethnicity which, to some extent does have validity with such groups as Muslims who have a higher chance of becoming radicalized toward terrorism or black people who statistically commit more crime in our cities. Profiling is unfortunate but it is simply a fact that certain groups statistically have a higher chance of certain types of behaviors which must be addressed for the safety of society.

Then along came the entitlement generation starting with President Franklin D. Roosevelt and continuing into the 1960s and beyond. Meanwhile countless reasonably dependable, good paying manufacturing jobs that did not require advanced levels of education employed many rural and minority people for well over an entire generation. Most unfortunately, many of these jobs either vanished due to technology taking their place or were outsourced to areas of cheaper labor overseas such as China in part due to union enforced wages and benefits which of course were excessive – not being commensurate for the type of work being performed or with the profits of the companies. Any business person with common sense, should they be offered 60 cent per hour wages for employees instead of $15.00 an hour wages plus benefits would move their company to the lower wage location. So we see why during the last twenty five years the "made in China" syndrome took over our country. Some of this lost money is returning in the form of wealthy Chinese investing in property here, the stock markets, tourism and education. And President Trump is doing all he can to bring more jobs back to the USA. Lowering the business tax is a good start.

How much employees are compensated must be based on how *profitable* a company is and their *skill level*, not on what they need to support their standard of living. Perhaps how wages are divided up within companies could be changed some such that there are less extremes but wages can simply not be set so artificially high that they kill profits or seriously burden tax payers either. I don't own and run a company to pay employees living wages; I operate it to make a profit. Am I merely being a greedy, selfish bastard to do so? Not at all! This is simply the nature of being in business and capitalism. The more profitable my company is, the more I can expand it and hire more employees and perhaps help enrich shareholders who then will spend their money generating more economic activity.

Should the government come in and raise the minimum wage excessively or a union leader declare that my machinists who are making $18.00 an hour must now make $24.00 an hour I will have to either lay off some employees costing the country jobs or raise the price of my products and/or services which will cost consumers more out of their pocket. *Either way there is a cost.* And let us get it straight that most all of us are shareholders, not only the wealthy. Most workers have some type of retirement plan available to them. These plans are all invested in the equity markets, often via mutual funds which depend on companies profiting and growing in order to increase in value over time. And for those without such plans the individual retirement account is available as explained earlier which also invests in such funds. Washington State raised its minimum wage to $15.00 an hour. No doubt now various products and services have gone up in price, some jobs have been cut and the workers most likely are still complaining that they "can't make ends meet". It is in the nature of humans to increase their spending in proportion to their income along with the griping that they do not have enough making the higher wage not necessarily improve contentment.

There seems to be a prevailing attitude mostly among liberals that most everyone is somehow entitled to live in a comfortable house, have a cell phone, use all the heat and air conditioning they wish, have virtually unfettered access to medical care, child care and attending whatever college one wishes more and more on the taxpayer's burden to pay. Indeed I am willing to assist some in helping via my taxes to provide *starting* opportunities to those with significant disadvantages in life to get them moving upward in prosperity. And if that initial boost launches such people to eventual success in life so much the better for society! However, if such initial stimulus is only very temporary we have failed. It is then time to assess the situation and determine to what degree individuals have taken responsibility for their lives. The less responsible they are the more they need to be financially squeezed and incented with less benefits as there is no better motivator to become self-reliant and ultimately successful than feeling hungry. It is amazing how fast people get moving when their phone service is cut off, the electric company is threatening to do so, their credit limit is reached on a credit card or they feel tempted to steal from the grocery store. I have been to countries with no safety nets at all and never have seen such hard working people.

As this less educated segment of the population lost work they tended to migrate into the inner cities if not already there and then social decay and unrest began occurring. The divorce rate dramatically increased as did the crime rate, drug use and violent teenage gangs. The better educated and white populations moved away from cities further creating class division in what used to be called white flight. A sort of new racism then developed in which mostly black and Hispanic minorities tended to be associated with illegal drug use, violence, shootings, victimhood and poverty, unfortunately still lingering today. I recall well people holding their bags and purses closer to themselves and locking their car doors when such people are near them in public. Even I was blatantly ripped off when in business for myself by such thugs, the license plate number of their getaway car being tracked by the police to a neighborhood they told me *they* would prefer not to enter.

## Race Means Nothing - Character Means Everything

I have since worked with people from practically every nationality one can imagine and largely left such feelings of distrust behind me though I know to avoid most ghetto areas of American cities. Racism and discrimination of all types is largely based on *behaviors* associated with a group which may be divided by skin color or some other ethnic trait. Certainly it is no surprise that many of us now conjure up images of terrorism when we merely come in close proximity to a person who is of Middle Eastern background or worse yet, mistakenly so. Acting in this manner is nothing more than our human instinct to guard and protect our personal safety and the safety of others even though rationally we may know that only a tiny percentage of Muslims are potential terrorists. Assuming we are mentally healthy we naturally gravitate toward others who are more likely to have a neutral or positive influence on us. Unfortunately in every society there are some people who will not conform to basic rules of civility, decency and self-responsibility and therefore will have to be isolated from the mainstream for the sake of the public's safety.

Many liberals and the majority of black Americans continue by choice to keep racism alive. Some such as the Reverend Jessie Jackson and Al Sharpton actually make their living from *perpetuating racism where it does not exist*. What we desperately need is more black leaders to put such people in their place and teach the black community that distrusting non blacks only helps blacks remain isolated, angry and impoverished. They should be teaching that color is *meaningless* and that whites clutching their valuables and snapping locks shut upon being near primarily young black men is simply due to the very poor reputation this segment of the population holds. Civil rights laws have been firmly on the books for a couple of generations now so it is long overdue that black and other poverty ridden groups pull themselves together and accomplish some solution oriented problem solving from within. According to government statistics 35% of black school children in grades 7-12 have been suspended or expelled from school compared to 15% for whites and around 80% of prisoners are black males in a majority white population so certainly it is long overdue for those responsible to take this major social problem into their own hands and stop burdening the remainder of the population to carry the weight. It is no wonder that police are biased toward stopping and arresting young black men!

According to the Bureau of Justice Statistics, one in three black men can expect to go to prison in their lifetime – and I ask whose fault is this. Various media outlets seem to relish in slanting statistics making it appear that racism is the cause of such higher incarceration rates. I have talked with black and white police officers who both simply say that they equally have far more problems communicating with, disciplining and arresting blacks than whites largely due to such extreme attitudes against authority. Color in of itself is meaningless but it is the *culture* of abuse, drugs, violence and fatherlessness that brings out the worst in anyone yet remains most prevalent among our poor black inner city neighborhoods. It is way past due for such people to look in the mirror rather than always casting blame elsewhere. Perpetuating division and racism along with the list of free handouts only maintains the status quo with minimal change. Worse yet doing so can reignite racism where it had not existed for many years as middle class people of all races keep watching murder, random knock out being played, drug crime and family abuse on their TV news primarily being committed by black youth. Profiling arises from reputation.

And what has our bi-racial president done about this problem other than to increase government entitlements rather than promote stronger family values and provide more employment? Though change often requires throwing money at a problem; money throwing in and of itself is analogous to kicking the can down the road, something the liberal end of Washington has done for decades with minimal positive results. The poverty and violent crime in our cities is an embarrassment to the world and inexcusable in our country of greater education and wealth! When we finally stop politicizing and finger pointing at social and economic problems and instead actually take action that generates real change we may finally see healthy outcomes. We know the underclass needs better employment, education, the drug life cleaned up, financial education and stronger families that care. It is easy for the rest of society to ignore this problem until we see drug and gun battles in our streets but it is time overdue to do things right in this area through appropriate social services and community based policing, quick care affordable health clinics and church involvement. These young people in our poor city neighborhoods need more than a basketball, gang leaders and rap singers to look up to. They need more solid male and female role models with strong work ethics that demonstrate why and how it feels good to clean up the streets, set goals, work hard, avoid drugs and early sex.

Black previous U.S. Attorney General Eric Holder was another obvious racist who sued states for implementing voter ID laws that only have the purpose of verifying legal citizenship with no regard to race whatsoever. And Loretta Lynch, his successor, is no better. Frankly, the obvious, common sense move to make would be for the federal government to *require* all states to require voter identification. Someone explain to me why simply requiring one to present a photo ID to vote in any matter discriminates against anyone! If one does not have a driver's license they can easily obtain a photo ID for *free*. I hate to say that those who oppose this are politically motivated but the indicators do point in this direction because those who are not easily able to obtain proper identification often are either poverty ridden in some form and/or an illegal alien – both groups who are statistically more likely to vote democratic.

And as for drivers licenses being an ID some states such as California are permitting illegal aliens to obtain them – giving illegal voting a green light, though they could simply say on such licenses that they are not valid for voter registration but they don't. And while at this topic I ask why *all states* don't agree to have the *identical* voting equipment and rules to streamline the system and not provide any advantages to either party. Isn't this an obvious action to take? Pew Research reports that the cost of processing a voter registration in the state of Oregon is $7.67 yet in Maricopa County AZ only 3 cents. How could there be such a difference within the same country? And for reference Canada processes voter registration at 35 cents per person and 93% register while only 75% of Americans register.

Even more pathetic is the obvious fact that we do not as a society implement the right incentives to create positive change toward individual accountability. Many of this underclass population are taking more free and discounted benefits than ever which are only an incentive to not change. Worse yet, keeping this population in such a holding pattern has political motivation as well. The more handouts they get the more they will tend to vote democratic which is the worst case scenario. The same political motive applies to supporting organized labor, gay rights and the overspending in Washington which keeps pumping debt created money into people's hands. The promoting of traditional family values, patriotism, more restrained sexual behaviors, keeping marijuana illegal, reduced excess spending, cutting health care costs and being more self-responsible with less insurance and toughening up on illegal immigration, border security and voter ID requirements does not win over many votes for conservatives.

This is why. It is human nature to take the easy and fun path while conservatives are asking for people to exert effort to restrain from the excessive use of government benefits which requires work. For most people it is more appealing to vote for someone who supports more government spending which ensures the security of fat paychecks of many who depend on countless government contracts. It is also more appealing to be able to legally purchase pot, have more sexual choices endorsed by society, be assured of endless amounts of medical care for all, for illegal immigrants to be freer, abortion to be more accessible and not have to be responsible all of the time.

The message of behaving more morally, responsibly, accountably and otherwise in a more restrained mode of integrity, regardless of the fact that doing so normally brings about the greatest long-term benefits to most any human society, does not have the immediate appeal to many, especially our young people. And the liberal media makes certain that it de-emphasizes such values. This situation was far less this way only one to two generations ago. This attitude prevails ever more today as people grab their cell phones and instantly begin taking photos and video of sensational violent events before even checking to see if someone is hurt. Acting in such a manner certainly says something about our emotional state and what we decide is important to us in the moment with such easy to use technology that permits us to record and instantly share. Is it more important to us to be the first person to upload some bizarre, violent scene to YouTube or Facebook than to rescue a person in dire need? If so we are in serious trouble! Conservative values are about human society living in ways that ultimately make our lives more rewarding, healthier and enjoyable. Liberal values are based on a lower level of maturity, largely promoting instant gratification and rights for everyone no matter how costly and inconvenient to others.

I have worked in the inner city primarily in schools with high populations of minority children, black and Hispanic. I have seen firsthand exactly how these mostly fatherless kids behave, experienced the anger many have and the distrust of me being white. I have had my life threatened, been hit and cursed by students, seen school administrators promote such kids to the next grade even though they hardly ever showed up to class and flunked, either due to district pressure to manipulate numbers, corruption or desperation. In 2014 Attorney General Eric Holder enforced laws to break down "racial discrimination" in child discipline in public schools. Statistics everywhere show that black students are about 30% more likely to receive disciplinary action than whites even though they comprise only 15% of the population. Liberals naturally wish to point the finger at racism when I ask how many of them have ever spent time in an inner city minority school. I say spend a week in such classrooms and then let us hear your response! It is solid, conservative leadership that is essential in promoting the values of a good society such as life-long marriage, strong family life, spirituality, going well beyond simply telling kids to say no to drugs, gangs and early sex but understanding the details of why such behaviors clearly lead to a dangerous, impoverished, terrible life which the entire society pays for.

The most successful blacks have learned to *ignore their color*, held their marriages and families together and have completed the hard work and taken the risks of leaving their poor neighborhoods in favor of a truly much better life. Am I suggesting blacks and other disenfranchised minority groups "become white"? Not at all! I am saying that they *must* improve their behavior should they wish to have a better life *regardless of race*. And let us not forget that we have many whites and Hispanics who are equally impoverished and need to take the same actions. Unfortunately having a *liberal-progressive* African American president who not only maintained the status quo and perpetuated racism and division but did nothing to slow black crime and in fact may have encouraged it due to ever more free or reduced handouts (from a basically bankrupt government) being available yet is not at all what the blacks need. As for racism Obama even blamed his lower approval ratings in early 2014 on his color yet a significant aspect of how he got elected related to his color. If only we were all the same color!

The Travon Martin case is such a classic example. The case was very carefully adjudicated in the fairest manner possible with every shred of evidence precisely researched and considered by an impartial jury but outcome the blacks and mostly liberal whites and Hispanics blaming racism. If Mr. Zimmerman was black it would simply be another black on black murder ignored by the media along with the several such murders that occur daily in our cities. And when a group of black teens murder a white man as happened not long after this case it hardly appears as a blip in most of the media. Progress will not be made until skin color is *innocuous* just as is hair and eye color, height, and other benign genetic features of appearance. Behavior is everything. When one behaves well they have a better life and when they don't they have a worse life – race aside, *period!* And taking personal responsibility for one's behavior is the hallmark of becoming a mature adult. Pity parties can only go on for so long. After a certain point in life if one has not learned the consequences of good vs. bad behaviors and they continue to not make good, healthy choices they must pay the price and not expect the remainder of society to share in the cost.

## Nothing Is Free

The liberal democratic establishment opened up the floodgates of government entitlements to the disadvantaged population segment without emphasizing practical education and job training enough as well as assistance in holding marriages together. They gave African Americans advantages with affirmative action laws that caused a backlash of reverse discrimination law suits by whites since employers and colleges were hiring and accepting some based more on their color than their ability while obviously it is ability that ultimately matters. For many receiving welfare, SSI, food stamps, Medicaid, discounted rent, college grants and loans, low cost legal services, etc. became an easier way of life than going to work and if with several children paid better than many jobs. I am not saying that republicans should have left poor people starving on the streets but certainly they stand more for self-reliance and accountability and providing a safety net to those who are in true need and unable to work. The more independently we can live relying on our own personal abilities, common sense, intelligence, intuition and moral standing the less we rely on government resources, thereby reducing the burden on everyone else.

Free things should almost never be given to anyone except the truly *desperate* poor and disabled. Surely certain areas of the economy such as college tuition and medical care are much too costly, but why not pressure higher education and the medical industry to lower costs rather than offer such services for "free or reduced" cost to consumers while raising taxes for everyone? There should be requirements to accomplish something for the good of society in order to receive things and money which President Clinton signed into law under congressional pressure – workfare over welfare. I do not care if someone has to sweep the sidewalks, shovel snow, assist their neighbor in a home repair, get EMS trained and volunteer for their local fire department, compile records online, or whatever but practically *nothing* should come free for those young and able enough to produce. Also, truly effective job training must be implemented that is known to generate results. Our government has spent $billions on job training yet results are hardly measurable. A working person is not only a productive person but usually a happier person. The fewer takers and the more producers, the more prosperous and satisfied a society will be, an irrefutable formula for economic success. The bottom line is that there must be accountability throughout the system which without the society will fail. With the fraud rate in various government programs such as Medicare, Medicaid, Welfare, Food Stamps, the IRS and others now climbing into the $100-300billion range annually we obviously are in serious trouble. Certainly we can do better.

Accountability begins at the top with our elected politicians who must take action on what is right over what keeps them in office. A couple of major changes could certainly be legislated to start. First, lobbying should generally be banned. Clearly, citizens and corporations should be calling and writing letters and e-mails to our elected officials regularly to express their concerns. However, we should not be able to use money as bait to persuade politicians and policy makers since doing so obviously opens the door to corruption because *nothing* is a greater force of corruption than money. Second, all politicians, leaders and high court justices *must have term limits* similar if not identical to the eight years presidents have. This being the case our leaders would clearly have far less incentive to legislate policy that promote their job security or political agenda but rather to make the world a better place for all to prosper and enjoy. Because Congress makes the laws they have no incentive to make such changes and they are far too comfortable in the endless Washington wealth to do otherwise. The only choice may be for the states to get together and have a constitutional convention which some are pushing for.

The problem here is that our congressional leaders do not have oversight though the president could at least raise the issue. Additionally we need to severely curtail to what level money influences and corrupts elections. Countless $millions have entered the coffers of campaigns from highly questionable sources to influence who becomes our elected leaders including much foreign money. Again, we should not be electing our officials from our checkbooks but from *our heart*. Additionally we should become more informed on important issues. I acknowledge that it clearly requires money to run an election campaign but I ask why any one candidate should obtain an advantage over any other merely because they have more money any more than a client with an expensive lawyer may bring about a better outcome in their case. A law simply limiting campaign funding would solve much of this problem. Let's make it happen!

There are many potential great leaders with firm moral compasses and great economic ideas who though usually not poor, may not be able to line the streets with hundred dollar bills as some can, nor are they known well enough to have influence. Certainly having campaign funding limits is an idea to consider as a way to level the playing field. A number of people who know me have suggested that I enter politics because they appreciate my "cut to the chase", common sense approach to numerous matters. However, I would never want to have to all but hold a gun to others to get things done properly and swiftly, be loved by one group and hated by others.

## Drug & Alcohol Abuse, A Real Drag On Society

Another area to explore is a multi-billion dollar business of illegal drug use and to what extent to legalize it. First, we must get at the root of why people are attracted to such chemical brain alteration. If we could ever stop the *interest* in using mind altering substances the whole business would collapse. Fixing the social ills of society that lead young people into drug and alcohol abuse and other decadent activities will not happen overnight. Of course promoting solid, traditional families is a good start since a truly caring mother and father who stay married, though not a guarantee usually is the groundwork for offspring being well-adjusted. Dependable family income can help as well but wealth and affluence in many cases may actually make matters worse in this area since then more money is available for such destructive activities. The *values* of the family mean far more than the level of family income. And I mean solid values with healthy boundaries where parents know who their children's friends are, where their children are, what they are engaged in, and in general how healthy their lifestyle is from eating, exercise, sleep, sexuality, finances, spirituality, orderliness and ability to engage in self-discipline and restraint as needed.

Obviously the need to alter one's mind must reflect that one is not satisfied in some way with the way their mind naturally is excluding the problem of addiction which comes as a result of repeated use in most cases. Child abuse, neglect, divorce or sometimes overly strict parenting, peer pressure, poor quality schools, depression, trauma and innate genes are the primary causes. Any combination of the above often leads to a sense of hopelessness in life as well which only exasperates the tendency for chemical highs. The good news is that most people can stop and rehabilitate and move onto a much higher quality of life though not always easily. There are many great examples of people who have overcome major obstacles in their lives and moved on to become highly successful and satisfied. Unfortunately a minority of young people even from the most wholesome of families will stray into substance abuse in part at least due to the natural emotionally difficult transitional years from teen to adulthood. This is the time in particular when young people need the regular support of loving – sometimes tough loving – parents as well as other family members, teachers and quality friends. Further regulation in the drug industry would also help along with destruction of drug agriculture.

## College Is Not For Everyone

Even among outwardly quality families questionable decisions are made by parents. There was in my teens and still is a strong pressure to attend a college or university in order to be accepted into the middle class or more which is quite unfortunate. Certainly one significant decision is this idea that once a child has arrived at the end of high school and reached approximately the age of eighteen that they are emotionally prepared to suddenly move hundreds or thousands of miles away to attend college to be left on their own. My freshman year of college was one of the top three lowest times of my life and I was only 100 miles from home. Ripping young people up from their high school roots of often closely aligned friends can be downright traumatic for some. And if they do not suffer from some form of homesickness they often view this as a free time to try drugs, excessive alcohol drinking and unhealthy sexual encounters while also balancing academic pressure – hardly a healthy combination. There are plenty of good colleges within an hour or two of most places that can meet the needs of students. Besides why pay double or more the cost for out of state tuition if attending a state school anyway?

We also must consider the *true value* of a college education and its ability to significantly improve life later on. A number of prominent educational researchers have been in the media recently seriously questioning the investment of college. Four year degrees are now frequently costing over $100,000 and more, deeply burdening families with ever greater debt in part due to the federal government offering more financial aid rather than placing pressure on schools to charge less. In addition, there is a cost of at least another $100,000 of lost wages for these years along with its lost opportunity costs so students better darn well graduate with a degree that is worth something. Sure it is nice to be able to say "I graduated from XYZ college" and learned a bunch of stuff that may broaden the mind. However, the practical aspect of being qualified for a professional occupation in which one can support oneself and perhaps a family overrides having the word "Harvard, Princeton, Stanford, University of ..." stamped in one's mind or sweatshirt.

There are plenty of plumbers, construction workers, auto mechanics, contractors, store managers, artists and self-employed investors that have a more prosperous life than those with a costly degree buried in debt for ten plus years. The standard model of four year degrees needs to be re-evaluated. Schools should offer other options which lead students toward careers perhaps in less time with courses more fine-tuned to their interests and career goals. It is a disgrace for college educated people to be cashiering, washing dishes, driving taxis and taking phone orders for little over minimum wage when such occupations do not require any college experience at all. Again, life is too precious to waste years of time and a pile of money for something that brings from a negative to zero return. Understandably for a temporary period of time many may need to work in such occupations no matter their qualifications but not long-term. If the economy is tough and low paying work is the only option for an extended period of time it is still best to find a way to live below our means and pay down debt, begin saving and acquire the American dream. There is always a way as I have done it.

# True Zero Tolerance on Alcohol and Drugs at Universities

The college drinking scene is an example of the dysfunctional behaviors in transitioning young people as we have many bright young people from quality families who when placed together away from home socially connect using alcohol, marijuana and sometimes hard drugs to get a buzz or high in order to fit in and reduce inhibitions. There are solutions to this issue as well which go beyond merely higher fines and criminal penalties. Remember that most young people don't believe they will be caught by the police for under age or excessive drinking. Generally, many young people are rather ignorant of the specifics of the laws and penalties. The removal of a student from their college or university for one to two semesters or permanently after one warning with no exceptions might speak with a louder voice than tougher policing.

College administrators have the ball in their court in this matter. I ask why not state on college applications as many employers do on theirs, "If you are a regular user of illegal drugs or abuse alcohol or intend to here you need not apply. If verifiably accused by an officer of the law of infringement of these rules either while on campus property or anywhere while being an enrolled student you will receive one warning. If a second confirmed offense occurs you will no longer be permitted to attend this college or university." Our leaders must gather up the courage to simply be firm no matter the whining of other parties or legalities – in this case perhaps the bar owners. Closing the bars earlier could also help some, though so many people of this age are very determined to mess up their minds and sleep patterns regardless. Unfortunately there is so much money involved in alcohol that early bar closing would be quite a fight. And there is also evidence that many college and university alumni give considerably higher donations who are graduates of big party schools so there is reluctance of administrations to crack down hard on the drinking – once again money causing corruption.

The root of this issue is our culture in which we have created something we call "the college life" which implies far more than going to class, learning, being tested, writing essays, doing internships and networking our way into a good career. As high school students reach their senior year and are accepted at various colleges and universities, they now anticipate the party life. This is primarily a western phenomenon because when I meet many foreign students they are confused and shocked at what they see upon attending our schools here. An African friend of mine recently explained to me that higher education is so respected in Nigeria and much of Africa that they wear a suit and tie to attend class, when the professor speaks students are fully alert and there is absolute silence and the entire party scene we accept here does not even exist. Attending college is a very serious, expensive matter and the bridge to a potentially good career in which one can support themselves and a family one day, a place to hit the books, not the bars.

Another problem that is arising is the legalization of drugs such as marijuana which has now occurred in Colorado and Washington State and no doubt others to follow which the federal government appears to be doing little to stop. This is happening despite the fact that federal law stands firmly against it as being illegal on the books which are supposed to supersede state law. Libertarians and others firmly believe that people should be free to mess their minds and bodies up with marijuana and hard drugs on their own time in the privacy of their own property. The trouble with such a belief is that as referred to earlier, the remainder of the non-drug using population pays for the ill effects caused by those who choose to engage in such behavior via higher vehicle insurance, health care and social service costs. They often argue that alcohol, cigarettes and even such seemingly more benign substances as cholesterol loaded ice cream, diabetes causing soda pop and junk food are legal, so therefore why not legalize most everything except sarin gas and cyanide. And there is always the temptation of money in the form of taxation of such substances.

I think the valid argument can be made that merely because some unhealthy substances and activities are legal does not justify legalizing more. Again, the trend to liberalize translates into the slow but sure progression of society toward boundlessness and therefore chaos. Whether it is legalizing marijuana, not firmly securing our borders and easing requirements for citizenship, opening up the definition of marriage to various relationships, elected officials ignoring laws they are required to support (For example, eliminating sanctuary cities.), relaxing standards of dress and use of language, permitting prescription drug ads on television, supporting the monstrous, corrupt health care industry with more insurance money, feeding into racism and minority victimhood instead of incenting self-responsibility, celebrating pop and hip hop singers whose lyrics belong in a cesspool and Christian churches straying from Biblical standards of ethics, we are losing the common sense and moral foundation this country was founded upon.

Yet huge segments of our population believe the relaxing of these standards is just fine with the younger generations being even more susceptible to such ideas despite such obvious evidence to the contrary. With liberals having largely hijacked public and higher education this is not surprising. How amusing it was to watch the left give public school students pet, music and aroma therapy and at the college level time off and psychological counseling for "Trump stress" when Donald Trump is merely a man who expects our country to live by the laws of the constitution and common sense as we always have until recently! How pathetic it is that the democratic party as of over a year into President Trump's term has still not accepted him as having legitimately won the election. Coming from a more serious direction perhaps disconcerting might be a better word to use than amusing since this situation was such a clear indication to what degree the left has negatively influenced our young people. And since Trump was elected most of the media continue to exaggerate and lie daily doing all they can to bring Trump down.

We all know of the failure of prohibition of alcohol and how deeply addictive and entrenched tobacco use is along with their health risks from auto accidents to cancer; yet, also common sense tells us that society is not going to totally ban either of these anytime soon or ever. But I certainly must ask why we should endorse the usage of other chemicals that have from very minimal medical benefit as with marijuana to the use of hard drugs. Such drugs have little purpose other than for people to alter their minds and place them in danger to both themselves and others in the society only adding further to health care, social service and criminal justice costs. Even if the substances are legal, if one messes up too seriously with others or their property it still becomes a law enforcement cost. One is always free to knowingly be a fool but don't ask others to take responsibility for the outcomes of one's mal behaviors. There is some pressure on the less responsible in society to curb their poor behaviors through raising auto insurance rates for those who are caught drunk driving and have excessive car accidents and increasing premiums for smokers but such policies are not always fair and quite limited in effect. Strangely some numbers show that it actually costs less to let people smoke because they die younger costing less in elder health care though I still insist though that reducing smoking is the morally correct action to take – money aside. If we permit money to be the ruler of every decision we are only headed for more trouble because finances are not the solution to every problem by any means.

Many say the War on Drugs which has been going on for the better part of thirty five years has not been successful and has cost the United States a fortune of our tax revenue. Indeed it has. Our government has spent fortunes sending equipment, airplanes and technical support to various areas of the world to stomp out the drug cartels with only moderate success at best. Illegal shipments of pot and drugs arrive almost daily packed inside truck tires, in hollowed out bricks, by air drop, ships and more despite our attempts at interdiction. Money is seized in various ways. So should we give in and throw up our hands and say it is hopeless since those who want drugs will always find a way to obtain them? Or should we legalize and regulate at least some as alcohol has been for many decades while following through with our temptation for profits and tax revenue?

Certainly our prisons and jails are overcrowded with a large percentage of inmates incarcerated for drug use, possession and sales of illegal substances and this is costing us tax payers a great deal along with rehabilitation. Just the cost of operating prisons according to the organization, Price of Prisons, is running upwards of $64 billion per year nationally as of 2012 with over 2.4 million people locked up. Between a quarter and a third of all incarcerations involve drugs. According to Action America $1,716.77 is spent every second on the drug war. According to the Schaffer Library of Drug Policy it costs $450,000 to put away one drug offender including all legal and related costs. Certainly the point can be made that legalizing drugs that are now not legal would significantly reduce our costs of operating our criminal justice system. And most certainly another proposition can be made regarding whether legalizing would in any way curtail usage. This is highly doubtful because the desire to engage in activities because they are taboo is exceeded by the curiosity and desire to alter one's state of being. It would most likely reduce prices and violence in the black market and raise tax revenue though.

On the negative side we must look at legalizing and legitimizing the use of other substances in addition to alcohol and cigarettes which themselves are a cause of a great amount of illness, wasted money, court and incarceration costs. Do we really want to add another substance that endangers ourselves and others while driving? And what about the rehab and health care costs involved from use of such drugs? As health care becomes ever more costly should the rest of us non users pay higher insurance premiums and taxes to cover drug addicts? And the excuse that smoking marijuana is less toxic to our system than cigarettes holds little weight and even if so does not justify adding another harmful substance to the legal marketplace. While it is true that cigarettes have been more scientifically studied there are enough studies to show that marijuana use has numerous health risks including increase in cancer as well. It should not take more than common sense to realize that inhaling the smoke from the combustion of anything whether it comes from pot, cigarettes, burning leaves or wood, factory smoke stacks or vehicle exhaust that this is not something good for us.

Those in support of drug legalization often say we already do pay for users habits and rehab, and up to a point they may be right but won't legalization only raise such costs even more? And what about the costs of impairment due to illegal usage whether from vehicle accidents, airplane crashes, cognitive and memory loss reducing productivity at workplaces and early dementia in our senior years? And how will we police age limits for not just purchase but usage? Do we honestly want our young children checking out our home for such stuff and experimenting with it which no doubt would happen more than it already does? Though I think some of the present consequences for drug crimes are a bit excessive and agree that this needs to be looked into further I believe that endorsing unhealthy mind altering substances to be available at the local Wal-Mart or convenience store is not the answer either.

Perhaps one of the values that brings about the greatest return for human life is reaching the ability to not merely look into the future, but realize the value of doing so to such an extent that behaving in the present in ways that help to ensure a brighter future becomes a regular habit if not a passion. And one must also become aware that some sacrifice in doing so can have enormous pay off. Sure, one can always rationalize by saying that they could be run over by a bus tomorrow, have a heart attack, be in a car accident or get cancer so why not just live for today, get high or drunk and deal with tomorrow when it arrives. If I was *certain* of running up against catastrophe shortly I most likely would live only for now but from life experience I know that I have a better chance of having to face tomorrow, next week, next month and many years from now than facing the end any time soon.

But the real question regarding drug and alcohol use is once again why people wish to alter their state of mind over merely only living in the moment and relishing in the natural environment they experience. I can understand engaging in some pleasures that we normally might delay if we knew our time is substantially limited such as driving that dream car, going on a vacation to a place we always had hoped to do, quitting work and starting a business we had only dreamed of, or engrossing ourselves in a hobby that we relish in, and spending more time with that special someone we cherish so much. But digressing from the natural way our bodies and minds are constructed and intended to operate via altering our state of consciousness has no significant appeal. And I don't mean harmlessly relaxing with an occasional alcoholic drink or two or a glass of wine with one's dinner a couple of times a week. As stated earlier most of the desire to alter one's perception of reality arises from emotional and psychological problems and rough, poor quality environments while growing up which is largely preventable.

Smoking, drinking or taking a pill to feel better is not the answer to our problems except in cases of diagnosed illness. Learning to deal more directly with our challenges and problems to find worthy solutions hard as it is at times, ultimately is the only and best method of coping with life. It is far more healthy and productive to spend time with a friend or counselor, take a nice walk or bike ride, get engaged in a favorite or new hobby, or play or listen to some great music than ingest some potentially harmful chemical. The high from the chemical only delays the inevitable confrontation with the issue which only adds further to the stress as the quality of life goes down. Life is always better when fires are stomped out fast while they are small and not delayed or covered up by temporarily altering one's mind. This brings us back to the principle I call "hard now easy later" or "easy now hard later".

You see, with some exceptions it is crucial issues such as these in our society which liberalism promotes that causes a human society to become ever more chaotic – movement from order to disorder. The ingestion of chemical substances other than healthy food, clean water and air are meant to be for the cure of illness and mild mood improvement, *not impairment.* War is a horrendous detriment to the order of the world and not something that can only be blamed on liberalism though liberalism puts us at the danger of further war via being overly soft and negotiable toward clear enemies.

I wish I could be such an idealist as President Obama and attempt to bring about peace via compassionate negotiation with our enemies but most unfortunately we have some enemies that will accept *nothing* other than our destruction. Such people simply must either be destroyed or severely isolated – There are no other choices which we must understand. Radicalized religion is an insane form of escape, gross misinterpretation of how life is to be lived, perhaps may be classified as a mental illness and often attracts the disenfranchised of societies such as those who have been neglected, abused or feel they have nowhere to turn to find an otherwise good quality of life. Yet there are many exceptions as stated earlier to this of solidly middle class people with good jobs and marriages who also become radicalized after exposure to ideas that create a perception of some type of inequality and/or devotion to extremism. As for North Korea we are dealing with a leader who wishes to start a war with no provocation from us, a very bad scenario. Such an insane regime cannot be permitted to have nuclear weapons and if he does not change course will have to be destroyed. The sadness is the people of that country who are on the verge of starvation while the government needlessly spends money on enormous weapons.

## Racism Is Pure Ignorance

Racism is unfortunately advocated by liberals despite the fact that they claim to be in such great support of diversity and equality by promoting affirmative action, political correctness and hate crime legislation. By keeping races separated politically and handing out excessive levels of cash and free or reduced items they obtain more democratic votes. As said earlier ideally all should blend into the society together and *totally ignore* their physical features such as skin color, eye color, tall vs. short height or blond vs. brunette hair. Remember, As Martin Luther King Jr. once said to judge people not by their color but by their character. And though dark skin may be a more noticeable characteristic, it in of itself has *zero bearing* on academic achievement, workplace and marriage success or any other features of becoming solidly middle class. This is simply because biologically the anatomical systems – brain and nerves, blood and circulatory, skeletal, digestive tract and skin have no significant difference – the darker skin being nothing more than an adaptation of higher levels of melanin pigmentation to tolerate the higher intensity of tropical sunlight where darker skinned people originated.

Sure, it is understandable that when a substantial sized group of people who enter a country and culture with differing physical features, especially one so noticeable as skin color and perhaps a different language, there will be a natural tendency to cluster together. This is nature's own method of generating feelings of security which is a natural and healthy response. Had I not had some ability to speak Spanish when I visited Peru I would have naturally gravitated toward other English speakers. However, once fully assimilated into a country and culture for the better part of ten generations as black people are in the United States and having equal rights laws in effect for over sixty years, separating by color and having distrust toward those other than of their own color should all but not exist anymore. But this is largely not the case. The reason is in part due to the federal government continuing to offer subsidization to many in the form of welfare, SNAP food benefits, Medicaid, subsidized housing, free or low cost phones, etc. which acts as a disincentive for them to focus, set goals, work hard, make marriages work and achieve a healthy status in the world. This is human nature when given things rather than having to work for them no matter the race, especially when such "entitlements" add up to more than many jobs pay.

# Achieving Success is Hard Work Not a Right

Then there is the victimhood mentality which only makes matters worse and should not be tolerated. We all have tough circumstances and hurdles to climb over in life no matter our color or socioeconomic level. Unfortunately a liberally controlled government tends to feed right into victimhood, again perhaps in part to obtain more democratic votes but also due to the overly bleeding heart mentality. Victimization is not due to someone else's success. People who perceive themselves as victims become victims while those who believe they can win become winners. I have lived on less than $5,000 a year yet never cried victim, asked for or received government benefits. In fact this experience actually motivated me to work harder and live smarter.

At heart we all must experience the fulfilling of other's needs to satisfy our own needs. I could go sit on my couch and grab the TV remote instead of writing this book but being "entertained" by the TV I find far less appealing than starting my own business giving slide shows of my travels and natural science interests and writing this book, both of which I produce to educate and share knowledge with others regardless if doing so increases the size of my bank account. While it is always rewarding and in many cases necessary to make money the real reward is the teaching and inspiring of others. It is essential to our human nature to feel productive and successful which in most cases translates into sharing and/or making other's lives also more productive. And no matter if working for oneself or employed by someone else one's mood improves enormously over living off of free handouts due to the brain being stimulated and incented into a necessary routine. I honestly ask – What we are here for if we choose to not be productive in some capacity. Sitting around on government handouts cannot motivate one to success. I particularly dislike the term "entitlements" to describe the free handouts as I ask when is anyone truly entitled to free money or things if they have not produced something. Life is about how we respond to it way over what happens to us.

# Judgment And Tolerance Must Go Both Ways

And as for political correctness I ask what is so wrong with judging others? If a segment of the population chooses to support and involve themselves in activities and agendas that are clearly unhealthy and/or immoral then don't they deserve to be labeled? What is wrong with calling someone mentally retarded when this is exactly what they are? Are we afraid that some will inappropriately call them "retards"? Perhaps. It can get worse calling dark skinned people "niggers", homosexuals "fags" or the handicapped "gimps" and by no means do I endorse the use of such language that is clearly derogatory in nature. A terrorist is the ideal word to describe a person who has the primary intention to cause mayhem and bloodshed and let us not be afraid to admit that most of them are of Islamic origin or have become radicalized due to perverted interpretations of Islam. Does this mean that most Muslims are terrorists or even support terrorism? Certainly not! And does the garbage man or trash collector somehow feel better and more respected because he is now called a sanitation engineer? Are we soon going to call prostitutes "professional sexual assistants" to give the trade more respect? Where does this nonsense end? The truth should never be delayed, muffled or covered up because as the ancient expression says, "The truth sets us free."

What is particularly aggravating to observe is how the liberal establishment so selectively creates protected groups that they benefit from by receiving more votes and/or money. Classic examples are minorities by skin color, homosexuals, the handicapped, the poor, those with special needs, illegal aliens, those of non-Christian religious faiths and even *criminals*. Yes, there are areas of the country where such pity is given to criminals that law enforcement is under pressure to permit them to leave prison to have sexual relations with their spouses. Is sexual intercourse a right that felons now have? Have we lost our minds? Yet a woman can walk down the street nearly naked dressed like the Pope with a Christian cross shoved into her vaginal pubic hair and a college professor can require a class to stomp on a picture of Jesus Christ (these are true examples) with no repercussions at all. Yes, we have free speech don't we. Certainly such acts are as offensive to Catholics and all Christians as speaking out against celebrating godlessness is to atheists, questioning some provocative warring language in the Koran is to Muslims or calling for illegal aliens to get the hell back to their country.

In the media we loudly hear about those who discriminate against these minorities and let the offensive, derogatory actions and comments against Christians, Jews, the wealthy and the classical family pass almost silently. The intolerance toward Christianity in particular is most noteworthy since it is by far the main religion of the United States yet we more than welcome religions of other cultures here. Law suits thrive against historical Christian symbols and the Ten Commandments posted in some public places or outside court houses while Muslim and other religious symbolism pass unscathed. The expression of intolerance is indeed permitted under free speech as long as it does not directly harm others though there is always some emotional and psychological scarring and arousal of anger created. The media so clearly leans far left in how it chooses which discriminatory stories to exploit which is simply not playing fairly. I thought liberals believed in *equality*? Yes, but only if the group in question is not perceived as being in a majority. It is also equality on *their terms* which negates the terminology.

The softening of terminology within the language softens our culture and what we stand for causing the society as a whole to weaken in relation to other societies in the world. The classic four letter swear words are ever more commonly heard in pop music songs unlike ever before. Such language that traditionally was only used under rare, extreme moments of anger or in some cases exuberance is now commonplace. And the use of online chatting, texting, tweeting and e-mail has only exacerbated the crudeness of communication due its necessitated briefness. This issue burns deeper than merely the obvious fact that our level of communication has roughened. Our threshold of toleration keeps moving down as we accept a wider and broader level of use of vocabulary previously retained for special occasions – again having less that is special and sacred. We are gradually accepting a more and more mediocre world not only in language use but in the acceptance of varieties of sexual expression, nearly limitless access to medical care and excessive levels of government safety nets. Such changes in how we live are generating too much complacency which demoralizes society and makes us more vulnerable and less secure.

Cal Thomas adds to these opinions of mine by saying "Today we have more information than ever, but less wisdom; more talk, but less listening; more things in the superficial showroom (celebrities are a good example), and less in the intellectual storeroom (that would be knowledge). We are either talking about relatively shallow trivia or tearing others down. Another aspect of this change is our ever growing culture of youth which sends the opposite message of our past when the young respected their elders, tapping into their treasure of wisdom from having lived 50-90 years." Now this view has reversed as those with some silver hair and balding heads are thought to be "old and stupid". Just because many of us older people may not be glued to smart phones all day hardly means that we are any the less wise than in the past. As always more life experience translates into a larger vault of knowledge to draw from, something that never will change and that younger people always can benefit from.

We can have dignity and respect in our society while also using language to create well-defined demarcation of what we tolerate and stand for. We must flunk a student if indeed this is what they have earned. Why should we be afraid of giving others brief moments of anger, shame, and frustration and by no means do I mean despise or humiliation? Everyone can not necessarily be a winner. Some are better hitters, slam dunk shots more easily, catch better and run faster, practically breathe A grades and are the first to complete exams, can build computers by the age of 12, blurt out perfect spelling every time, have five professional job offers months before graduation, obtain 20% annual returns in the stock market, have exceptionally attractive girl or boyfriends or have ideal social networks in place. Of course we should encourage all to become content and successful in some form regardless but we cannot deny natural born innate talent and personality that leads some to success in a variety of ways over others. We are not all able to be winners and feel good all the time and besides, those who we perceive as winners are not necessarily feeling good all the time because what makes us feel good is all relative anyway.

Liberalism of course promotes abortion and birth control for most anyone who wants it regardless of age or length of the pregnancy. Now instead of the good old days when there was strong shame on teen girls that got pregnant we have public school day care centers and well-baby classes along with girls as young as age fourteen being able to get birth control for free without parental permission – hardly good for the order of modern day society. I doubt even the most liberal of parent does not want to know that their early teenage daughter is legally going to the pharmacy to buy birth control, morning after pills or getting an abortion unbeknownst to them. Most parents I know highly discourage serious teenage dating as they should for this immature age group.

As we stray from values that have been accepted as the default of common sense structure and order, civil decency and a sense of the sacredness of life, sexuality, and the ultimate grand forces of the universe or God, respect for our country and reasonable limits to personal freedoms toward boundlessness and moral relativism, society becomes eroded with decay moving toward disorder and ultimately civil unrest. I ask if this is honestly the direction we wish to go. Pathetically liberals want their values of limitlessness and the endless pity party for minorities no matter how minuscule, to become entrenched to the point of inevitability – something that must be fought with tooth and nail to preserve civilization as we know it. How pathetic it is to have to all but fight a war to merely keep our culture and country the best it can be!

As stated elsewhere to receive something one must produce something – it's really that simple other than perhaps those who receive lottery winnings or large inheritances or are disabled to the extent that they are unable to produce. Entitlements that have not been paid into must be slashed – union pensions being one ideal example. Contrary to what liberals believe, people will find other methods to survive without taxpayer money inconvenient as it may be for a period of time. I will say it again – *hunger is the best motivator!* In Sierra Leone in Africa where I visited this hunger was evident because there are no government safety nets. People simply don't have the time or energy to waste on demanding the government help them or fight over race (they are all of the same race anyways) or whether someone is Christian, Muslim or not religious. When people are all in survival mode they put such foolish differences aside and get along more peacefully though there are some exceptions as with terrorists who have a defined, strict, vicious agenda. We can observe similar behavior during catastrophes such as earthquakes, hurricanes and fires. We come together peacefully when we all must work to survive. If only we could apply the same peace all the time!

This pity party for the poor and/or minority races all started with the softening of vocabulary to political correctness many years ago as described a couple of paragraphs back. And affirmative action entered the scene which often forced employers and schools to hire people of different skin color or be accepted to school more by their race than their qualifications only bringing down standards for a variety of professions. While I support helping the downtrodden move up, lowering standards and qualifications for them is *never* the answer. Doing so is essentially a form of cheating them of the necessary requirements to properly and professionally perform in a profession and cheating customers of the quality they pay for and expect while using the services and products they produce. Real compassion involves helping those with less free themselves from government dependence. As the ancient expression says, "It is more productive to teach a man how to fish than to give him fish." Unfortunately when anyone in the media offers this type of opinion it is always politicized by the liberal side that highly exaggerates and distorts it to portray this sensible concept as one of harshness on the poor so nothing changes. And worse yet, our politicians are not willing to "rock the boat" with major changes should they risk losing votes and their jobs.

Extreme greed has ruined societies in past history, still is in many corrupt countries and has the power to ruin ours as well while the cost of health care gradually consumes a greater and greater share of the economy. Meanwhile liberals feed the system even more cash to waste by insisting that the young and healthiest of our population pump more cash into the system through being required to purchase health insurance. Removing the endless checking account of cash from insurance for most medical care would kill off much of the excess greed almost overnight once all but the most active protesters who are largely overpaid in the system from hospitals to medical suppliers calm down and accept more reasonable compensation or quit to a line of job seekers happy to take their place.

And paying cash for most care would certainly incent more people to take charge of their own health while saving the system, employers and themselves a fortune. Just imagine the employee pay increases, greater profitability and increased share prices corporations could reap without having to pay for health insurance! For example, the EpiPen drug which administers a shot of epinephrine worth about one dollar for allergic emergencies made my Mylan cost $57.00 for a set of two in 2007 yet in

2016 suddenly rose to over $600.00 for the same. Why? Because Mylan knows they have a monopoly on it, people can be desperate for it and of course that *insurance will pay*. A building without a foundation will fall and so will the price of health care and medicine if only we would wake up, stop the flow of insurance cash and maintain our health.

And the excessive use of technology has us interacting less and less in person which is reducing our social and literacy skills. What happened to the warmth of receiving a genuine voice phone call instead of an abbreviated text message and paying about $10 a month for the entire family's phone service via a land line? Wow what people are willing to pay for convenience! For those who can afford to kill their paycheck due to buying health insurance, having smart phone service and cable TV, they certainly are not poor or they are significantly paying in lost opportunity costs.

## The Environment and Energy Usage

Is there anyone on the planet who wants to have dirty air, polluted water and soil and climate change? I don't believe so. The conflict arises on *how* to maintain and utilize resources to within healthy limits while also maintaining prosperity. Liberals tend to believe that drilling for oil and the burning of coal and other fossil fuels will continue to pollute and cause global warming while conservatives also acknowledge these detrimental effects though tend to minimize the potential seriousness of them. And indeed we all must face and appropriately deal with the negative consequences of our choices to obtain energy. Liberals idealize alternative energy sources such as hydroelectric, solar, wind, geothermal and ocean waves which don't directly pollute yet produce only a small fraction of needed energy.

Sure, it would be wonderful if we could harness enough energy from such clean sources to fill up millions of motor vehicles, heat, air condition and light up our homes and businesses, fly airplanes, run the internet and telecommunications infrastructure and more. Most certainly everyone would love to have this type of energy production become the new norm. However, the basic laws of chemistry and physics are such that doing so is *not feasible*. Enormous amounts of land would have to be covered with solar photovoltaic panels and/or mirrors at very high cost to generate electricity from the sun, the panels and mirrors would need regular cleaning and maintenance, and extended periods of cloudy weather would obviously be problematic. And of course the sun is at a much lower angle during the first couple of hours in the morning and last couple in the evening and during winter which significantly reduces absorption plus obviously there is nighttime to contend with when zero energy is being produced. Storage batteries are costly, do not last indefinitely and can be very toxic to dispose of. And more recently there have been reports of birds being singed to death flying through the paths of concentrated, reflected solar energy and hit by wind propellers.

As for wind energy this is also very limited. Wind is very sporadic and where it does blow more consistently it is not always convenient to place wind power machines or people don't want them "littering" the landscape. Geothermal is also another great source of free energy but costly to implement in buildings and homes and not going to easily fill the gas tanks of cars and trucks. Nuclear is a mixed bag as well. If built properly in an earthquake free zone (nowhere is completely free but very close in some areas) nuclear plants can provide electric power for many years to thousands of homes and businesses quite efficiently. However, the initial cost is well into the $billions, nobody wants such a power plant "in their backyard", and disposing of the very toxic radioactive waste is very costly and leaves some unanswered environmental concerns.

So what is left if we want to continue to heat and light our homes, watch TV, use the internet, drive cars, fly, cruise, etc.? Guess what? We are right back to burning fossil fuels. Obviously nobody wants to cause climate warming or endanger the future of life but hell if we are all going back to the dark ages. We can and should use energy as efficiently as possible, conserve when and where we can and certainly use free, non-polluting sources where we are able to but the vast bulk of energy for the time being must continue to arrive from the combustion of coal, oil and gas. At this time in history these are the cold facts. Fusion energy, the process of how the sun continually burns for a couple of billion years, has not yet been able to be re-created in the laboratory and does not appear to be on the near horizon in terms of being an energy source we can harness for everyday use. And hydrogen fuel cells are costly to produce.

Another issue regarding energy is becoming independent from the Middle East where we have been receiving a considerable amount of oil for a number of decades. Certainly it is to our benefit to be energy independent and not need a resource from anyone else, particularly from such an unstable part of the world. So if we wish for our economy to continue to prosper, at this time we honestly do not have a choice but to accept that we must extrapolate more fossil fuels from the ground. As for energy independence hydraulic fracking has changed things considerably in recent years with the United States now producing more than it needs. The offshoot of this industry has more recently caused Saudi Arabia to increase its oil production along with Iran back online as well which has flooded the market for oil bringing the price down and largely killing the fracking industry since a higher price of oil is needed to make it economical.

This issue should not polarize liberals and conservatives as it does. Conservatives understand that we must explore for more fossil fuels and most certainly accomplish this using the best technology that is least disruptive to the environment and using what energy we obtain in the most efficient manner we can. Meanwhile if improved methods of receiving energy from the sun, wind, ocean waves, geothermal, algae farms or whatever can be accomplished economically then by all means they need to be implemented wherever and whenever they can. A gallon of gasoline has an amazing amount of energy in it for $2-4. However, the amount of energy consumed to produce an equivalent amount of energy constructing infrastructure to harness alternatives actually is more consuming and costly at this time. Placing ethanol into gasoline has been a boondoggle to say the least as all we have done is hardly altered the cost of gasoline yet raised food prices while reducing the energy in gasoline with this lower energy additive. Liberals need to *acknowledge the facts* of the science and economics of energy instead of highly exaggerating that conservatives do not care about the environment. Life is about making it the best it can be rather than politicizing practically everything!

# Illegal Immigration & Solutions

This issue is different from the environment. And in some ways it is more complex. Placing every person in the United States who is not a legal citizen onto buses and airplanes and sending them home immediately is not the simple solution it may sound. Sure, we mostly agree that the thugs, criminals and just plain mooch offs generally do not deserve to be here. But most illegal immigrants are not trouble rousers. They came for a better life than they have elsewhere. Some married Americans. Others have been highly productive students and workers in the U.S. for ten to twenty years or more and many have created families here. And some claim to do the work that few Americans are willing to do with limited truth to this.

Liberals lean toward letting all but the worst criminal offenders stay while conservatives tend toward enforcing existing laws or altering and making exceptions in a more limited manner. Again, it goes right back to the conservative side leaning toward staying within the boundaries of laws designed to protect the integrity and national security of our country and liberals tending to offer rights to "the disadvantaged". I ask what rights someone has if they are not legally in the country? The first right an illegal immigrant should exercise is the right to return to their country of origin! I simply expect them to *obey the law* so if they are not legally entering they do not stay – no matter their disadvantages – because I know that we cannot save billions of needy people and that it is up to their countries to maintain population control, create more peaceful, better economies, improved infrastructure and health care and eliminate corruption and crime on their soil. I even support some of our resources going to assist those poorer countries but only with strict accountability.

Our borders are not secured properly at all. The fact that over 12,000,000 immigrants have entered the U.S. illegally over recent years demonstrates this well. Thanks to President Trump finally enforcing the law illegal immigration is down considerably now. Many are utilizing our education and health care systems basically for free at U.S. tax payer cost which is not right in my opinion. Some schools in California have to deal with *dozens* of different languages being spoken within their buildings! Some are also costing our criminal justice system a fortune as well. Others are involved in drug running operations and a few may be terrorists infiltrating our country. And as just mentioned, many are here for a better life. We obviously should have constructed a hardened, high tech border system many years ago but it is not too late. Again the real problem is our attitude of *pity* toward others who are less advantaged than Americans. It is true as Americans we have more advantages than many others have around the world. But even so, this does not mean it is our duty to hand them our freedoms and opportunities. I would be immediately arrested in any other country without my passport and or visa and a stated purpose of my presence. Why should it be any different here? The pity party and obsession with rights has got to stop!

## National Voter Identification Cards are Common Sense

The question that keeps arising is: What level of American rights they should have if they are not legal citizens. I think it is rather clear that while we do not threaten their personal safety and provide them with a minimum of sustainable resources temporarily we must properly identify them and explain to them exactly what their rights are and clarify their status. Certainly deportation is a strong possibility for those not married to an American, who do not have minor children, do not have a job or high enough paying job to not depend on the tax payers, are criminally minded and are costing our country money. They most certainly should not have the right to vote but because of the lack of voting identification laws some fraudulently do. This is why I obviously support having a national voter identification law such that anyone voting anywhere in the U.S. must simply show an official free photo identification based on correct information stating that they were born in the U.S. And chain migration must stop.

This is an area where again liberals and conservatives disagree which puzzles me some since this is so basic. Liberals claim that conservatives want such a law because more liberal democrats apparently have no identification cards or have lost or cannot locate their birth certificates. It may well be true that the poor, elderly and handicapped as a class may be more liberal and do not have driver's licenses and birth certificates but forcing everyone to obtain a free ID card at no cost is not a significant burden, especially if only having to get one every so many years. It is only fair and legal that strictly U.S. citizens should be voting. Having such a law in place would make it easier to weed out the dead from the voting rolls as well as those who try to vote more than once in different states. Liberals have politicized this issue by allowing illegals to break the law and vote while continuing to play the pity party game for the extreme minority that have problems obtaining photo identification cards, knowing that such people are more likely to vote democratic. Are we ever going to do what is *right and proper* instead of for our self-fulfilling needs? According to Pew Research 24 million voter registrations are inaccurate or 1 in 8 which is very significant and enough to alter the results of an election.

## We Can't Save the Whole World

I always feel sad that so many millions of other people around the world are suffering, starving, war torn and desperately poor compared to the lives of most Americans. However, I have the common sense to realize that we have limits on how much we can help them. The United States of America hands out more money, food and resources for infrastructure and technological development around the world than any other country despite the fact that we are so deeply in debt that we cannot pay our own bills without creating more debt. We are an incredibly generous bunch with many non-profit, charitable organizations and churches contributing to help world poverty as well. We let in thousands of legal aliens every year including desperate refugees. At some point *limits must be drawn* since even we have only so much to give. We can be just as generous by using the same level of resources to settle people in safe areas of their own countries rather than bringing them here and risking some committing terror acts and other crime. And let's not forget that we have enough Americans suffering here who need to be helped first.

Most certainly the obvious place to start after securing our border is to make certain that everyone here is identified and legal and those that are not are appropriately dealt with which in many cases may mean deportation. And going so far as to create "sanctuary cities" which break the law, permitting illegals to stay is wrong and unfair to the legal American tax payers. I do not know of any place in the world in which I can cross into their border without proper identification and just plop myself and expect to be taken care of – actually quite the opposite as I most likely will be arrested and imprisoned. Maybe Trump should send in the federal police and arrest those who are supporting sanctuary cities and get the illegal immigrants out. Illegal immigration is not a matter of liberal vs. conservative despite the issue being politicized. It is simply a matter of *legality* which our federal government should be enforcing but has not in recent times. Ironically, the government under President Obama has sued states such as Texas and Arizona for enforcing federal laws. I did not know the Federal Government could sue against the enforcement of its own laws!

## Get Rid of Organized labor

I predicted public backlash against labor unions many years ago when it became so blatantly obvious that unions had become an outdated concept. When young children were forced to work sixteen hour days for pennies per hour in coal mines and other workers in hazardous places with minimal safety protections unions were most certainly all but essential to force employers to improve working conditions and wages. This period of time when business exploited capitalism to its worst potential was truly horrendous and quite naturally workers fought back and organized. And I can thank unions for helping to create reasonable wage laws, overtime rules, and vastly improved safety in workplaces. But by the 1960s and into the future they carried things far beyond merely the enforcement of reasonable living wages and safety. It was not long before they demanded far better wages and other benefits than non-unionized workers which have created a huge divide in workers, class envy and horrendous burdens on tax payers. In addition union dues are often used for political gain which is also unfair to the majority non-union workers. This has now gone way out of hand.

We have non-union workers doing *exactly* the same job as union workers for less than half the wage and no other benefits. Is there anyone who considers this fair? Is it fair for United Auto Workers to earn over

$40 an hour on an assembly line for work that does not even require a high school diploma when many PhDs do not earn this much? Is it fair for home owners to pay absurdly high property taxes to pay for excessive union wages and cheap high quality benefits for school teachers, police officers, fire fighters, and state and municipal workers when many of them don't receive such benefits themselves? In Austin Texas not long ago all public school personnel received *entirely free* health insurance at tax payer expense with only a $5.00 copay per use and zero deductible while obviously most of these tax payers did not get such benefits, nor should anyone in my opinion.

Now most employers charge in the $300-$500 a month range for medical coverage with annual deductibles of over five times what I have spent in my whole life on all of my medical care. However, the school teachers in the state of Pennsylvania receive better coverage for as little as a tenth of this cost, yet I have to pay for theirs. Certainly something is terribly wrong here! And worse yet us tax payers have to pay for guaranteed big pensions for teachers, police, municipal and state workers while I, working for a private corporation, am guaranteed *nothing* other than what I personally save from my paycheck. I naturally ask why I as a tax payer should fund the pensions of other workers when I don't even come close to receiving such a gravy train when I retire. Taxpayers are way over burdened with this matter. I am happy to pay something toward our schools, police, fire protection and having my streets well-maintained, leaves and snow removed, etc. But such workers can pay far more as private sector non-union workers do for benefits and *save their own money* for their retirement using 401k plans and IRAs.

Also, working for private industry makes workers more productive and responsible. If I don't show up on time, work hard and follow the rules I will simply not have a job or not get as high a raise when that time arrives. And this is how it should be. The more responsible one is, the better their life is. When one works hard, shows up on time, is pleasant to others on the job, shows interest in learning the job and is accountable for their work they are compensated accordingly. However, once in a union much accountability is out the window. Work quality often goes down, employees become lazy, arrive to work late and unless they very flagrantly commit an act of high indiscretion, their job is all but assured.

Look at the teacher strike in Chicago in September of 2012. The Chicago School District, as it should, demanded that teacher pay and raises to some extent be tied to their performance evaluations. The union comes in and does all they can to water this down when in most industries I know wages and raises are most certainly tied to work performance and should be. If we seriously care about our children's future us tax payers should most certainly be attending school board meetings and giving our firm opinion that merit pay for teachers should be a certainty and unions must be abolished.

Teacher unions in particular are among the most pernicious. In the states without right to work laws teachers are *forced* to join a union, normally the American Federation of Teachers (AFT) or the National Education Association (NEA) which strips substantial amounts in required dues out of each paycheck to the tune of $billions over the decades which are largely given to lobbyists and various primarily liberal organizations. I ask about the teachers who would prefer to have those dues in their own pocket to improve their personal lives or that do not support how their dues are being spent. Meanwhile tax payers nearly have to remortgage their houses to pay school property taxes which unlike state and federal taxes, always rise virtually every year. Did you know that you *never* actually own your home since if property taxes go unpaid one loses their house? This system is deeply antiquated and in desperate need of change. We need regular people to get the wheels turning faster, not liberal politicians.

Exactly as I assumed years ago various towns, cities and states are either bankrupt or close to it largely due to labor unions forcing artificially high wages and benefits on public workers while tax payers are totally fed up. And worse yet, many of these union contracts are non-negotiable meaning that their obligations "must be met". I ask by whom will this be when bankrupt? No doubt tax payers again in some form, if not from local taxes the basically bankrupt federal government will step in and/or bonds will be issued merely increasing debt and "kicking the can down the road" further until it is too heavy to kick. Again, this issue should not be politicized but it most certainly is since traditionally labor unions have been supported by the Democratic Party.

I cannot help but tend to believe that liberals must relish in self-sabotage. Yet they also believe so firmly in fairness and socialist policy.

Fairness means police officers do not receive $55,000+ per year pensions and practically free medical benefits for the remainder of their lives at tax payer expense starting at age 50 while the rest of us must work our brains out until at least age 65 or more with few if any assurances beyond Social Security. Fairness means school teachers must pay for more of their own health insurance just as private workers do and have wages and raises based more on performance. Fairness means we all pay for education via tiny increases in sales, income and other taxes, while eliminating school property taxes, which translates into the wealthier paying more since they spend more and those with lower incomes and less purchasing power paying less. Fairness means eliminating labor unions *entirely!*

## Public Education

Obviously I realize that there are many dedicated teachers who change their curricula each year and put to use what they learn in summer workshops and more. Certainly knowing that one's compensation is tied to performance is a great incentive to be fresh and creative with each new school year. It is pathetic that in order to get around union requirements taxpayers now have to fund charter and cyber schools. And then there are parents who demand that their children learn alternative languages or specialize in greater individual instruction in perhaps science or some other area with practically no boundary on what they expect. Frankly I think they should pay some extra tuition for such specialized desires. Tax payers can simply not pay for every whim parents and the school districts want!

## More Money is Not Always the Answer

Largely due to teacher unions the quality of public education in America has not significantly improved in many areas of our country over the years. As alluded to above, unions have kept teachers too cozy in their niche for too long. Unions have prevented charter schools from spreading despite their well-documented better performance over standard public schools. And they offer no solution to the poverty ridden inner city schools other than to blame poverty itself which they offer little hope for other than simply throwing more money at it which after 50+ years has done nothing to create measureable improvement. Numerous schools devoted solely to poor, black children such as Columbia's Dunbar High School, the first black high school in the United States, Xavier University Prep in New Orleans, the Marcus Garvey School in South Central Los Angeles, Marva Collins' Westside Prep in Chicago and Eva Moskowitz who runs the Success Academy Charter Schools around New York City serving 6,700 students all have proved this *not* to be true. I have seen the paper notebooks of children in Africa where they pay $8.00 a month for school, have no property taxes, unions, electricity, running water or computers yet the work in these notebooks exceeded the level of math, science and history that I have ever learned in my upper middle class towns in the U.S.

## School Choice Improves Schools

Liberals have the assumption on various issues, education being a major one, that throwing more money at the problem is the solution. Changing people's values, attitudes and assumptions are the keys – not higher teacher salaries, fancier buildings, or more technology in the classrooms. In fact more money actually often has the reverse effect, causing teachers to be more complacent rather than innovative just as welfare and food stamps often do the same for many poor people who would be better off with jobs or at least tasks that must be completed in order to obtain a welfare check. In addition to limiting charter schools teacher unions have fought hard to stop school voucher programs in which school property tax money is given to families to send their children to private schools of their choice over the public schools despite the obvious advantages of doing so for the students.

Students are the number one priority in a school, right? At least that is what I always thought but if one examines the agendas of unions one will be shocked to find that they do not see it this way. Patrick Wolf of the University of Arkansas who was hired by the U.S. Department of Education as an independent evaluator of the Washington DC school voucher program noted that recipients of vouchers had graduation rates of 91% in 2011 versus 56% for D.C. public schools and 70% for those who put in for the lottery to obtain a voucher but did not receive one.

And another study showed that in Milwaukee the high school graduation rate at 94% for those using vouchers over 75% for those in the standard public schools there. Additionally those who make use of vouchers have been shown to have higher test scores and in 2013 a study was done that demonstrated that college enrollment for blacks who used vouchers rose by 24%. Better yet vouchers save tax payers money since public schools cost more to operate, again in part due to unions overly inflating salaries and benefits for teachers. Naturally the unions support the endless spending for schools and wish to protect teacher's jobs no matter what happens to students.

I have taught school for a few years in a variety of classrooms around a large city from higher income areas to poor areas and observed a lot. As expected generally in the higher income parts of town where families are more educated and intact achievement is higher and classroom behavior is better with some exceptions. The exceptions in the poor areas are noteworthy since observing high achievement and quiet, studious classrooms in the ghetto tells us a lot. The clear message here is that income is not necessarily an essential ingredient of higher achievement, but *values* are. Poor families with strong values that maintain their marriages and single-parents with the same value system keep their children away from drugs, crime, early sexual contact, the gang life, etc. can produce quality responsible adults as well. Naturally they are more challenged in doing so due to the stresses of the environments they live in, however.

The point here is that all the fancy new impressive buildings, updated technology, higher teacher salaries, etc. has minimal effect on how seriously students take their studies and the learning taking place. *Parents and families* are always number one. Children who come home to a quiet place to study with parents who preferably have a solid marriage and encourage learning have a huge advantage over those who arrive home from school to broken up families, chaos, alcohol and drug abuse in and/or near the home, roving neighborhood gangs, early sexual temptations and the sounds of gun shots and screaming ambulance and police sirens. They honestly are much better off sitting on the ground under a canopy in school with a pencil and notebook than living in such terrible conditions.

# We Need National Teaching Certification & National Student Standards

How we evaluate both teachers and students is nowhere near unified enough. The teacher certification system is a horrible and a *totally unnecessary* mess with each state having differing laws and requirements and not honoring each other. We are the *United* States so other than perhaps having some knowledge related to one's state which can easily be learned in one course there most certainly is no reason why we cannot have *one national* teaching certificate. There literally are fully certified teachers that when they leave their state, cannot teach without – in many cases – obtaining an entire teaching degree all over again. This obviously is *absurd* but it happens regularly. Some states honor teaching certificates from any other state while others only from some or not at all – complete chaos with no good reason whatsoever – increasing the coffers of universities while wasting the lives of many. Also the content of teaching degrees varies significantly from one state to another as do tests.

Clearly our resources could be used far more efficiently and effectively and teachers need not have their entire careers destroyed simply because they move across a state boarder! It is hardly a picnic to have a $52,000 a year teaching job, move and then have the door slammed one's face and have no choice but to either be a retail cashier for $18,000 a year and/or go back to college, perhaps not be able to work costing another $125,000 in lost income and only maybe end up back in the classroom three to four years later with a pile of college debt. This scenario is not far-fetched. So naturally I propose that all states have the same teacher certification system, most of the same course work and the same final exams. A panel of educators from various parts of the country could certainly create such a system – please no excuses. Unification is power! Don't believe me? Just check out Japan, Korea and some other Asian countries.

As for the students most of what takes place in our classrooms should also be streamlined so that from coast to coast all American children are held to the *same standards* in the core areas of math, science, writing and English, U.S. and world history, a foreign language and basic personal finance. Understandably some students will have to work harder than others to meet the mark but after a couple of generations such a mark will become the essential standard requirement and accepted norm. We cannot keep flexing and dumbing down assignments and requirements for those with fewer advantages other than those with truly special needs. For those who come here and don't know English they had better buckle down hard and learn it ASAP and understandably such students could be given a temporary period of flexing requirements to learn it well enough to compete in all subjects.

## Language Teaching Must Begin in First Grade

I am especially concerned about how science and languages are taught. It is well-known now that to properly speak a foreign language with minimal accent one must learn it under the age of twelve or so when the brain is best able to do so. Language teaching should start in first grade so by middle school students in theory could be nearly fluent in a foreign language rather than starting to teach at the middle school level which is still done in most public schools. We also should consider thinking out of the box in terms of what languages we teach and teaching the most spoken and useful – leaving the standard model of only Spanish, French and German behind. Certainly with well over a billion Chinese in the world and China being such a major world power we might consider teaching Chinese though not at the expense of losing Spanish. I have Chinese neighbors whose five-year-old daughter can fluently speak Chinese and English simply from speaking it and now starting to read and write both.

## Science Teaching Must be Hands on and Inspirational

As for science I recall having great science teachers and boring ones. The great teachers taught science in a manner that truly inspired me by provoking the wonder, awe and mystery of atoms and molecules, microbial life, human physiology, chemistry, the laws of physics and mind boggling extremes in astronomy. The boring teachers taught science mostly in dry mathematical terms and endless formulas that while necessary up to a point would hardly inspire a child to want to become a scientist. If I were

231

a science teacher I would complement the mathematics aspect of science with taking my classes out to swamps with their boots on while gathering water samples, observing, photographing and taking notes on animal and plant life.

I would not merely teach the basic math formulas for astronomical calculations but have a class telescope building project and take my classes out at night to meet the local astronomy club using their telescopes. I would describe in lucid detail what Albert Einstein was contemplating while riding the train imagining how the train would appear to a passerby if it was traveling at or near the speed of light. I would demonstrate centripetal forces by taking my class safely out into a playing field. Then I would set up a rotating spindle with a rope wrapped around it with a disk attached at the top perhaps with a miniature digital camera at its edge. I would attach the rope to a car and have someone floor the accelerator. I might set up a field trip to chase severe weather. I would make the mystery of black holes come alive and would encourage my kids to complete projects and papers on the most esoteric aspects of science they could find. We are severely lacking in *inspirational* science!

Many of our greatest scientists and engineers of all time spent their spare time mixing chemicals, stretching, bending and throwing things, grinding lenses and mirrors and seriously visualizing how the world and universe behave under conditions far out of reach of ordinary observation. To truly be unique in the world and highly passionate about a subject one must *test limits* via researching more deeply, take risks and go to extremes others have not. For this is the ultimate expression of the human spirit! It is the extremes in life that make life exciting and interesting. When we look back in time we do not recall stretches of time in which went simply went to school or work every day, did our work, came home, made dinner, watched a relatively benign TV program and went to sleep. We remember those special times with those we care the most about, great adventures and vacations and other experiences that are *out of the ordinary.*

# Technology in the Classroom

I ask if we are carried away with technology in the classroom. I recall at the end of my senior year of high school in 1976 the placing of a Wang computer about the size of a small car into our school library which probably had less than 100 megabytes of storage capacity that virtually nobody knew how to use. Then as I attended college it seemed to generally be assumed by most people that computers were primarily tools for scientists, mathematicians and engineers to use and that was it. I would see graduate students "pulling their hair out" staying up all hours of the night working with Fortran and other programming code. I thought that I would probably never use a computer and did not for many years until the 1990s when of course they became an essential tool in offices and homes everywhere with a huge variety of uses – especially once the internet became available.

Computer labs became the norm in high schools, then middle schools and then down into the elementary level. Now even more recently in many schools they are getting rid of computer labs and every student is being given a laptop to carry around all day. Perhaps next textbooks will be out the door since they could be simply downloaded into the student's computers easily reducing the weight of student backpacks by over 75%. I really wonder if libraries may even be necessary much anymore with most everything available online though many still enjoy having a paper book in their hand and prefer to read paper over a lit screen. Cursive handwriting is becoming a lost art. The term smart phone is now ubiquitous and I suppose smart schools will be next. I live near a major university and am totally fed up with nearly bicycling into students who are constantly staring down at their darn phones totally oblivious to their environment. I love my dumb phone!

And then there is the cell phone problem in classrooms with kids constantly communicating, often quietly by text. I frankly do not see why parents let their children have phones before their teenage years. They are a terrible distraction in the classroom and in an emergency there is always a phone within a couple of minute walk within the school or the teacher has one. Parents will say they need them for calling for rides home from after school activities. I ask what worked to ensure rides home from such activities in the pre-cell phone era? It is amusing to me how we reach the point where we think we cannot do without certain technologies, just what the phone companies want of course as they reap large profit margins with surprisingly minimal resistance. If companies made this level of margin on food, refrigerators, cars, TVs and tools the public would practically be burning down buildings in protest!

## Firm Consistency & Uniformity Works

Perhaps the toughest challenge for many teachers is classroom discipline. The three strikes and you're out rule is quite dependable for the most part. This involves one warning, then either a firmer warning or action and on the third offense action is taken with zero exceptions, I repeat *zero!* Kids learn very fast what zero means. Such consistency and firmness must be fully supported by school administrators, the school district and preferably the parents as well with *no regard* to race or sex. If children of a particular race or sex happen to misbehave more than others this is *just the way it is*! Teachers with the most successful discipline outcomes normally begin the school year very firm so the law is laid down giving children an immediate impression that they will not get away with poor behavior with this teacher. When this occurs classrooms function much better. Just as with quality parenting, *consistency* is absolutely crucial to good outcomes. Though they will obviously test limits children thrive on predictability and knowing their boundaries while also being given the freedom to be creative – within reason.

So to summarize, when families, school administrators and teachers get on the same page keeping students well focused on why they are in school does not have to be particularly challenging. In addition there must be an absolute requirement to learn English fluently as quickly as possible for foreign students. And we must have total uniformity in testing in the major academic areas for *all* regular education students for all states. The more differences in how different states and localities operate, the more chaotic and costly education is. Temporarily some students will have to work harder than others to reach the same playing field but what uniform great results we will have upon completion of high school. The big problem with the federal government laying down the rules for all is that they tend to always make such issues far too complex with too many exceptions and have the tendency to dumb down curricula and politicize some subjects.

The Obama administration is proposed the new "Common Core" for public education which Texas and some other states are already exempted themselves from due to controversial teaching methods in mathematics and anti-American history and English reading material. One of the agendas of the progressives is to downplay the greatness of our country. And we don't need some long winded explanation of why $13 - 7 = 6$. Again we end up with the liberal philosophy in general – constantly making exceptions for this or that reason which clearly leads the country to ever greater disorder and chaos in the name of political correctness and fairness. I do not think it is unfair to make some students work harder than others. Just because we are all not equal in intelligence, abilities and pre-requisites does not mean we should not expect most everyone to reach the benchmark, hard as it may be.

Look at most Asian countries and we will find true uniformity. Understandably the U.S. has a far greater diversity of people from many backgrounds, ethnicities and socioeconomic levels but becoming more uniform in education with strong standards is one way we will be able to unify and compete better. And while I certainly do not support religion being directly taught in public schools, I fully support it being incorporated into our history since it has played a very significant role. Also are we literally in fear now of simply assuming that a family is a mom, dad and the children as liberals pressure the schools to tell children that a family can be anything one wants – that having 2 moms, 2 dads or choosing what sex you wish to be and actually living it is healthy, normal and acceptable when reality tells us differently. What parents want their children being taught that denying reality is acceptable? To deny reality is to delude and lie to oneself.

# Crime

The crime rate in the United States is absolutely deplorable. For being perhaps the most advanced country in the world we have the highest per capita crime rate. Comparatively poor developing countries have much lower rates but this does not necessarily reflect the precise risk one might have in touring around. It really depends on where one goes. My risk of being robbed or murdered is multitudes higher in the poor inner city areas of most U.S. cities, especially at night, than it is in rural or suburban towns. Cities most everywhere tend to attract more crime in part because crime is easier to get away with among large, concentrated populations where criminals can vanish or in areas where potential witnesses will turn their cheek and keep walking.

Crime naturally tends to occur in densely populated areas and where socioeconomic division and perceived injustice are the greatest though of course there are exceptions. And as has always been the case the amount of crime, type of crime and level of violence can be divided along sex and age lines with younger males tending to be at the greatest risk. And in the U.S. and some other countries race plays a significant role in crime statistics as well with those with the darker skin colors as a whole at far more risk. I personally observed the classrooms of black children almost all talking, fighting, romancing, being extremely antiauthority and racist toward me and frankly doing almost anything but their assigned work. Meanwhile when I taught over on the other side of the city in primarily white, Asian and some other races as a minority there was comparative order, quietness and considerable learning taking place. With some exceptions of course this generalization is undeniable.

Race itself is innately irrelevant but due to a whole complex set of issues from distant times of slavery, racism, and more recently the entitlement programs from the government are disincentives. Due to the lack of the desire to work and higher quality employment for those with less formal higher education, an entire culture of crime ridden poverty has manifested itself. Then add in the ability to make big money fast selling drugs, television and internet and the overall emphasis on materialism and consumerism along with government leaders who encourage further class warfare and we naturally create more envy among the poor and therefore, another reason for crime.

We are born having a brain with a clean slate and though we have some personality traits that are inherited, we generally are good people with positive feelings. It is our *environment* that can bring out the best, worst or somewhere in between. Being handed real weapons and told to hate under the age of ten will most certainly bring about entirely different outcomes than those raised in peaceful, loving homes with two caring parents who support curiosity, creativity, self-initiation, hard work and academics. Obviously these examples are extreme. Children being brainwashed and given guns is really an attribute of terrorists, not everyday shoplifters, burglars, car thieves, drug thugs and murderers though some minority parents do plant racism into their children, if not directly, indirectly through clustering together rather than randomly integrating into the population. Sometimes we observe what appear to be exceptions to this rule as we see teenagers falling deeply into decadent, criminal behaviors from what we outwardly believe are good homes but usually upon closer inspection it can be determined that there are severe communication problems within the family and other substantial stresses. Or often parents are not aware of who their children have associated with.

## Fathers are Important!

But let's examine the number one cause of crime, fatherlessness. Perhaps a required reading before young people leave school should be the Case for Father Custody by Daniel Amneus, Ph.D (1999), which is now online for free along with his other excellent book, The Garbage Generation. This is one of the greatest eye opening works I have come across in my research for this work. His points are extremely well-researched and founded making it ever so clear that the matriarchal household which from an evolutionary standpoint was with us for countless thousands of years, in present day society is the perfect recipe for marital separation and divorce, promiscuity, black male low self-esteem, anger and crime. Under the same conditions the white race or any race follows the same pattern. The launch and aggressive push of feminism giving women the message that they are no longer "property of men", are in control of their reproductive sexuality and with birth control can have all the men they wish, great academic degrees and careers, while correct in the sense of fiscal and sexual equality, gives women a sense that the only purpose for men is impregnation. Add in government entitlements and who needs a man around? I will tell you exactly who, *the children!*

Peggy Orenstein, author of School Girls: Young Women, Self-Esteem, and the Confidence Gap (1994) said black women have traditionally been a source of strength and prized for the girls in their communities but the boys have been deprived of fathers or know they might be easily deprived of them. This matriarchal pattern is rapidly spreading to the larger society, whereas Senator Moynihan tells us, "the breakup of family inevitably, predictably … will lead to the growth of large numbers of predatory males. We saw it coming. It has come." Feminists saw this as progress. Well-known feminist Mary Ann Mason said "For many women the route to liberation from domestic drudgery was liberation from the family. The only chance for true equality with men lay outside the patriarchal family structure....In the real world of the seventies full-time housewives were ending their careers on the rocks of divorce in astonishing numbers."

The white feminists acknowledged that they would prefer living in patriarchal upper class neighborhoods over the ghetto, yet denied that matriarchy and female sexual promiscuity have any connection to the ghetto life with the patterns that permit women to free themselves sexually and to marginalize men and make themselves heads of the "families" which generate the social pathology of the next generation. Feminist Naomi Wolf, author of Promiscuities: The Secret Struggle for Womanhood (1997) said "We are living in what feminist Naomi Wolf calls a "post-divorce, post-sexual revolution, post-moral relativism world." These three alterations of society are purposeful; they seek to overthrow patriarchy, to marginalize males and to restore the female kinship system. But they require the cooperation of the males whom they victimize. They require that men consent to allowing the legal system, responsible for enforcing contracts, to instead make marriage a fraudulent contract which guarantees husbands nothing, but guarantees wives the right to deprive husbands of their children." Judges of divorce cases continue to give custody to mothers the vast majority of the time only further perpetuating fatherlessness. Our association with mothers giving birth to their children probably plays a significant role in such decisions along with higher employment and lower crime rates among women but these decisions only keep men down and maintain the ghetto mentality only keeping crime more active among such men. This is a terrible cycle that must be broken which requires much higher levels of awareness of the problem. Just look at these statistics from the Families Civil liberties Union below for a real truth shocker!

85% of all children that exhibit behavioral disorders come from fatherless homes (U.S. Center for Disease Control);

90% of all homeless and runaway children are from fatherless homes (U.S. Bureau of the Census);

80% of rapists motivated with displaced anger come from fatherless homes (Criminal Justice & Behavior, Volume 14, p. 403-26, 1978);

70% of juveniles in state-operated institutions come from fatherless homes (U.S. Dept. of Justice, Special Report, Sept 1988);

85% of all youths sitting in prisons grew up in a fatherless home (Texas Dept. of Corrections 1992).

Fatherless children are:

5 times more likely to commit suicide

32 times more likely to run away

20 times more likely to have behavioral disorders

14 times more likely to commit rape

9 times more likely to drop out of high school

10 times more likely to abuse chemical substances

9 times more likely to end up in a mental institution

20 times more likely to end up in prison.

Fatherless children are also, according to one British study, about 33 times more likely to be abused. In 1983, the US Department of Health and Human Services found that 60% of child abuse is inflicted by mothers with sole custody of their children. Almost all of the rest comes from other members of her entourage, especially boyfriends and second husbands.

## Solutions do Exist

So just what is the solution? Fifty plus years of free handouts has certainly done nothing to help and in fact added to this problem. This is because poverty in and of itself is not the primarily cause of the problem. There are plenty of poor people here and around the world who do not commit crime in the name of envy of the wealthier out of class warfare though significant class division does not help. Extreme discontent strong enough to cause some people to rise up and commit crime derives itself from dysfunctional families – fatherlessness being a major component as just discussed, poor economic policy, poor educational policy, government corruption and lack of directly addressing the problem. Perhaps we need to offer neighborhood venues where meetings with local citizens can be regularly held in secure, peaceful places in which we emphasize the importance of the family unit staying together and discussing these statistics as well as trying to break down racial barriers.

Something is surely wrong when black people terrorize a town when a white police officer shoots a black person and the media trumps up such news while if the officer is black and does the same or kills a white person we hear virtually nothing. Within a couple of weeks after the Michael Brown shooting in Ferguson Missouri August 9, 2014 a black police officer killed a white/Hispanic man in Utah yet none of the mainline media reported it. Death is death no matter and racism is a total waste of energy from all parties involved! Another possibility is church involvement. We need gap bridging, team building and local employment way more than welfare and SNAP handouts. And we must examine successful inner city schools and model after them. We have to make it cool and hip to strive for As, start small businesses, work, maintain our health, grow some of our own food, avoid gangs that notoriously bring young people down, visualize the future to create hope, set goals and by all means do what we can to pull people out of the drug use and sales life. Ghetto citizens must become educated on these issues via community leadership and perhaps more peaceful mingling of the police with these citizens. Even teaching something as simple as right from wrong may come into play because some young people have very poor judgment.

Deliberate mingling of races through bussing children from ghettos to wealthier areas has not had a good success rate either. And I know of several cases personally in which poor black children have been adopted by white parents and raised to adulthood yet a high rate of them end up as democrats following the pity party routine again for their black counterparts. And many turn racist against white people as adults. Certainly in theory groups that have tended toward crime, teenage pregnancy and the violent gang and drug life should be better off if scattered among those who do not engage in such lifestyles but good outcomes from such placement have been limited. I continue to believe that placing pressure on those who continually engage in illegal and immoral behaviors via less and less financial support, improved quality of local education including the atmosphere in schools and appropriate job training skills, that we may see significantly improved outcomes.

The criminal justice system is another component that needs some fixing as well. There are way too many methods that lawyers can use to drag out cases, waste time and money. Death row is a joke. And please nobody tell me that simply putting the most heinous of murderers to death has to cost more than decades of prison time. Also, though I most certainly do not support illegal drug use or sales it does appear that some tough sentencing by judges is not having its intended effect. Perhaps cutting the strings of how drug money is funneled and moved around may have a stronger effect because let's face it; the dollar remains an incredible motivator. If someone can't make money selling drugs the flow halts and the users stop buying. Unfortunately much of this trade in the black market is in cash. A similar comparison can be made in regard to countries that support us bombing terrorists while at the same time accepting terrorist's big money for weapons. Healthy family life and duel parenting remains the best cure. Another choice for ghetto people who are burnt out from this horrible life is to relocate out.

So let's make is clear. The main causes of crime are far more related to socioeconomic and cultural problems than simply moments of passionate anger and the desire for the big TV one's neighbor has. In fact in most burglaries items are stolen to resell for cash over taking them for self-use. And the majority of rapes are not the stereotypes of men lurking behind trees with out of control sex drives ready to grab any women they can get their hands on. However, crimes of revenge are often fairly well planned or at least extremely violent due to pent up anger over time from being tormented and bullied by others or perhaps being unfairly fired from a job which one is totally dependent on to feed their family. I have had to exert restraint from taking revenge out on people several times in my life, knowing firsthand how powerful this anger can get. The price of doing so is far too high.

# Health Care

More than fifty years ago medical care in the United States was not a major issue of concern. People simply went down the street to their small doctor's office and paid a reasonable, affordable fee for an office visit. Hospital care was $10-40 a day back in the 1950s to 1960s. Even adjusted for inflation what is being charged now is *totally absurd and unnecessary*. There are now people literally spending over half of their income just for medical insurance, deductibles and co-payments! Yes, some are spending the equivalent of a mortgage or car payment and saying good bye to family vacations to pay these outrageous amounts. Medical bills are the number one cause of bankruptcies, even for the insured. Surely we have spent fortunes on research and development of many technologies and pharmaceuticals but it still doesn't add up to what the medical industry is charging for its services. As one surgeon I heard speak recently said, "Everyone wants a piece of the pie for themselves whether it is medical schools, medical textbook publishers, malpractice and health insurance companies, equipment manufacturers, drug companies, hospital suppliers, medical software companies and even some doctors themselves." One opinion of Dr. Norton Hadler, MD, author of the excellent work, "The Citizen Patient" among several other great books is, "If healthcare could take the moral high ground the nation would be rewarded with better health at a very tolerable cost." I could not agree more!

I also support profiting and capitalism and have my own business but I am selling my photography, a *non-essential* product. However, medical care is *life saving* and obviously very essential and therefore in a totally *different category* – one where I believe we really should not be profiting significantly. It simply is *not right* to profit off of people's illnesses and injuries! Unfortunately because of the essentialness of medical care business exploits our need for it to the max. We spend more per capita (50% more than France, Israel and Britain) than any other country in the world yet our outcomes are no better and actually worse in many cases. Medication prescription errors, fraud, billing errors, unnecessary procedures and waste are rampant in the industry to the consumer's detriment with Obamacare only stirring the pot and making it more costly – if not to consumers directly then indirectly through increased insurance costs and higher taxes. With less cash available certainly less hands would be grabbing.

# Reducing or Eliminating the Third Party Payer

I ask why the medical industry should be so insulated over others. It is way overdue for the whole health care industry to consolidate, slash its costs and charges and truly deflate to the reality of what the market will bear based on what patients can afford to pay in *cash*. Tevi Troy, former deputy secretary of Health and Human Services, I will quote saying in the April 19th 2010 edition of National Review as follows; "When a third party – such as the government or an insurance company – picks up the bill, doctor and patient have little incentive to avoid excessive or inappropriate costs. When the patient pays out of pocket, by contrast, he takes careful note of the expenses he bears, with the consequence that the market becomes more efficient. Moving away from third-party payments would therefore not only reduce waste and fraud, but reduce the cost of legitimate services. Perversely, President Obama's health care reform further entrenches the third- party system." And he ends the article saying "Ultimately, however, only the repeal of Obamacare – and a decisive move away from third-party payment – will solve the problem that the president has just exacerbated." At the time of publishing this work, Obamacare has just about died. Yet so far President Trump is not making much progress in significant change either, partly due to the democratically controlled senate but primarily from the deplorable power of the medical industry.

Practically everyone I talk to about the health care issue believe I am too radical in recommending abolishing health insurance in its present form. I actually believe it is practical, sensible and morally correct to do so and the best incentive for people to take more charge of their own health along with greatly helping to reduce fraud, waste, greed and a sense of patient entitlement of receiving "the best". Forcing everyone to purchase health insurance is merely a handout to the lower income people so they can obtain insurance at a much lower cost when such pressure from the government should be emphasis on taking better care of ourselves.

Meanwhile young, healthy people at the beginning of their work lives who often are buried in college debt, struggling to buy their first car, saving for buying a house and perhaps marriage and a family – let alone a nice vacation once in a while or funding retirement accounts – are being asked to significantly burden their lives through purchasing health insurance that very few will make use of.

Why not demand that the health care industry carry this burden since they have been riding the gravy train of insurance money long enough? When will people finally reach the point where they are angry enough from overpaying for health insurance and health care that they fiercely revolt and stop the heard of sheep mentality? At least if we don't get rid of the third party system we should make insurance premiums based on a sliding scale but only at the health care industry's expense. I saw this crisis coming way back in the 1970s as a teenager when my family was on the Harvard Community Health Plan HMO in which we could pay $1.00 for unlimited care yet as of 2018 I meet few that are willing to take any action. From my many interviews with others they all believe that it is hopeless, that the health care industry has us over a barrel despite agreeing that medical care is way overpriced.

I will make it glaringly clear how the system works with an ideal hypothetical example. Picture yourself the owner of a bicycle shop that has been selling a particular model of bike for $500 that cost you $230 each in quantities of ten which has been selling regularly at this price with the customer paying this full amount with minimal price resistance. Now consider how you might price this bike if customers only had to pay a $20 co-payment and a $200 deductible for this same bike while the other $280 is guaranteed to be paid by the customer's insurance company. Certainly the obvious temptation would be to price this bike at a minimum of $780 knowing that customers were happily paying $500 and still will with their insurance. In health care the dollar numbers become astronomical with average people paying over $1,000 a month for health insurance ($600,000 over 50 years plus opportunity of investing which could easily be several $million) in combination with their employers to pay perhaps $2,000 in co-payments and deductibles for an appendectomy or broken leg once in 50 years or less whose actual cost before the staggering profits is under $5,000 yet billed to the insurance company at $37,000 hoping to get reimbursed at least $28,000. This is the multi-trillion dollar scam on the American people! Abraham Lincoln said "You can fool some of the people all the time and all of the people some of the time" but I think most unfortunately the healthcare system here has managed to fool all of the people all of the time.

Engaging in better health habits and preventive care is actually number one in terms of cost reduction – estimated by numerous health care experts to be worth a full 75% cost reduction of the entire health care system, over a *trillion dollars* a year. This explains why President Obama's idea of forcing everyone to buy health insurance just keeps health care costs moving ever higher, clearly a recipe for a worst case scenario. We saw horrendous price increases as the plan became implemented in part because insurance must cover more procedures and pre-existing conditions and the medical industry seeing an ever larger pot of insurance cash to dip into. Numerous insurance companies bailed out of the Obamacare plan adding to its demise.

Just imagine how much higher our paychecks could be and stock share values without the employer costs of these benefits – no doubt plenty. We buy things on sale in stores and often can negotiate prices. Why should hospitals be any different? Well, when we shop at the grocery, home improvement or furniture store we don't have grocery, home improvement and furniture insurance do we. If we did one can be certain that prices would be sky high with virtually no negotiation, coupons or sales since there would be no incentive to be price conscious to the consumer when the consumer is carrying the ticket to riches, the insurance card. I look forward to the day I see hospital commercials on TV promoting sales on medical procedures instead of grossly overpriced, dangerous designer drugs with minimal efficacy rates.

Clearly it is unethical to make someone who happens through no fault of their own to be born with negative hereditary traits or is involved in an accident be all but imprisoned by medical bills for the duration of their lives. Yet when we supply any industry in the capitalist world with a perceived bottomless stock of cash via a third party payer the sad but true nature of being human, that of greed at some level, will manifest itself by exploiting that third party's money to what level it can. As another example just imagine if one had "grocery insurance" and could purchase $600 worth of food for a $20 co-payment. Does anyone reading this honestly believe that grocery retailers, wholesalers, food processors or farmers would desire to lower their prices? No doubt quite the opposite! Well, this is how we are paying for health care now. And those paying for expensive insurance premiums naturally tend to feel more complacent about taking charge of their own health habits so are more likely to seek medical care rather than engaging in more self-responsibility, only leading to increased costs in the health care system. Therefore, having the system of third party payers whether the government or private insurance companies, causes financial dysfunctionality at both ends with minimal incentives to save on costs by both consumers and providers. This is the train wreck happening as we speak. Nothing will change in health care until *it is affordable to the consumer in cash* based on supply and demand like other basic commodities without a third party to pay!

## Pricing Often Based on Fear

Worse yet many are fully indoctrinated by the medical and insurance industries into believing that they "could lose everything" or be "put out on the street" without insurance. Keying into our fears is the greatest way to market insurance of all types. And yes, catastrophes do occur occasionally, but just how much are we willing to sacrifice to pay to cover a potential catastrophe? And what can we do to significantly lower our own risk of a negative occurrence? Taking charge of our own lives more through greater levels of awareness in every area of our lives whether it be what we eat, educating ourselves on our health, being on top of our driving habits and increased consciousness of just how the world works in general may pay off far more than dropping fat checks to insurance companies on a constant basis. For healthy people who conscientiously make a regular effort to maintain a low risk lifestyle and do not have enough income to both fulfill their dreams in life and purchase insurance, their statistical risk of never having those dreams filled while buying insurance is many fold higher than their risk of an actual occurrence requiring insurance to cover it.

# Ethics, Morality & Compassion VS. Profits

The real issue comes back to ethics and morality here. As already stated medical care is lifesaving. Human life is sacred as far as I know and issues that are sacred involve humility, compassion and love. However, the millions of people who work in the health care industry have bills to pay just as all of us do and cannot work for free, nor should they, since they are providing a service that requires considerable education, effort and time. The question that arises is how to deal with the obvious conflict that occurs between what should clearly be an act of compassion toward another human being who is suffering regardless of ability to pay and the fact that doctors, nurses, utility companies warming the office or hospital, medical supply companies, liability insurance costs, drug researchers and equipment designers must be paid.

The only answer we have arrived at to solve this conflict is the creation of insurance which spreads out the costs of the few who need services among those who rarely or never use the services. The obvious problem with this system is that the majority pay a fortune over time for the insurance – *way more* than the care they ever receive. One person receives a million and half dollars of care for their major car accident, diabetes and cancer while another may live 100 years and only receives occasional checkups costing perhaps $800 combined while paying $700,000 in insurance premiums over their lifespan (Lost opportunity cost could easily quadruple this actual cost.). Is it ethical for the less fortunate to cost fortunes that the fortunate pay? – hence the conundrum of insurance. It is particularly noteworthy that those with the lowest incomes and least education statistically cost the most to insure since they are more at risk for medical problems while they are least able to afford insurance or care.

There really is a solution to the healthcare crisis; one that will not be without pain for certain components of the system. Just imagine if everyone placed every penny they pay in health insurance including employer portions, to themselves into a savings account of some type (preferably an account that is invested in a manner that assures at least a break even with the approximately 3% general inflation rate). The very healthy would be well rewarded over time since one aspect of the plan should be that after a certain number of years one may get access to these funds or a portion of them, for most any use they wish. Those that make poor health choices would use up their money or at least more of it. And hopefully from the savings due to the natural incentive of saving money from staying healthy, the cost of providing care to rare birth deformities, cancer and major injuries could be provided by government risk pools paid by perhaps a negligible income tax increase. Additionally paying primarily in cash would provide great incentives for providers to stop overprescribing drugs and other procedures. And just imagine the fortunes companies would save rather than providing grossly overpriced insurance plans!

Hospitals price services by the "chargemaster" rates which are unjustifiably high, often 10-25 times higher than enough to cover their costs – their excuse often being that they have to cover those who cannot pay which holds little justification. And oddly enough hospitals that call themselves non-profit actually make more profits than for profit hospitals because they get a tax exemption for being non-profit while charging about the same prices for services. Also, keep in mind that retirement accounts, annuities and certain types of trusts can be set up that cannot be touched by medical providers. Remember, we work hard to earn our money and certainly we should reasonably pay for services but not be ripped off.

If we want a good life we must do what we can to hold onto what we have while not stiffing doctors and hospitals or way overpaying for their services and insurance. Health savings accounts are a better compromise but the bottom line is that the medical industry simply must "take the hit" as they have been riding the gravy train far too long. Rather than buying insurance most people should be saving at least half the cost of the insurance in an emergency fund to pay for medical services in cash in effect creating one's own medical savings account. Also keep in mind that it is far cheaper to negotiate a fairer price and make normally interest free monthly payments toward a medical bill than to buy insurance. Another issue is the absurd cost of liability insurance for doctors though some doctors are waking up and opting out.

The little bit of good news is that if we are savvy enough with regard to our health and dealing with the medical system we can seriously negotiate saving big bucks. This even includes those with insurance since now typically the insured even must pay around $5,000 a year out of pocket should they have a significant medical procedure because the deductible amounts, copays and procedures not included are so high. Many medical procedures vary by as much as thousands of percent which translates into tens of thousands of dollars. Yes, it is common for one institution to charge as much as $60,000 for exactly the same treatment as another who will charge $4,000. Need I ask which we would prefer given the same quality of care? Such enormous discrepancies are obvious proof of the rampant scamming in this industry. Unfortunately money rules over concern about our care and lives in most circumstances so we must be smart in dealing with the health care system. As for doctor quality and experience we always can check many out at zocdoc.com. One customer of medibid.com was quoted $72,000 for hip replacement surgery by her local hospital who upon realizing that she had no insurance offered her a price of $45,000 while at Medibid she found an offer of $13,000.

Cataract surgery which only takes an eye surgeon about an hour to complete can rack up a bill from as little as $3,000 to nearly $20,000 in some places again shows an incredible price discrepancy. Often doctors contacted directly will drop perhaps another 10% if asked about paying by check or cash instead of credit card since this reduces their cost of dealing with insurance companies. Newchoicehealth.com is another site that allows price comparisons. And sites such as needymeds.org or the Goodrx app offer drug discount coupons that are well worth our time. Sometimes even drug manufactures offer great coupons. And chains such as Walmart, Target and Walgreens offer certain medications at standard rates of around $4-$10 which may come to less than insurance co-payments. And let's not forget to take full advantage of our employer flexible spending account (FSA) which permits up to $2,500 of pretax money to be used for medical related and child care expenses – subject to change under the new tax law.

So do we regulate the industry and tell all of the businesses in the medical and health industries that they can only break even and not make a profit? In the U.S. I most certainly don't see this happening anytime soon. But there are solutions to significantly deflate health care costs without such direct regulation. The most obvious solution is for the population to use medical services far less frequently than they do now. It is more than coincidence and perhaps some good genes that I have spent an average of about one dollar a month on my medical care and drug prescriptions during my life. I take *conscious control* of my health. I regularly practice good health habits. And by good health habits I don't mean maintaining a life of deprivation. Sure, I eat a healthy, daily regimen of fruits and vegetables along with appropriate amounts of protein and starches, maintain a healthy weight, exercise almost daily, try to handle stress appropriately though this can always be challenging, rarely drink alcohol, do not smoke and get that 7-8 hours of sleep. I still fully enjoy a delicious piece of chocolate cake or hot fudge Sundae occasionally. I do avoid consciously engaging in activities at high risk for injury. So should we charge more for insurance for those who knowingly leave themselves at higher risk of needing medical care and will doing so actually alter their behavior for the better? This is another ethical issue that does not have simple answers though on the surface appears sensible to a degree.

Of course anyone including the healthiest can fall on the ice in the winter, end up in a car accident or become seriously ill with cancer or some other debilitating illness. A small minority of people are born with congenital problems which require regular or advanced medical care. But if we as a society would simply take on the basics of good health habits that I just mentioned above, numerous medical professionals and health economists who I have listened to in the media say over and over again that the U.S. would reduce its health care costs by nearly a $trillion per year. Just a small portion of that savings would easily cover the serious illnesses and injuries. I am often amused at others responses when I mention that I have no health insurance. I hear the endless stories of injuries and illness that "would have killed or bankrupted me" without my insurance yet it is the insurance in the first place that makes prices so high.

One person recently told me that their son had taken his motorcycle roaring through trails out in the woods and smashed into rocks and trees and now has a $200,000+ medical bill yet only has to pay $6,000 because insurance covers the rest. To be polite I did not say what I wanted to and this was, "Why the hell did your son do something so foolish that the rest of the insured people now have to subsidize?" Another involved the sixteen-year-old drag racing drunk with his friend late at night in the rain who ended up upside down in a creek barely alive which will cost upward of a $million in medical and rehabilitation care. How about the fool who dove from a high cliff into a lake with rocks only six feet under the water's surface? What about parents to be who knowingly give birth to a baby that is so severely disabled that it will cost $millions in care, live only a couple of years and be miserable? Should we all have to pay for such care?

And what about the elderly whose doctors and/or children want to squeeze out every minute more of their parent's lives – giving them major surgery and dozens of pills a day into their nineties? Somewhere there must be limits whether it is limitations of care provided and limits to what insurance will pay or else health care will simply bankrupt everyone. Yes, even sacred human life has some limits on its preservation in certain circumstances. Remember, it is *limits that provide freedom* for without them we remain indecisive, in chaos and cannot think clearly, respectfully and honestly. Now I do realize that there are exceptions with healthy people who become injured or seriously ill through no fault of their own but reducing risk only makes good sense.

Just the co-payments insured people now pay for doctor visits equal what the entire doctor's fee was when I was growing up back in the 1960s and '70s! The average annual cost of health care for an individual in 1970 was under $400 while by 2016 it passed $10,000! Inflation alone does not nearly account for this level of increase. A person paying for employer provided family coverage over thirty years at $250 per month ends up having a loss of $519,822.80 had it instead been invested obtaining a 10% tax-free annual return – minus the value of any claims. And let's note that this amount is only a rough estimate of the only employee contribution. Employers normally pay far more which translates into higher costs for whatever the employer produces in products or services and lower wages for employees. In fact it is now estimated that the cost of health coverage averages between $150 and $235 *a week* for each employee!

According to eHealth, the nation's largest private online health insurance exchange in 2018 the average annual total cost of a health insurance premium is $4,716 plus a $4,238 deductible for an individual and an unbelievable whopping $12,252 plus a $8,352 deductible for family coverage – as much as several new cars are priced at. Yes, now this last figure exceeds the take home pay for an entire year for someone earning minimum wage by several thousand dollars! These figures are before subsidies but subsidies should not exist since they only fake the real cost and ensure the absurdly high costs. And with Obamacare increases these amounts have grown even worse. And let's get it straight that *insuring*

*or subsidizing anything only keeps the price of that product or service high.*
Note that cosmetic surgery is comparatively low compared to surgery for
injury or illness. Why? Because insurance does not cover it so it can be
competitive with market supply and demand.

## Endless $Billions in Waste, Fraud & Useless Procedures

Fraud and waste continue to haunt the system. An example of this is the
statement by James Mehmet, retired chief investigator of Medicaid fraud
in New York State in which he said that fraudulent claims wasted 10% of
Medicaid money while 20-30% was spent unnecessarily on treatments of
no value. Medicare, the program for the elderly, has about the same fraud
rate with both combined loosing around $60-80 billion annually to fraud
according to the National Health Care Antifraud Association. Perhaps even
sadder is the U.S. Senate Permanent Committee on Investigators admitting
in 2008 that dead physicians were paid for 478,000 claims costing $92
million from 2000 through 2007. Private insurance companies have a
better record with private companies tending toward greater efficiency than
the government due to their obvious incentive to generate profits. I am
generally against significant profits being made from people's misfortunes
but if a profit can be made at less cost than the government then so be it.
We need is a system in which costs are paid only for providing decent care.

Medical care *must* be provided. Therefore, if we take away the insurance
component for most care the care would still have to be provided but there
would simply be a whole lot less money available to pay for it so the price
would *have to* come down. The $1,500 MRIs and CAT scans that only cost
the hospital under $100 would drop like a rock along with the $5 aspirin
pills that cost hardly a penny each, surgeons earning $1,000 a minute,
dentists charging upwards of a week's pay for many merely to fill one or
two cavities, $20 for a box of tissue that cost $1, Medicare being billed
$850 for a $132 back brace (The same  back brace which is probably
available at Walmart for $59 but Medicare will not reimburse Walmart so
the patient gets it from some specialty medical supply company charging
the $850 which Medicare is dumb enough to pay $625 for), etc.

Elimination of most health insurance could not happen overnight as it would "pull the carpet" right out from the whole industry but it should be phased out and we should phase in paying for health care in good old cash on an as needed basis, *affordably* largely based on a sliding scale in proportion to one's ability to pay. Sure the medical industry would reel for a while but the money would just flow to other segments of the economy over time. Those entering the medical field would do it more for the love of human biology and compassion than the pay as they used to. And it is not right for one particular sector of the economy to receive *guaranteed payment* over any other. And why should Americans pay triple or more for the same drugs marketed in other countries? This nonsense must come to an abrupt stop!

So, to sum up there *are solutions* to making medical care affordable to all. By far the greatest savings could come from self-prevention, taking care of one's health at home by being more aware and well educated on health, using home tests and good old common sense. It does not take much intelligence to realize one is overweight, should quit smoking, not drink too much alcohol, get a good sleep, eat well, take a mile or two walk a few times a week, know their family health history, manage stress appropriately and not engage in foolhardy high risk activities. Second, we largely eliminate the third party payer as already explained above. And third, a system of ability to pay when needed must be established by mandating that a certain portion of one's pay or other income be set aside for paying for medical care which if not used within perhaps 10-15 years receives a partial withdrawal option to use as one wishes. This would be essential since I know all too well that the funds people are presently paying for insurance would find a way to be spent otherwise. It would obviously not require nearly as much to be saved as insurance costs but it is essential for people to have a medical fund of accessible cash for primarily catastrophic problems with minor office visits and exams to be paid in cash. There could also be a requirement for more to be saved after the age of 60 or so since one is more likely to need medical care with age.

Under such a more simplified system waste and fraud would naturally be reduced considerably. With prevention being the greatest area of saving yet necessitating behavioral changes this is where the greatest challenge is. What do we do with the millions upon millions of diabetics who keep gobbling down ice cream, cake and soda, teenagers who start smoking and adults who will not quit, alcoholics and drunk drivers, drug addicts, daily inner city gang violence, eighteen-year-old drag racers, the obese who refuse to change their eating habits and all those who will not alter their behavior for the better? It has been shown that penalizing them by charging more for their insurance has minimal effect. However, obviously such behaviors should be discouraged in whatever way possible since they are a drag on the productivity of society. Health classes in schools can emphasize such issues but ultimately it is up to friends and relatives, particularly parents, to highly discourage such behaviors. Here is one figure that says a lot about our behavior as a whole. It is recommended that people over the age of 60 take part in 150 minutes of moderate physical activity each week to stay healthy or 75 minutes of vigorous exercise. But Department of Health figures show that just 17 per cent of men and 13 per cent of women over 60 manage that amount, while 60 per cent do no exercise at all. It is way overdue for our health care industry to base their philosophy on *prevention* over treatment and profit.

We still are a country of compassion enough that we don't permit human beings to literally die on the street because they are without money. Also there are borderline areas in deciding exactly what constitutes irresponsibility or self-abuse as the true cause of some illnesses or injuries. Should we punish junk food, cigarette and soda drink companies? Is it really their fault for making poor quality, illness inducing substances that attract our taste buds or the consumers fault for not saying no to it? I believe most of the responsibility lays in the consumers hands for if the consumer says no to behaviors that are not healthy the industry will market healthier products. At least we as a society must do all we can to *promote* good health habits. Even the greatest health ethicists do not have simple answers because this is honestly where we arrive at crossroads with our own ability to exert self-control. All I know is that I expect to continue to enjoy the rewards of my comparatively low risk, healthy lifestyle and not be required to pay for those who make poor choices. Therefore, I chose to avoid participation in the system and pay a negotiated cash price if and when I need care.

# Let's Finally Tackle Tort Reform Head On

In the climate of defensive medicine this can be challenging since the need for certainty beyond all doubts in diagnosis of conditions and fear of law suits permeates the atmosphere in medical offices. And indeed patients expect nothing less than the maximum of attention to their medical problems with the "latest and greatest" of procedures, equipment and pharmaceuticals. This attitude arises naturally since nothing is more precious than knowing for sure if that headache and fever is simply our immune system responding to fight off a relatively common germ or a brain tumor. And then add in being insured and of course we demand ever more since we don't feel it hitting us directly in the pocketbook. Some doctors even view not testing for every possible ailment violates the Hippocratic Oath they take.

We also must engage in tort reform regardless of the fact that the amount spent on medical malpractice law suits is comparatively low in percentage terms to the cost of the whole health care system – presently estimated to save about $11 billion per year. A basic rule of mathematics is that numerous small amounts add up to a large amount especially over time. Over ten years $11 billion is $110 billion which is more than pocket change! Rationalizing that "It's only a couple of bucks" or "It's only 1, 2, 3 or 5% of a budget" is groundless. I ask if any of the readers here would ignore picking up a $1, $5, $10 or $20 bill drifting across the grass or sidewalk in front of them because such amounts are only a tiny percentage of their work salary or savings. Small amounts *always* matter whether at the personal level or in cutting the federal budget, deficit and debt. The bottom line is that every dollar counts.

Except for the most egregious acts of extreme negligence on a doctor's part law suits should be very limited in extent and all medical suits should have significant limitations on what can be requested. Most studies have shown that the majority of patients who suffer from a medical error are not even compensated, a few obtain oversized awards of which 54% goes toward legal and overhead costs and the typical wait period to receive payment is close to five years. Tort reform would reduce the rates for doctor liability insurance premiums which have risen at nearly twice the rate of health care, especially for surgeons and obstetricians – some who are paying as much as $300,000 a year. Doctors should also arrange their finances in ways to protect their assets from such suits using trusts, perhaps overseas accounts or other legal methods as should most everyone who has significant assets to preserve. Another idea is to have some type of medical dispute resolution board to settle matters out of court, therefore substantially reducing legal costs. Also waivers that patients sign should hold far more weight making it even more difficult to sue. All but the most gross and intentional negligence should generally be thrown out of court.

## Is the Distribution of Wealth too Extreme?

While on the topic of legal costs I believe it is worth giving my opinion on this topic. While I certainly do not like to emphasize class envy much I firmly think there is something very wrong with lawyers being in this class with hourly rates equaling or exceeding what most people earn or at least take home in an entire week of full-time work. Should they earn more than food service and janitorial workers make? Of course! But must they earn multitudes more than other professionals such as teachers, professors, engineers, nurses and others? Understandably not all lawyers earn huge six figure incomes but most certainly a $19,000 a year worker should not have to pay $200-400 an hour or have to sacrifice the quality of their legal defense merely because they don't have enough money. Nor should one have to unload a three-figure dollar amount to see the face of a doctor or dentist or more than a whole year's salary for a couple of hours of surgery. Capitalism cannot properly function without reasonable moral and ethical boundaries that maintain less resentment and envy among the masses. Without such boundaries the distribution of wealth causes ever increasing division among a society and, understandably, growing frustration among those who have a lot less, especially those who responsibly use their resources to try to live well. At the worst extreme civil unrest and war may ensue.

# Should we Have a Quality, Affordable Single Payer?

I propose that we put on our thinking caps and figure out ways to be healthier, use the health care system far less and tear down the absurd profits in the industry. In addition to becoming far more active and responsible for our own health we could all simply pay a very modest tax to a *single entity* for major and chronic conditions. All basic exams, preventive care, birth control, abortions, and easily treatable illnesses we would pay for almost entirely in cash under controlled prices. Illnesses that are determined to be primarily our own fault from consciously engaging in preventable, risky activities as mentioned would largely not be covered by this single plan. Sure, there would be some sticky areas to deal with but a board staffed by a variety of professionals who have no personal economic interest would be hired to make these decisions with consumer rights to appeal. This could perhaps be a panel partially financed by this tax we all pay and maybe be a quasi-federal run program like the Post Office.

The Post Office is a good example since unionization has made it too expensive to operate and it sunk horribly in debt while electronic communication took the place of snail mail. But it is the cost of providing the union mandated health insurance for retirees that has most seriously burdened it as I have said all along. The tax could be perhaps a combination of both income and sales taxes. Another idea is to give people "medical vouchers" which can be used toward care and if not used traded for the more seriously ill. And of course this tax would give every legal American access to any licensed physician at any medical facility or hospital – no more of this "in-network" nonsense that most present day insurance plans have in place and prices would generally be about the same everywhere. Nobody can deny that such a system would be fairer than what we have now and obviously way better than the Obamacare nonsense. And all parties must be able to demonstrate accountability to reduce waste and fraud. Doing so would have two positive effects – one to incent people to take more charge of their own health and second to lower insurance costs. Should we not, the cost of employer provided medical coverage could equal or exceed some employees entire salaries!

## A Medical Website For Everyone

Also I propose having an internet site that operates with a "tree" for every American citizen in which a main page with a photo and basic information on the patient such as sex, age, address, spouse or whoever for emergency contact, siblings, and children exists with numerous branches with drop down menus for family history, previous medical conditions, medications being used, allergy information, medical history all the way back to birth, physician information and a place for doctors to add new data. Of course, it would take good information technology people to set it up, maintain it and be certain of its privacy and security but this would largely eliminate paper and streamline efficiency with all parties – patient, doctors, nurses and perhaps pharmacists having access.

I am shocked that in today's world of such constant internet based technology that so many medical offices remain immersed in swamps of paper and even still using FAX machines. Rand Company study estimates that if 90% of medical facilities had electronic record keeping that it would save $77 billion per year after initial costs. I am a bit cynical as to why installation costs for medical offices are so high at around $30,000-$40,000 when, from what I believe, is only a well-managed internet site which if shared among all medical offices would only cost about one to two thousand dollars a year. Just a couple of high quality storage hard drives to copy records also stored online would be the main cost at under $500 per office. Some advertising, though not in patient records, could also offset some costs.

# CONCLUSION

I HAVE NOW SHARED my ideas, opinions and suggestions on how life can truly be enjoyable, productive, exciting, loaded with adventure and ultimately very satisfying. It is more than luck and coincidence that I am now sitting here in my mid to late fifties, feeling as healthy as my twenty-nine-year-old son while having never been hospitalized, am celebrating my thirty-sixth anniversary this year, traveling a couple of times a year around the world, have been debt-free for twenty years despite my relatively low income, have work that is my own choice which I love, pursuing my passions of photography, writing and more and otherwise *fully enjoying* life. I firmly believe that anyone who reads and applies the principles of living that I have presented here can equal or exceed my quality of life and better yet, obtain it at an even younger age than I have. May everyone be at peace and acquire the best possible life that can be had!

# SUMMARY OF HIGHLIGHTS

1.  Having the genuine desire to receive the absolute maximum possible from life and being willing to persevere, no matter the obstacles to reach this goal.
2.  Acknowledging that *all* human life is sacred and that our lives are only a one-time event. Every hour, day, week, month and year have value.
3.  Understanding that all resources whether it is money, time, energy, talent, and intelligence all have limitations, therefore how they are managed and utilized directly effects the outcome of their use. All resources should be used to their absolute maximum potential.
4.  Knowing that in order to receive one must give. To receive most anything in life we must produce. Nothing is free. If a person wants something they do not have they must place effort and intelligence out in order to obtain desired results.
5.  Applying the concept of "hard now easy later" by prioritizing that which is most challenging so that life only improves with age along with setting realistic goals. This offsets procrastination which there is nothing positive about.
6.  Realizing that reality/nature/god makes the final and ultimate decisions. This means having a solid, practical understanding of our physical environment and how it works with the most basics of science. Additionally we must deny that which is fictional because not doing so will only take us down a dead end road and lead us to confusion.
7.  Arriving at a peaceful understanding of our spiritual feelings and beliefs. This involves deep thinking and an ultimate conclusion that human kind has created organized religions and that no

matter which one, if any that we chose to adhere to, that there may or may not be a conscious god. Also we have no choice but to acknowledge that we are a mere speck in the universe both physically and in time and that there are grand, mysterious forces and processes that may never be fully comprehended.

8. We must arrive at an understanding and commitment to moral integrity which without human society falls into decay and mayhem. This means maintaining order and accountability to our lives that generally follows the principles of nature itself. Rejecting reality/nature/god only produces short-term satisfaction at best and most of the time generates long-term suffering in some form.

9. Accepting and tolerating other's differences that are healthy or incurable is critical in a human society. From a personal standpoint we may not be able to closely identify with some other's lifestyles. However, if they are living legally and not significantly generating a cost to others let's be at peace with them.

10. Reaching an understanding of how our minds and bodies work to the best of our ability and taking action to maintain our mental and physical health, which without, not only we suffer but so does the whole society.

11. Realizing that we can negotiate with the health care system and many other operations within our lives. It is a moral abomination for the sick and injured to have to either go bankrupt due to their misfortunes or significantly compromise their lifestyle from buying insurance which the vast majority of the time will cost far more than the actual cost of care.

12. Being willing to stand up strongly against others when seriously threatened and firmly and decisively eliminate such threats as required to maintain human freedom and social order. And understanding that there are times when placing negative judgment on others is the *right* choice to make.

13. Keeping abreast with world news and information in order to maintain a broader understanding of how we manage our lives in relation to others and to apply such information in electing our leaders.

14. Understanding the importance of voting and the integrity of each person's vote by voter identification in our government of democratic principles and that in many countries one has no voting rights at all.

15. Knowing when one has enough money and material possessions at which point the greatest satisfaction can be attained.

16. Being educated and applying the basic principles of personal financial management in a healthy and balanced manner in order to create a more prosperous life.

17. Realizing when we are being exploited by others, businesses and government policy and firmly speaking out upon becoming aware of this while supporting fairness and equality. And knowing under what circumstances we must legally protect our assets.

18. Arriving at an understanding of the complete ignorance of racism and realizing that while a significant amount of crime and poverty may coincide with certain racial groups, it is not race itself that causes crime, but poor government policy by misguided leadership that has created a long-term ghetto culture.

19. Becoming more aware of the value of higher education which in many cases does not raise our standard of living while also being keenly conscious that four years of lost wages and tens of thousands of dollars of debt for a credential of minimal marketability has some serious draw backs.

20. Awareness of quality parenting and the need to not protect our children from experiencing failure and to acknowledge the disadvantages we place upon our children should we engage in sexual indiscretions, divorce, child neglect or abuse.

21. Being on top of ourselves or anyone we know who is or has fallen into the trap of chemical dependency. This is a life of hell and very curable much of the time.

22. While supporting fair compensation for work well-done we must do all that we can to abolish labor unions as they largely support corruption, rob tax payers excessively. They offer unrealistic wages and benefits that the majority of others are not compensated equally for comparable work.

23. Learning and applying good communication skills. This is critical throughout life from dealing with our friends, parents and other relatives, teachers and professors, employers and coworkers to our spouses. Note that we judge others and others judge us within the first five second impression we make.

24. Understanding true balance in our lives. This means knowing when we are out of balance which could take the form of drug abuse, being overly focused on our productivity to the point of not having a healthy social life, not eating or sleeping well or obtaining enough exercise, neglecting our spouse and not fixing our marriage or our job being on the rocks.

25. Being solution oriented. For life to improve we must solve problems regularly. Whether it is a relationship, a broken window, a car that must be repaired or a dead tree that has to be brought down safely, *everything has solutions*. Delaying, ignoring and procrastinating taking care of issues only lets problems grow worse. Find a solution, set a goal on how it will be taken care of, and fix it – now, not later!

26. Travel! Yes, travel and go places. See your local sites and scenes, check out other states and if you have the resources see the world. The experience and education one receives from being exposed to different people, other languages and cultures, varying geography and climates, new varieties of trees, flowers, bugs and animals is unforgettable and a great education. And you just may meet the person of your dreams at a bus or train station, airport or any other place.

27. Staying in contact with our leaders. Contact government officials and voice your opinion so that they know the concerns of their constituents. Always hold them accountable for their positions and voting records. Fight waste and fraud, support efficiency and the enforcement of laws that have been legislated.

28. Learning and applying the true nature of mercy and compassion toward others while also integrating practicality, sensibility according to the irrefutable laws of nature and knowing where to place limitations.

29. Supporting lawfulness and understanding that boundaries are essential for our society to ethically and morally function for the

greater good of the maximum of the population. Understanding that stretching, bending and molding laws to suit every imaginable exception – even creating exceptions in some cases – only generates further chaos and cost to all without significant positive outcomes.

30. Unifying many of the practical necessities of life. We should firmly encourage more universal adaptability in software and hardware as well as long-term reliability no matter a little extra initial cost. Additionally all countries should move toward using the metric system of measurement and perhaps temperature Celsius. Unifying many laws among the fifty states also would create much greater effectiveness in the country.

# BIBLIOGRAPHY

Angela McGowan, Bamboozled: How Americans are being Exploited by the Lies of the Liberal Agenda, Thomas Nelson Press Nashville TN, 2007.

Bruce Bawer, While Europe Slept: How Radical Islam is Destroying the West from Within, Broadway Books, New York NY, 2006

Carol Gilligan, In a Different Voice: Psychology Theory and Women's Development, Cambridge Massachusetts, Harvard University Press, 2016.

Dinesh D. Souza, What's So Great About Christianity, Tyndale House Publishers, Carol Stream IL, 2009.

Jason L. Riley, Please Stop Helping Us: How Liberals Make It Harder for Blacks to Succeed, Encounter Books, 2015.

John Mackey and Raj Sisodia, Conscious Capitalism, Harvard Business Review Press, Boston Massachusetts, 2013.

Lyn Mikel Brown and Carol Gilligan, Meeting at the Crossroads: Women's Psychology and Girls' Development, Random House, New York City, 1993.

Marie Wilson and Idelisse Malavi, Mother Daughter Revolution From Betrayal to Power by Elizabeth Debold, Da Capo Press, Boston Massachusetts, (1993).

Mark R. Levin, Liberty and Tyranny, Simon and Shuster, New Nork NY, 2010.

Nortin M. Hadler, MD, The Citizen Patient, University of North Carolina Press, Chapel Hill, 2013.

Peggy Orenstein, School Girls: Young Women, Self-Esteem, and the Confidence Gap, New York, Anchor Books, 1994.

The Case for Father Custody, Daniel Amneus, By Daniel Amneus, Ph.D., Primrose Press, Los Angeles California, 2000.

The Inevitability of Patriarchy, Professor Steven Goldberg, William Morrow and Company, 1974.

http://www.personal-development.com/chuck/self-sabotage.htm
http://www.personal-development.com/chuck/
http://www.spiritual-happiness.com/soshc.html
http://tlc.howstuffworks.com/family/stupid-people-happier1.htm
http://www.nhs.uk/news/2009/02February/Pages/Facebookhealthstudy.aspx
http://voices.yahoo.com/how-deal-problems-adulthood-regardless-3174087.html
http://www.salon.com/2011/12/27/why_we_make_bad_decisions/
http://www.psychologytoday.com/blog/evolution-the-self/200806/laziness-fact-or-fiction
http://psychcentral.com/library/procrastination.html
http://blogs.discovermagazine.com/notrocketscience/2010/04/01/scientists-discover-gene-and-part-of-brain-that-make-people-gullible/
http://atheism.about.com/od/aboutskepticism/p/Gullibility.htm
http://ogcwebb.hubpages.com/hub/WHAT-IS-DESTINY-SHOULD-WE-BELIEVE-IN-FATE-ARE-OUR-DOINGS-LEADING-US-TO-OUR-DESTINY-OR-WHAT-WE-DO-IS-AS-PER-OUR_1
http://www.fueleconomy.gov/feg/ethanol.shtml
http://www.cbsnews.com/8301-3445_162-57418495/the-cost-of-a-nation-of-incarceration/
http://www.drugwarfacts.org/cms/Prisons_and_Drugs
http://www.actionamerica.org/drugs/wodclock.shtml
http://suite101.com/article/financial-cost-of-the-war-on-drugs-a53068
http://www.heritage.org/research/reports/2013/03/why-marriage-matters-consequences-of-redefining-marriage#_edn2
http://videos2view.net/tax-fraud.htm
http://depression.about.com/b/2008/09/23/homosexuality-strongly-linked-to-depression-and-suicide.htm
http://www.topix.com/forum/city/glendale-ca/TT3L3F0UJH9UHT4OC
http://individual.utoronto.ca/james_cantor/blog1.html
http://www.nobeliefs.com/exist.htm
http://www.unesco.org/new/en/social-and-human-sciences/themes/international-migration/glossary/poverty/
http://ish-tmc.org/wp-content/uploads/2013/10/PositiveNegativeEffects_of_Relgion_on_Health_and_Healing1-13-11mJKG.pdf

http://en.wikipedia.org/wiki/Psychology_of_religion

http://www.latimes.com/local/la-me-brown-bills-parents-20131005,0,7226241.story#axzz2pdqdkg2k

http://townhall.com/columnists/rebeccahagelin/2013/10/29/california-strips-privacy-from-kids-the-coed-bathroom-law-n1732783/page/full

http://www.heritage.org/childpoverty

http://www.cnn.com/2013/06/26/politics/scotus-prop-8/

http://www.naacp.org/pages/criminal-justice-fact-sheet

http://www.huffingtonpost.com/2013/10/04/racial-disparities-criminal-justice_n_4045144.html

http://www.bankrate.com/brm/news/credit-scoring/20031104a1.asp

https://www.annualcreditreport.com/requestReport/requestForm.action

http://www.myfico.com/crediteducation/rights/fixinganerror.aspx

http://archpedi.jamanetwork.com/article.aspx?articleid=346930

http://www.renewamerica.com/columns/fischer/111027

http://socialinqueery.com/2013/03/18/no-one-is-born-gay-or-straight-here-are-5-reasons-why/

http://dougsaunders.net/2013/04/muslim-immigrants-terrorists-jihad-terrorism/

http://www.fathermag.com/news/Case_for_Father_Custody.pdf

http://www.foxnews.com/opinion/2015/02/19/why-does-government-consider-this-grandmother-public-enemy-no-1/

https://www.psychologytoday.com/blog/the-science-success/201208/how-keep-happiness-fading

http://www.thenewatlantis.com/publications/number-50-fall-2016

http://news.vin.com/vinnews.aspx?articleId=31369

http://borngay.procon.org/view.answers.php?questionID=000019#answer-id-003897

https://www.forbes.com/sites/danmunro/2016/05/24/annual-healthcare-cost-for-family-of-four-now-at-25826/#1acb83201f52

https://www.zanebenefits.com/blog/affordable-care-act-policy-costs-up-in-2017

https://www.today.com/health/arianna-huffington-collapse-exhaustion-was-wake-call-2D79644042

h https://concernedwomen.org/images/content/bornoibred.pdfttp://amazinghealth.com/13.06.24-identical-twin-studies-prove-homosexuality-is-not-genetichttp://www.telegraph.co.uk/news/science/11922975/The-latest-gay-gene-study-gives-no-comfort-to-homophobes.htmlhttp://www.josephnicolosi.com/published-papers/

http://www.josephnicolosi.com/published-papers/

http://www.ejfi.org/family/family-57.htm

http://archive.is/RnTTx